ANIMAL COGNITION

Also by Clive D. L. Wynne

Models of Action: Mechanisms for Adaptive Behavior
(co-editor J. E. R. Staddon)

Animal Cognition

The Mental Lives of Animals

Clive D. L. Wynne

First published 2001 by
PALGRAVE MACMILLAN

Palgrave Macmillan in the UK is an imprint of Macmillan Publishers Limited,
registered in England, company number 785998, of Houndmills, Basingstoke,
Hampshire RG21 6XS.

Palgrave Macmillan in the US is a division of St Martin's Press LLC,
175 Fifth Avenue, New York, NY 10010.

Palgrave Macmillan is the global academic imprint of the above companies
and has companies and representatives throughout the world.

Palgrave® and Macmillan® are registered trademarks in the United States,
the United Kingdom, Europe and other countries

ISBN–13: 978–0–333–92395–5 hardback
ISBN–10: 0–333–92395–2 hardback
ISBN–13: 978–0–333–92396–2 paperback
ISBN–10: 0–333–92396–0 paperback

This book is printed on paper suitable for recycling and
made from fully managed and sustained forest sources.
Logging, pulping and manufacturing processes are expected
to conform to the environmental regulations of the
country of origin.

A catalogue record for this book is available
from the British Library.

Library of Congress Catalog Card Number: 2001052322

10
10

Printed in China

For my parents

Contents

List of Figures

The illustrations at the head of each chapter are by J. J. Grandville and accompanied an 1838 edition of the fables of Jean de La Fontaine.

Preface

This book wants to convert you to a different way of looking at animals. It wants you to be amazed at what animals can do – but amazed with a critical glint in your eye. This book wants to convince more people to find out what makes animals tick.

If you have an interest in animal cognition but have not studied animal behaviour before, then this book is for you. You may be studying psychology and wondering how much of our human cognition is shared by other species. Or you may be studying biology and wondering how complex animal behaviour can be. Or you may just be curious about the animals you see around you or learn about through TV documentaries. Though I have assumed no specific prior knowledge of psychology or biology, the tone I have adopted is a somewhat critical one. I think the truth about animal minds is interesting enough without having to embellish it with fanciful stories that are unlikely to stand closer scrutiny.

As a textbook, this volume is probably best suited to undergraduate students in the first three years of their degree. Combined with study of the further reading for each chapter it could stand alone as a text for a course on animal cognition. Alternatively it could be combined with a standard learning text for a class on animal learning and cognition, or with a behavioural ecology text for a class on animal behaviour and cognition. More advanced students could use this text as a framework to identify topics of study, and then follow these up by means of the original research papers I have cited. Alternatively advanced students could find this book useful preliminary reading to acquire an overall feel for the field of animal cognition before launching into more detailed study.

I have tried not to bog down the text with citations of every single research paper pertinent to the topics discussed. Rather the citations in the text are generally to major contributions to the field. At the end of each chapter I suggest further reading and, where possible, interesting websites. There are now a few very good websites on animal cognition, including some that exploit the multimedia possibilities of the web in interesting and animated ways.

This book may show only one author on the cover, but it owes its existence to the willingness of a number of people to lend a hand. First I want to thank John Staddon and Kevin Durkin for their encouragement in the early stages ('Try it – I think you'll like it,' John said). Next I owe a debt of gratitude to Herb Jurkiewicz for his help with the images, as well as to the many researchers who contributed images. Kevin Durkin, Mark Randell, Rosalind Sadleir and several anonymous reviewers read individual chapters and made most helpful comments. Cecilia Heyes, John Pearce, Bernard Wynne, Tom Zentall and an anonymous reviewer read the whole thing in draft and made many constructive suggestions. My editors at the publishers – Frances Arnold and Philippa English – were always helpful and supportive. All these wonderful people share the credit for what went right – the blame for any errors that remain rests with me. Most of all I thank my wife, Rosalind Sadleir, for her support, especially on the bleaker days. Without her this project might still have been possible, but it wouldn't have been so much fun.

I thank the University of Western Australia for a research award in 1999 that gave me the time to start this book, and a sabbatical leave in 2000 that enabled me to finish it. I am also grateful to Duke University for hospitably accommodating me during that sabbatical. Grateful acknowledgement is also due to the Australian Research Council for supporting the research on marsupials mentioned in Chapter 9.

CLIVE D. L. WYNNE

Acknowledgements

Figure 1.1, reprinted by permission of Harcourt Brace and Company from Pfungst, O. (1965). *Clever Hans: (The horse of Mr. von Osten)*; figure 2.2, copyright F. Kanchi reprinted by permission; figure 2.3, reprinted by permission of The Experimental Psychology Society from Heyes C. M., and Dawson, G. R. (1990). A demonstration of observational learning in rats using a bidirectional control, *Quarterly Journal of Experimental Psychology: B, Comparative and Physiological Psychology*, **42**, 59–71; figure 3.8, copyright 1962 by the Society for the Experimental Analysis of Behavior, Inc. reprinted by permission from Skinner, B. F. (1962), Two pigeons playing ping-pong. *Journal of The Experimental Analysis of Behavior*, **5**, 531–3; figure 4.2, copyright © 1976 by the American Psychological Association. Adapted with permission; figure 4.4, copyright © 1998 by the Psychonomic Society. Reprinted by permission from Reid, S. L., and Spetch, M. L. (1998). Perception of pictorial depth cues by pigeons. *Psychonomic Bulletin & Review*, **5**, 698–704; figure 4.7, copyright © 1980 Springer-Verlag reprinted by permission from Wallraff, H. G. (1980) Olfaction and homing in pigeons: Nerve-section experiments, critique, hypotheses. *Journal of Comparative Physiology*, **139**, 209–24, figure 6; figure 4.9, reprinted by permission from Wallraff, H. G. (1990). Navigation by homing pigeons. *Ethology, Ecology and Evolution*, **2**, 81–115; figure 4.10, copyright © 1996 Company of Biologists Ltd. Reprinted by permission from Papi, F., and Luschi, P. (1996). Pinpointing 'Isla Meta': The case of sea turtles and albatrosses. *Journal of Experimental Biology*, **199**, 65–71; figure 4.11, reprinted by permission from Dyer (1991) Bees acquire route-based memories but not cognitive maps in a familiar landscape. *Animal Behaviour*, **41**, 239–46; figure 5.1, copyright © 1994 American Psychological Association, adapted by permission; figure 5.2, copyright © 1988 Psychonomic Society, reprinted by permission from Wright, A. A., Cook, R. G., Rivera, J. J., Sands, S. F., and Delius, J. D. (1988). Concept learning by pigeons: Matching-to-sample with trial-unique video picture stimuli. *Animal Learning and Behavior*, **16**, 436–44; figure 5.11, reprinted by permission from Boysen, S. T. (1992). Counting as the chimpanzee sees it. In W. K. Honig and J. G. Fetterman (eds), *Cognitive Aspects of Stimulus Control* (pp. 367–83). Mahwah, Hillsdale, NJ: Lawrence Erlbaum and Associates; figure 5.12, copyright © (1989) American Psychological Association adapted with permission; figure 6.4, copyright © (1988) Psychonomic Association reprinted by permission from Spetch, M. L., and Honig, W. K. (1988). Characteristics of pigeons' spatial working memory in an open-field task. *Animal Learning and Behavior*, **16**, 123–31; figure 6.5, reprinted by permission from Sherry, D. F. (1992) Landmarks, the hippocampus, and spatial search in food-storing birds. In W. K. Honig and J. G. Fetterman (eds), *Cognitive Aspects of Stimulus Control* (pp. 184–201). Mahwab, NJ: Lawrence Erlbaum; figure 6.6, adapted with permission from Vander Wall, S. B. (1982). An experimental analysis of cache recovery in Clark's nutcracker. *Animal Behaviour*, **30**, 84–94; figure 6.7, reprinted by permission of Blackwell Wissenschafts-Verlag Berlin, GmbH. from Fersen, L. von, and Delius, J. D. (1989). Long-term retention of many visual patterns by pigeons. *Ethology*, **82**, 141–55; figure 7.3, from Cortical destruction of the posterior part of the brain and its effect on reasoning in rats. Maier, N. R. F., 1932, *Journal of Comparative Neurology*. Copyright © 1932 John Wiley and Sons. Reprinted by permission of Wiley-Liss, Inc., a subsidiary of John Wiley and Sons, Inc.; figure 7.4, copyright © 1925 Springer-Verlag reprinted with permission from Köhler, W., 1995, *Intelligenzprüfungen bei Menschenaffen*, Skizzen 3 and 4; figure 7.5, adapted with permission from Poucet, B., Thinus-Blanc, C., and Chapuis, N. (1983). Route planning in cats, in relation to the visibility of the goal. *Animal Behaviour*, **31**, 594–9; figure 7.6, reprinted by permission of The Society for Experimental Psychology from Chapuis, N., and Varlet, C. (1987). Short cuts by dogs in natural surroundings. *Quarterly Journal of Experimental Psychology. B, Comparative and Physiological Psychology*, **39B**, 49–64; figure 7.7, copyright © 1925 Springer-Verlag. Reprinted with permission from Köhler, W. 1925 *Intelligenzprüfungen bei Menschenaffen*, Tafel IV; figure 7.9, adapted with permission from Hood, B. M., Hauser, M. D., Anderson, L., and Santos, L. (1999). Gravity biases in a non-human primate? *Developmental Science*, **2**, 35–41; figure 7.10, copyright © 1981 The American Psychological Association. Adapted with permission.; figure 8.5, copyright © 1983 Springer-Verlag. Reprinted by permission from Terrace, H., 1983. In J. De Luce and H. T. Wilder (eds) *Language in Primates*, NY: Springer-Verlag; figure 8.6, reprinted from *Cognition*, **16**, Herman, L. M.; Richards, D. G. and Wolz, J. P., Comprehension of sentences by bottlenosed dolphins, 129–219, copyright © (1984), with permission from Elsevier Science; figure 9.1, from *Evolution of the Brain and Intelligence* by Harry J. Jerison figure 2.4, copyright © 1973 by Academic Press, reproduced by permission of the publisher and author. All rights reserved.; figure 9.4, reprinted with permission from Passingham, R. E. (1981) *Primate Specializations in Brain and Intelligence*, Symposia of the Zoological Society of London, **46**, 361–88.

1
The Mental Lives of Animals: Introduction

> Let man visit Ourang-outang in domestication, hear expressive whine, see its intelligence when spoken; as if it understood every word said – see its affection – to those it knew – see its passion and rage, sulkiness, and very actions of despair; and then let him dare to boast of his proud pre-eminence. (Darwin, 1987, p. 79)

We live with animals (of course people are animals too, but for ease of reading I shall stick with the tradition of calling humans 'humans' and the rest 'animals') – we always have and we probably always will. As a city dweller at the start of the twenty-first century, I share my home with a cat (sweet and cuddly), occasional mice (shy and fast), regular spiders (scary but harmless), cockroaches (I don't want to think about these) and many other smaller hopping, scurrying and biting things. Over the last few thousand years farmers and agriculturists have lived among many large domesticated mammals and a few birds. Before agriculture humans hunted – and were in turn preyed upon by – the various beasts that surrounded them. There is evidence that even the earliest hominids were accompanied by at least one domesticated animal – the dog. No matter what our attitude towards animals, they are always among us.

But what are we to make of them? Do they think? Do they have minds? Are they conscious? What is it like to be a bat (as the philosopher Thomas Nagel famously asked)? Or a cat? Or an ant? Going back as far as the records allow, people have treated animals as if they were people – a little simple, perhaps, but people nonetheless. This tendency to view animals as people is called 'anthropomorphism' (from the Greek, *anthropos* – human; and *morph* – form), and it seems to be an ancient and irresistible urge. Some of the earliest artworks in the world – paintings on the walls of caves in southern France dating back over 30 000 years – depict human bodies with animal heads, suggesting that the people of those times viewed their animals as having human-like qualities. I defy anyone, no matter how hard-nosed, not to adopt an attitude towards our cat, Sybille, that involves treating her as a small child. I believe I could write a computer program (and not a very long program at that), that could convincingly simulate Sybille's behaviour (to be called 'SimSybille'), and yet I could never for one moment treat her in the same way as I treat a computer. The tug of anthropomorphism is just too strong.

Anthropomorphism, then, is our most natural, spontaneous and everyday way of considering animals. And yet anyone who has ever observed and reflected on the behaviour of an animal for a little while knows this cannot be right (Box 1.1). Animals are not little people. Sybille is not a baby; a dog with a grey beard is not a wise old man (or even a foolish old man). It may be emotionally satisfying to treat them that way, but we know it cannot be true. Cats and dogs, and all other animals, have their own mental lives to lead. In the case of domesticated species, these may overlap quite satisfactorily with the roles we have created for them, but reflection tells us that anthropomorphism must be wrong. We must consider the psychology of animals in their own rights.

When we look at animals, we may recognize that they are not people but we still can't help seeing them from our human perspective – this is called 'anthropocentrism'. Just as tourists visiting a new country make the foreign more manageable by comparing it with home ('they use dollars like we do; but they drive on the left'), so, when considering animal psychology, we inevitably start with our human minds and compare what animals do to what we do. Are they intelligent or conscious? Do they think or feel? All these are anthropocentric questions. We know we are intelligent and conscious, we think and feel, therefore we

---

Box 1.1   The popular view of animals

The other day a friend came to me with a story he had read in a newspaper. Dolphins, chimpanzees and humans are the only species to indulge in sexual activity solely for pleasure, and not for procreation, said the newspaper report. Had I heard of this, my friend wanted to know, and was it true? As so often, I was astonished at the absurdity of the popular presentation of animal minds. What does it mean to say that some species indulge in sex for recreation not procreation? It would seem to imply that all the other species of animal on this planet only engage in sexual activity when they want to have offspring – that they know the connection between sex and pregnancy – surely a wildly improbable conjecture.

What is known of sexual activity among dolphins? In bottlenose dolphins, male groups – typically of two or three individuals – harass groups of females and young until they have separated a female from the group. They then keep this female captive, taking it in turns to have sex with her over a period of several days or weeks. In an in-depth study of 255 cases of dolphin mating behaviour in Western Australia, Richard Connor and his colleagues (1996) reported that 82 per cent of these cases involved coercion on the part of the male dolphins. As for the remaining 18 per cent, they could not be certain that some coercion had not taken place beneath the water's surface where they could not see it.

It would be anthropomorphic to claim that female dolphins do *not* experience pleasure in sex under these circumstances just because human females would not, but Connor *et al.*'s findings do not encourage the belief that female dolphins are uniquely privileged in terms of their opportunities for sexual pleasure.

ask whether other species share these talents. Anthropocentrism is a more subtle problem than anthropomorphism. Since we are human we can probably never be entirely free from anthropocentrism. But just as astronomers gradually came to recognize that the Earth was not at the centre of the solar system and developed a cosmology that placed our planet in its appropriate place, at a particular point in a particular galaxy, so we may hope that we can develop an animal psychology that moves humans from centre stage and sees each species as being at the centre of its own world.

On minds, thought and intelligence in animals

So what of 'minds', 'mental life', 'thought' and 'intelligence'? Are these anthropocentric terms, to be avoided by a mature animal psychology? That depends on what these words mean. If by 'mind' you mean something different from your body, something like a non-physical soul in which your intimate essence resides even beyond the death of your body, then the question of whether animals can have minds becomes one for your spiritual adviser, not an animal psychologist. In this book I use the terms 'mind' and 'mental life' in a more down-to-earth manner. Here they refer simply to the totality of the behaviour of an animal and the operations it performs to create those behaviours. That includes perception: seeing, hearing and senses we do not share, such as the magnetic sense of pigeons; simple behaviours, such as having a sense of when dinner is coming, through to the most complex cognitions such as what psychologists call 'theory of mind' – the sense that other individuals have characteristic patterns of behaviour – minds – too.

I am less convinced that the term 'thought' is useful to modern animal psychology. Although colleagues whose views I respect disagree (for example Hauser, 2000), to me 'thought' implies language. Although there certainly are mental operations that do not involve language, I would not consider these as 'thought'. Furthermore my assessment of the attempts to teach language to apes is that this enterprise has been unsuccessful (see Chapter 8). Consequently I do not believe that animals think in the way we mean that word when we apply it to other members of our species. In my view it is unhelpful anthropocentrism, verging on anthropomorphism, to talk of 'thought' in non-humans. Talking about 'thinking' animals tricks us into believing we understand animal mental life better than we really do.

'Intelligence' is another problematic term for animal psychology. Even in our own species arguments rage over what constitutes intelligence, where it comes from and how to measure it. But even if we accept that, for humans, there exists a package of problem-solving skills that can be effectively measured and labelled 'intelligence', it is not clear what this means for non-humans. Talk of 'intelligence' is often linked to attempts to form a single scale of 'intelligence' with some species at the top (humans, inevitably), and others down at the bottom (usually marsupials). Modern comparative psychologists take the more Darwinian view that each species has its own problems to solve, and has therefore evolved its own skills to solve them. Each of the species that we see around us today has adapted to its own unique niche. As we shall see in the chapters that follow, different niches make different demands on their occupants, and these include different cognitive demands.

To take an example from the Australian bush, are rabbits more intelligent than wallabies because they are smarter at evading foxes? A fox is a very unfair challenge to a wallaby. There were no foxes in Australia until they were introduced by Europeans in the early nineteenth century. Consequently Australian marsupials have only had 200 years to try to figure out how to evade foxes, after millions of years adapting to the challenges of a climate that, though often harsh and very dry, was without fox-like creatures. Should we call the wallaby smarter than the rabbit because it can go for longer without water and feed on drier grasses?

However, as long as we stay away from attempts to rank the 'intelligence' of different species, the term might still be a useful one. Used carefully, as a shorthand term for 'wide-ranging problem-solving abilities', intelligence seems like a very natural way of describing an important aspect of behaviour.

Finally, what about 'cognition' – what does that term mean? In this text 'animal cognition' means the full richness of animal behaviour. It does not necessarily mean that the behaviour has to be especially complex, nor that, even if the behaviour is complex, the explanation for that behaviour need be terribly complicated. By using the term 'cognition' (rather than, say, 'behaviour' or 'learning') I am signalling that complex behaviours are within the range of topics I intend to cover – not any doctrinaire adherence to one or other school of psychology.

Historical background: Darwin, Wallace and the minds of beasts

Although, as we saw above, an interest in the behaviour of animals is evident in the earliest human artworks, the modern study of animal behaviour began with Charles Darwin and his theory of evolution (1859). Darwin's originality lay not so much in arguing that all living things had evolved from earlier forms – other people, his own grandfather Erasmus Darwin included, had suggested as much before. Rather Darwin's unique contribution was to propose a plausible mechanism for how such evolution could have taken place. In each generation, Darwin observed, more young are born than can survive to have offspring of their own. These young are very variable – they are not simple clones of their parents. Inevitably some of the offspring vary in ways that make them more or less likely to survive and have young of their own. In modern terms, they vary in 'fitness'. Darwin reasoned that if some of the qualities that make some individuals better able to have viable offspring are inherited, then we have a mechanism for evolution. Those individuals with greater fitness will tend to leave the most offspring, and consequently the species will come to contain more fit individuals. Of course, just as in any game of chance, environmental conditions can change abruptly, so those which were previously less fit may suddenly find themselves better suited to the environment. But on average, over long periods of time natural selection ensures that only the most fit organisms survive and have young.

In general, then, we can say that the Darwinian mechanism for evolution is a process of variation (many different offspring are born); selection (some of these offspring survive to have young of their own); and variation again (the survivors from one generation are the parents of the next). The outcome of this process is a species continuously improving its adaptation to the environment around it (or seeking environments to which it is better adapted, or at least struggling to keep up with the rate of environmental change).

From the beginning Darwin believed that behaviour and psychology were part of the evolutionary process too. He expanded on these thoughts in his private notebooks and letters (see Box 1.2), in *The Expression of the Emotions in Man and Animals* (1872) and in *The Descent of Man and Selection in Regards to Sex* (1877). What struck Darwin were the commonalities between human and non-human psychology. In his private notebooks he allowed his feelings to show more than in the works he prepared for publication. The quote at the start of this

---

Box 1.2   Charles Darwin, Alfred Russel Wallace and mental continuity

Darwin would never have thrived in the 'publish or perish' atmosphere of contemporary academia. Between his first sketch of the theory of evolution by natural selection in 1842 and the final publication of *The Origin of Species* in 1859 lies a gap of 17 years. In that time Darwin only disclosed his theory to a handful of his closest confidantes. Historians wonder whether Darwin would ever have found the courage to publish his theory had it not been for a letter he received from another biologist and explorer, Alfred Russel Wallace, in 1858. Wallace, who was on his way to Borneo, was recovering from malaria in the Spice Islands when the idea of evolution by natural selection came to him. He immediately wrote to Darwin, who was stunned by the similarities between his own theory and Wallace's and was overcome with anxiety as to how to deal with the difficulty he now faced. How could Darwin be fair to Wallace and yet maintain his own position as the originator of the theory of natural selection? Two of Darwin's friends, to whom he had shown earlier drafts of his theory, proposed that Darwin and Wallace jointly present their theory to a scientific society in London. This was done, although neither Darwin nor Wallace was present at the meeting: Wallace was still overseas and Darwin was mourning the loss of a son to scarlet fever.

In most published accounts of the origin of the theory of evolution by natural selection, at this point Alfred Russel Wallace disappears from the story. It is less widely known that, in at least one crucial respect, Darwin and Wallace differed in their thoughts on evolution. Darwin believed that the theory of evolution by natural selection applied to humans as well as other species. And not just to our physical characters, but to our thoughts and feelings, to our minds. Wallace on the other hand drew a line at humanity. He wrote:

Box 1.2   (cont'd)

Neither natural selection nor the more general theory of evolution can give any account whatever of the origin of sensational or conscious life. The moral and higher intellectual nature of man is as unique a phenomenon as was conscious life on its first appearance in the world, and the one is almost as difficult to conceive as originating by any law of evolution as the other. (Wallace, 1869, p. 391)

We know that Darwin disagreed with this statement because his letter to Wallace has survived:

If you had not told me I should have thought that they [Wallace's remarks on man] had been added by someone else. As you expected, I differ grievously from you, and am very sorry for it. I can see no necessity for calling in an additional and proximate cause in regard to Man. (Quoted in Marchant, 1975, p. 243)

Wallace's position, that the theory of evolution can tell us nothing about the interesting psychological qualities that human beings have, is by far the dominant position among academic psychologists and lay people today. Take, for example, this introductory statement from a textbook on cognitive psychology:

Whenever higher mental processes are involved, we heartily disagree that human and animal behaviour are necessarily governed by the same principles. We regard the human as a specialized product of evolution, as an animal whose cognition is also specialized. (Lachman et al., 1979, p. 42, cited in Wasserman, 1993)

This was not Darwin's view, and it is not the view I will be exploring here. The evidence gathered in this book indicates that the mind has evolved and is still evolving. Sure enough, there are differences between the minds of humans and those of other animals – just as there are differences between the mind of the mother digger wasp that supplies her newly hatched offspring with a stunned but living cricket for them to feed on, and the mind of the pigeon that finds its way home after being displaced hundreds of miles from its home loft. There are differences between the minds of different species, just as there are differences between the heads, arms and feet of different species. But the minds of animals, just like their bodies, are adapted to the environments in which they live, and the minds of closely related species are more similar to each other than to those of their more distant relatives. Both these points indicate that minds, just like bodies, are the product of evolution by natural selection.

chapter shows how impressed Darwin was by the human-like behaviours of the first orangutan at London Zoo.

Darwin's proposal of a plausible mechanism for evolution, his detailed analysis of how evolution could account for the then-known facts of biology, and his belief that human psychology was also an evolved trait in which some commonalities with other species could be expected, combined to launch a new science of comparative psychology. 'Comparative' here means the comparison of different species.

One of the first to pick up the challenge of studying the psychology of non-human animals from a Darwinian evolutionary perspective was one of Darwin's closest acolytes, George Romanes. Unfortunately, rather than develop controlled ways to study animal behaviour Romanes relied on anecdotes collected from others' observations. Where Darwin was a masterful compiler of observations from correspondents all around the world, Romanes was a far more gullible collector. At the start of his 1884 book, *Animal Intelligence*, Romanes describes how he had considered restricting himself only to anecdotes about animal intelligence that had been recorded by 'observers well known as competent'. This essential constraint, however, he dismissed as too limiting; 'I usually found,' Romanes continued, 'that the most remarkable instances of the display of intelligence were recorded by persons bearing names more or less unknown to fame.'

Not surprisingly Romanes' claims of fellow feeling among ants, fetishism in dogs and intelligence throughout the animal kingdom raised not a few hackles among his more careful contemporaries. In 1894 another early British animal psychologist, Colwyn Lloyd Morgan, published his *Introduction to Comparative Psychology*. In it Lloyd Morgan dismissed Romanes' over-vivid interpretations and argued for more careful interpretations of animal behaviour. It fell to an American, however, Edward Thorndike, in his *Animal Intelligence: An Experimental Study of the Associative Process in Animals* (1898), to introduce experimental method into the study of animal psychology. Just two years before the start of the twentieth century, with the introduction of experimental rigour, animal psychology became a science.

The story of animal psychology in the twentieth century can be told in two parts. For the first half of the century, psychologists in the English-speaking countries developed the laboratory experimental method for studying animal behaviour that had originated with Thorndike. They took a particular interest in the kind of animal cognition covered in Chapter 3 – learning about cause and effect. They found that many species' abilities in this direction were remarkably similar, and so they concentrated on a limited number of easy-to-work-with species – particularly rats and pigeons. It was during this period that behaviourism came to the fore. Behaviourists believed that a science of psychology should confine itself to the study of the only thing that could be observed – behaviour. Some behaviourists went further and prohibited all forms of speculation about anything other than observable behaviour, thereby excluding from consideration concepts such as 'memory' or 'attention'. Meanwhile, especially in continental Europe, other scientists were taking an interest in more complex behaviours such as counting (Chapter 5) and reasoning (Chapter 7). It was also European scientists who developed a particular interest in studying animal behaviour in the wild. Strong fieldwork-based traditions developed in Germany, Austria and the Netherlands. It was through this tradition that great discoveries were made, such as the dance language of the honeybee (Chapter 8). The Europeans' interest in complex

Box 1.3 The ethics of studying animals

Animal psychologists live in interesting times. As species are driven extinct by human activity at unprecedented rates, so popular interest in the mental lives of the animals that remain grows to ever higher levels. What do animals think? Do they experience pleasure and pain? Are they conscious? Are they clever? Along with the fascination with animals has come a growing respect for other species. Across the Western world, people no longer find it is acceptable to force beagles to smoke cigarettes, or for rabbits to have cosmetics dripped into their eyes. There is a growing feeling of regret for the damage our species has done to others, and a desire to redress the balance.

Ironically and unfortunately, some of this energy – this desire to redress the balance – has made it more difficult to do psychological research on animals. Some animal rights groups have decided that all research on animals is wrong – even research aimed at better understanding the animals themselves. Some animal psychological research has come under violent attack from extremist groups of this persuasion. In other cases animal rights activists have succeeded in influencing national regulations on animal research in such a way that all animal research has become more expensive to carry out. This additional expense is readily absorbed within the major branches of medical research, but in the low-budget world of animal psychological research it can be the kiss of death.

The irony of animal rights groups restricting the activity of animal psychology researchers is that many of the arguments put forward to show that animals deserve respect derive from the work of psychological animal research. The argument of the Great Ape Project, for example, that our closest relatives (chimpanzees, pygmy chimpanzees, gorillas and orangutans) deserve basic human rights derives from research that has been done on language and consciousness in other species (reviewed in Chapters 2 and 8). Without this psychological research the arguments of the Great Ape Project could never have been mounted. Without psychological research, arguments about the cunning, resourcefulness, ingenuity and playfulness of animals are just so much hot air. Indeed without psychological research we would not even know what kinds of human action cause the most distress to a species – and consequently arguments about how to minimize distress would be quite vacuous. People who care about animals need psychological research so that they can avoid unintentional distress and discomfort to animals, or, in situations where some discomfort is unavoidable, minimize its impact.

behaviours and field studies led to an emphasis on the diversity of behaviour in different species and a diversity of theoretical approaches. The school of animal psychology that grew out of the fieldwork tradition is known as ethology.

The development of animal psychology in the second half of the twentieth century is a story of the opening of communication between the two originally distinct traditions. Behaviourism lost its pre-eminent position in animal psychology in the 1960s. Scientists studying animal behaviour in laboratories in the English-speaking countries began to absorb the more biologically informed views of their European cousins. Around this time also, cognitive psychology began to take centre stage from behaviourism. The rise of the cognitive approach freed animal psychologists from their concern mainly with learning (in the sense of learning about cause and effect, as in Chapter 3) and enabled them to study a much wider range of phenomena.

Many who work in animal cognition feel the need to line up with one school of animal psychology or another. They may be behaviourists, who disparage the wild speculations of cognitive psychologists or object to the lack of control in most field studies carried out by ethologists. Or they may be cognitive psychologists, who criticize behaviourists for not permitting themselves to look at the more interesting and complex aspects of animal behaviour. For their part, ethologists sometimes argue that only their work, because it observes animals in their natural habitats, can be considered as the 'true' science of animal psychology. But science is not sport. We do not have to cheer for one team or another. On the contrary, this tribal attitude is quite antithetical to a scientific frame of mind. Since the purpose of this book is to come to a well-rounded appreciation of the minds of animals, I borrow what I find useful from all three schools of animal psychology. From the behaviourists I take a concern with finding watertight experimental designs and an impatience with unnecessarily complex explanations. From the cognitive psychologists I take a willingness to consider very complex behaviours as part of my field of interest. Finally, the ethologists give me an awareness that behaviour is part of a tool kit of adaptations that animals use in the wild in the daily struggle for survival.

Two cautionary tales

Clever Hans: the horse with the intelligence of a 14-year-old child

Clever Hans was a horse who lived in Germany at the end of the nineteenth century. Hans's trainer was a schoolteacher, Mr von Osten, under whose tutelage Hans was able to answer a great variety of questions put to him by his trainer and other interested people. Hans was most famous for his ability to answer arithmetical questions. By stomping his foot the appropriate number of times he was able to answer questions involving addition, subtraction, multiplication and division, with both integers and fractions. If asked, for example, 'what is two fifths plus one half?', Hans would stomp his foot nine times, followed after a pause by 10 stomps to indicate nine tenths. Hans's mathematical abilities went beyond simple arithmetic to calendar reckoning ('If the eighth day of a month comes on Tuesday, what is the date for the following Friday?') and clock reckoning ('How many minutes has the large hand to travel between seven minutes after a quarter past the hour, and three quarters past?'). He could also answer questions requiring words as answers, such as 'What is this lady holding in her hand?' and 'What does this picture represent?' Hans provided word answers by reference to a table of letters, whereby each letter of the alphabet could be identified by Hans stomp-

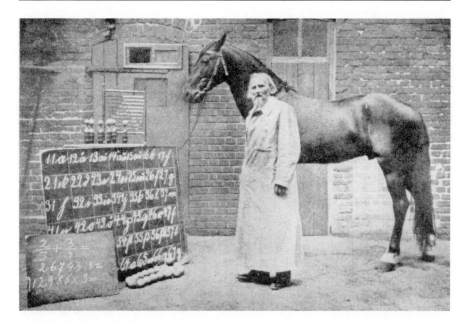

Figure 1.1   Clever Hans with his trainer, Mr von Osten. Examples of the kinds of arithmetical problems Hans could solve are shown on the small board in the bottom left-hand corner. The larger board behind it is the table of letters used when Hans answered questions requiring a word answer (from Pfungst, 1911/1965)

ing his foot the requisite number of times to indicate the column and row of the letter required. Clever Hans, von Osten and the table of letters are shown in Figure 1.1.

Hans was no fairground spectacle, trained to hoodwink the unwary for profit. A group of experts called on von Osten and his horse, put them through their paces and declared there was no trickery involved – Hans the horse had the intelligence of a 13- or 14-year-old child. This committee of experts included an African explorer, the director of Hanover Zoo, the leading psychologist of the day (Professor Stumpf of the University of Berlin) and two experts on horses from the Prussian cavalry. All were convinced of the horse's ability to count and solve arithmetical problems. According to one newspaper:

> Concerning the question of whether the horse was given some sort of aid, Professor Stumpf expressed himself freely. He said: 'We were careful to state in our report that the intentional use of the means of training, on the part of the horse's teacher, is out of the question, . . . nor are there involved any of the known kinds of unconscious, involuntary aids.' (*Frankfurter Zeitung*, 22 September 1904)

Despite this committee of experts' unanimous acclamation, others were still suspicious. Oskar Pfungst, a research student working with Stumpf, decided to make detailed observations of Hans and his trainer. Pretty soon Pfungst began to notice some strange things about Hans's performance. For one thing, although Hans could answer questions put to him by many different people (which was one of the aspects of Hans's performance that had convinced the commission that his feats were genuine), he could only do so if the person in question already knew the answer, and if that person was visible to him. Pfungst put von Osten in a tent to question Hans, and Hans's performance collapsed. These observations led Pfungst to think that the horse was relying on visual cues from his interrogators. Careful observation of the behaviour of those testing Hans led Pfungst to the latter conclusion. For example:

> As soon as the experimenter had given a problem to the horse, he involuntarily bent his head and trunk slightly forward and the horse would then put the right foot forward and begin to tap, without, however, returning it each time to its original position. As soon as the desired number of taps was given, the questioner would make a slight upward jerk of the head. Thereupon the horse would immediately swing his foot in a wide circle, bringing it back to its original position. (Pfungst, 1911/1965, p. 47)

The crucial detail here is the 'involuntarily' in the first sentence. It is not surprising, or remarkable, that a horse could be trained to tap its foot in response to very slight movements on the part of the questioner – circus animals are routinely trained in this way. What is remarkable and important about Hans is that there was no suggestion that von Osten knew he was making these signals, nor did the many other people who questioned Hans successfully. The horse was picking up very slight movements of the head that his questioners did not even realize they were making.

The involuntary, unconscious nature of the signals that Hans's questioners gave him is very important for two reasons. First, it shows that Hans really was very clever – just not in the way that von Osten believed. Hans's ingenuity lay not in understanding arithmetic, spelling, the calendar and so on, but in an astonishingly acute eye for the body language of the people around him. Who would have thought that the way one nods one's head gently while watching a horse tap its foot could be used by that animal to guess how many taps are required? This was indeed a clever horse. The second reason why what has become known as the 'Clever Hans phenomenon' is important to anyone interested in animal cognition is what it implies about studying animals. Whenever a human experimenter gets together with an animal subject to test some aspect of that animal's cognition, steps must be taken to ensure that the animal does not have the opportunity to pick up signals that the experimenter gives off unintentionally. It is not enough for the experimenter to go into the experiment with the honest intention of not giving any signals – the story of clever Hans tells us that, for a signal to be picked up by an animal, it is not necessary for the experimenter to intend to give this signal, or even to know he or she is giving it. The only conditions in which we can be certain that unintentional cueing is ruled out are those where the experimenter cannot be seen (or heard, or picked up in any other way) by the subject, or where the experimenter does not know the correct answer. Nowadays these conditions are usually built into the critical tests in all experiments, but this cannot simply be assumed and it is always important to check.

Lloyd Morgan's canon – the most awesome weapon in animal psychology

Colwyn Lloyd Morgan published his *Introduction to Comparative Psychology* in 1894 in response to the appearance of Romanes' *Animal Intelligence* ten years earlier. Morgan was concerned that Romanes' rich interpretation of fanciful anecdotes had got the fledgling science of comparative psychology off to a bad start. For one thing, no science can be based on facts that are unreliable. Furthermore it is a principle of science that simpler explanations are always preferable to more complex ones. The reason for this is that an unlimited number of complex explanations always exist for any observation. The trick is to find the most parsimonious, or efficient, explanation for what we see, otherwise science would rapidly become impossible. It may seem easier at first to use more complex and interesting explanations for what animals do. However if these turn out to be red herrings, much time will have been lost. In the long run it is far better to be safe, secure and plodding but confident that the knowledge we have amassed so far is reliable.

> In no case may we interpret an action as the outcome of the exercise of a higher psychical faculty, if it can be interpreted as the outcome of the exercise of one which stands lower in the psychological scale. (Morgan, 1894, p. 53)

This statement has become known as Lloyd Morgan's canon or principle. It is certainly not without problems of its own. How, for example, can we tell what is a 'higher psychical faculty' and one that is 'lower in the psychological scale'? The whole notion of a psychological scale is now considered outdated. Nonetheless, if we take Lloyd Morgan to be saying that we should not get carried away with what may look like astonishing animal performances, but experiment carefully to find the – quite possibly simple – explanation underlying the behaviour, then his canon can continue to do useful work in comparative psychology.

Now and the future

If just one dog finds its way home from 20 or 30 miles away you can be sure that the story will be all over the papers and the evening news. However, every weekend pigeon fanciers release thousands of pigeons over much greater distances, the majority find their way home, and nobody sees any need to comment on it. Stories about animals in the media emphasize the improbable, the rare and the downright untrue. And yet, as I hope this book will show, the truth is often far stranger than fiction. The amazing skills pigeons use to find their way home are just one example of that.

Animal cognition – the study of the mental lives of animals – is a very new science. Unlike the older sciences there is no great mass of accepted facts through which students must wade before they can hope to make a novel contribution. There is no reason why any reader of this book could not make a contribution to our understanding of the minds of animals. I hope that reading this book will inspire some to do so.

FURTHER READING

Plotkin, H (1998) *Evolution in Mind: An Introduction to Evolutionary Psychology* (Harmondsworth: Penguin). This book offers an excellent and thoughtful introduction to evolution and psychology.

Boakes, R (1984) *From Darwin to Behaviourism: Psychology and the Minds of Animals* (Cambridge: Cambridge University Press). Boakes' (unfortunately now out of print) work is a fascinating history of animal psychology and includes many interesting photographs of historical figures and their animal subjects.

Hauser, M (2000) *Wild Minds: What Animals Really Think* (New York: Henry Holt). Hauser's stimulating book offers a quite different view from mine on the relationship between animal thinking and intelligence.

Mithen, S (1997) *The Prehistory of the Mind: The Cognitive Origins of Art, Religion and Science* (London: Thames & Hudson). This book offers a very stimulating account of the evolution of the human mind.

Desmond, A and Moore, M (1991) *Darwin* (London: Michael Joseph). Darwin's life, including the dispute between Darwin and Wallace mentioned above, is recounted in this book.

Cavalieri, P and Singer, P (eds) (1993) *The Great Ape Project: Equality Beyond Humanity* (London: Fourth Estate). The views of the members of the Great Ape Project, who believe that great apes should be given some human rights, are set out in this volume.

WEBSITES

The following attractive multimedia site considers different forms of animal intelligence http://www.pbs.org/wnet/nature/animalmind/intelligence.html

Robert Cook's site contains carefully selected readings from important historical figures http://www.pigeon.psy.tufts.edu/psych26/history.htm

2
Other Minds, Other Matters

What is matter? – Never mind.
What is mind? – No matter.
(Anonymous, *Punch*,
vol. 29, 1855, p. 19)

Consciousness in mind

The philosopher Daniel Dennett, in his optimistically titled book *Consciousness Explained*, describes consciousness as 'the last surviving mystery'. After discussing some difficult problems that became at least a little more tractable in the twentieth century he states:

> With consciousness, however, we are still in a terrible muddle. Consciousness stands alone today as a topic that often leaves even the most sophisticated thinkers tongue-tied and confused. (Dennett, 1991, p. 22)

Dennett, of course, is only considering human consciousness. If it is so difficult to come to grips with consciousness in humans, where we at least have some personal experience to guide us, how are we to consider consciousness in other species? It seems positively foolhardy for an animal psychologist to rush in where even philosophers fear to tread. Sometimes, however, a question is sufficiently interesting and important that, having been appraised of the risks, we still want to proceed. Several animal psychologists have taken up the challenge of trying to understand animal consciousness through the use of a variety of experiments that appear to capture at least part of what consciousness means to us as human beings.

At their core the studies considered in this chapter are concerned with assessing how much one animal understands of the motivation of another, and how much insight it has into its own motivations. Psychologists know this form of consciousness as 'theory of mind', or the theory of what underlies the behaviour of another individual.

To make the notion of theory of mind more concrete, let us first consider some examples from everyday human experience.

- A friend phones you from a call box to apologize for running late for dinner – she is having trouble finding your house. What do you do? You first ask her to describe where she is (what she can see from the call box) and then you describe how to get to your house. Even though you are south of the river looking north and she is north of the river heading south, you succeed in putting yourself into her shoes and giving directions that are correct from her perspective. You have a theory of her mind – an idea of how the world looks from her perspective – and you are able to use this to provide helpful directions.

■ A crowd of people is gathered by the delicatessen counter in the supermarket. What do you do? Like most people you go over to see what the fuss is about. Consciously or not, you reason that these people may have seen something (a really good special offer, perhaps) that you might like too. You have an idea that their motivations may well be similar to your own. You have a theory of their minds.

■ A colleague you do not trust tells you of a way of impressing your boss and positioning yourself for promotion. You decide not to follow this advice. You reason that this colleague is not motivated by anything but his own advancement, and therefore advice from him that appears to be to your benefit cannot be trusted. Again, you have a theory of your colleague's motivations – a theory of his mind.

As these examples show, theory of mind means having ideas about what goes on in the minds of other individuals. Another aspect of theory of mind is having ideas about one's own motivations. When you ask yourself, 'Why did I do that?' you are developing a form of reflective self-consciousness – a theory about your own mind. We call this self-awareness.

As you can probably guess from these examples, tests for theory of mind in non-humans have not been easy to develop. Some aspects of the behaviour of several species, observed in the wild, have suggested that these animals might possess a theory of mind and self-awareness. These observations have in turn inspired a series of controlled experiments attempting to ascertain the extent to which these species really have a theory of mind.

Deceitful behaviour is one type of action that suggests an understanding of others' minds. To be deceitful means to provide false information for one's own advantage. To know that placing a false belief in another's mind could be advantageous to oneself implies an understanding that others act on the information they receive – this implies a theory of others' minds.

Dorothy Cheney and Robert Seyfarth (1990), in their extensive study of vervet monkeys in West Africa, observed that some monkeys appeared to act deceitfully in order to gain an advantage. Cheney and Seyfarth's work on the communication system of these monkeys is discussed in more detail in Chapter 8. For now it is sufficient to know that vervet monkeys can produce a range of alarm calls depending on the predator they have seen. Cheney and Seyfarth observed that one low-ranking male monkey, Kitui, was in the habit of uttering a leopard alarm call whenever a new male attempted to transfer into his group. Kitui was of such a low rank that it was reasonable to assume he would take a lower rank than any new male monkey that might join the group. Consequently he would be motivated to prevent any new males from joining his group because that would increase the number he would have to compete with for food and access to females. When Kitui gave his leopard alarm the monkeys – the established members of his group and the newcomer – all scattered into the trees and the newcomer was kept at bay. This might be evidence that Kitui had an understanding of the minds of other monkeys: he understood that any monkey hearing a leopard alarm call would think a leopard was nearby and would run into the trees for protection. If this was what Kitui was thinking then it would imply that he had a theory of mind.

Kitui's subsequent behaviour, however, makes this interpretation somewhat less likely. Once Kitui had frightened the intruding monkey into a tree with his leopard alarm, he would leave his own tree and cross over to make his alarm call closer to the intruding monkey. Presumably Kitui wanted to be certain that the intruder had got the message. However if Kitui really had had a theory of mind of the other monkey, he would have appreciated that by climbing down from his tree he was showing that he did not really think there was a leopard in the vicinity. This weakens the account of Kitui's behaviour in terms of a theory of mind, and makes it more likely that he had simply learned to associate alarm calls with monkeys fleeing into the trees. (Learning about the consequences of an action is one of the kinds of associative learning considered in the next chapter.) Perhaps once, when a new male had been trying to join Kitui's group, there had been a real predator threat and this had disrupted the new monkey's attempts to join the group. Perhaps Kitui had been the first to notice the predator and sound the alarm. He had then simply associated his leopard alarm call with the consequence of the intruding monkey retreating into the trees. This is a form of learning that does not imply a theory of mind on Kitui's part.

Another intriguing story of animal deceit also comes from Cheney and Seyfarth (ibid.), this time from their study of baboons. Among baboons, subordinate females typically raise their tails when approaching a more dominant animal. This seems to act as a gesture of submission and reflects the subordinate animal's anxiety about being in the vicinity of a more powerful individual. Cheney and Seyfarth observed that a particular female baboon attempted to press down her rising tail as she passed a dominant male. This may have been because she recognized that her raised tail signalled anxiety and she wanted to conceal this from the male. If this really were the reason, then it might imply she had a theory of mind of the dominant male. But, as is so often the case, this anecdote raises more questions than it can answer. For example if the subordinate female really did have an understanding of how the male would interpret her rising tail, why didn't she keep it in check before she came into the male's view? How do we know that she didn't just feel an itch in her tail at the point when she passed the male? It is also not clear why she would want to hide her submissive tail gesture from the more dominant male in the first place – submissive gestures usually function to reduce aggression in more dominant animals. Was she trying to provoke trouble with the more dominant troop member?

The problem with anecdotes from the wild is that they are always open to different interpretations. Those who believe that the animals under observation have a theory of mind can always pick observations that best support their case. But those who doubt the existence of theory of mind in animals can always find an alternative interpretation for what was observed. Consequently we need to move to experimental tests in order to gain a more detailed understanding of the possibility of non-humans having a theory of mind. Some of the best known studies in this respect are those which have addressed the question of whether different species recognize themselves in mirrors. An interesting series of tests has looked at how much animals understand when they watch people hiding food. Do they comprehend that you have to see something being hidden to know where it is? Probably the most interesting and effective studies of theory of mind in animals have been simpler ones – studies of imitation. It is to these that we turn first.

Imitation – the sincerest form of flattery

> I wanna be like you
> I wanna talk like you
> Walk like you, too
> You'll see it's true

> (*The Jungle Book*, Disney Corporation)

Imitation might seem like a very simple thing to study. We just watch two animals and observe if one copies what the other does. Unfortunately real life is not that simple. For one thing, without careful experimental control it can be very difficult to be certain whether imitation really has taken place. Take for example the famous case of the potato-washing Japanese macaques (Box 2.1). The original researchers were convinced that they had observed imitation in these animals. Subsequent, more sceptical, scientists have demanded that these results be looked at more critically. The results obtained, they claim, are more compatible with the idea that each monkey learnt independently. Even if we are convinced in a particular case that learning through imitation has taken place, there are several ways in which animals can imitate each other and not all of these are equally significant for an analysis of how much animals understand of each other's motivations. Imitation becomes most interesting to an analysis of theory of mind when it shows evidence of an understanding of others' motivations.

In some cases of imitation – we may call them 'true imitation' – one animal observes another obtaining some desired object or outcome. The observing animal desires that object for itself and therefore copies the action. This shows that the observing animal understands the motivation of the other animal – it understands that other animal was performing the action in order to obtain the desired outcome. This ability to understand another's motivations is an indication of possession of a theory of mind. Many other forms of behaviour, however, can easily be confused with this true imitation. I may, for example, turn right at the lights at the bottom of the hill, just like the four cars in front of me. This does not imply that I am imitating them – simply that we are all coincidentally following the same route.

A slightly subtler case that can also be easily confused with imitation is called 'stimulus enhancement'. When I type in the front office at home, very often our

Box 2.1   Potato washing in Japanese macaques

In the early 1950s in Japan, people studying a wild population of macaques started to provide them with potatoes to eat (Nishida, 1987). In September 1953 a young female monkey, Imo, was observed to wash one of these potatoes in the ocean before eating it (Figure 2.1). This washing removed unpalatable sand from the potato. A month later a second monkey was observed to wash potatoes in the same manner. Two more monkeys started washing potatoes two months later, and over the following few years many more monkeys took up the potato washing habit. The question of interest here is whether Imo was the only monkey to learn to potato wash for herself and the others merely imitated her because they wanted the beneficial consequences of potato washing (sand-free potatoes) for themselves. Or did each monkey figure out for itself how to wash potatoes, perhaps encouraged, but not directly enlightened, by observing other monkeys taking potatoes to the water? The answer is not straight-forward. The original reports claimed that imitation had taken place among these monkeys, in which case this imitation would certainly suggest that the monkeys under-stood each other's motivations. 'Why would she be washing a potato?' the observant monkey might ask itself – a question that implies a theory of mind.

Subsequent commentators on the potato washing saga have been less convinced that imitation learning was taking place. One detail that has proved to be important is just how many monkeys knew how to wash potatoes at any point in time, and how quickly the habit spread. If imitation was taking place, then the habit should have spread through the group of monkeys only slowly at first, but increased in rate of transmission as time passed. The reason for this is that the social transmission of a habit is similar to the social transmission of a disease. At first, rather few

Figure 2.1   A Japanese macaque washing potatoes in the ocean to get the sand off them (picture courtesy of F. Kanchi)

Box 2.1   (cont'd)

individuals have the habit: since you can only catch the habit by meeting an individual who already has it, your chances of catching it are small and the habit spreads
slowly. As more individuals become infected with the habit, the chance of your
meeting somebody who already has it goes up dramatically, and consequently the
rate of spread is much higher. Critics argue that the rate of spread of the potato
washing habit among the Japanese macaques did not show this slow-at-first, quicker-
later pattern. Rather the rate of acquisition of the habit was fairly constant. This is
more like the pattern that would be expected if the monkeys had learnt to wash
potatoes independently of each other. The original research was done so long ago
that it is now unlikely that a definitive answer to the question of whether the
macaques learnt socially or independently will ever be reached.

---

cat Sybille jumps up on my desk and tries to get on the keyboard. Now, highly
as I rate Sybille's intelligence I cannot in all honesty claim that she is trying to
imitate my typing activity. It is much more likely that she finds the keyboard
interesting because she has seen me interact with it so energetically – she has
experienced stimulus enhancement with respect to the keyboard.

The first to recognize stimulus enhancement was the great Austrian etholo-
gist Konrad Lorenz (1935). In 1973 Lorenz, Nikolaas Tinbergen and Karl von
Frisch shared the only Nobel Prize ever awarded for research in animal behaviour (Lorenz and Tinbergen had earlier cofounded the discipline of ethology –
the scientific study of animal behaviour in the natural habitat). In a study of ducks,
Lorenz observed that an individual duck was more likely to escape from its pen
through a hole in the fence if it happened to be near another duck in the act of
jumping through the hole (Figure 2.2). Rather than making the tempting inference that the ducks were imitating each other in the true sense, Lorenz recognized that it was more likely that seeing a fellow duck jump through the hole
attracted the other duck to the hole – the other duck experienced stimulus
enhancement of the hole.

Another type of behaviour that can easily be confused with true imitation is
social facilitation. People, being social animals, seem to have a fairly spontaneous
tendency to imitate each other without there being any need for a deeper reason,
and certainly no understanding of the motivation one individual has for performing an action before deciding whether to imitate it or not. Consider the
delightful infectiousness of yawning and laughing, for example. It is strange how
difficult it is, when sitting at a table surrounded by people laughing at a joke
in a language you don't understand, not to join in their laughter – despite not
having the faintest idea what they are laughing at. Many examples of imitation
in animals, such as birds feeding in flocks, probably come from the simple and
automatic process of social facilitation.

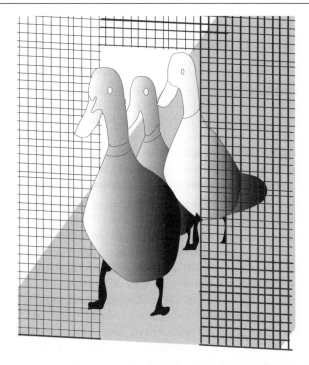

Figure 2.2   The front duck has found a way through the fence. The two ducks
behind it may be imitating their leader but it is more likely that they are just
showing stimulus enhancement – their attention has been drawn to the gap by
the action of the first duck

Identifying true imitation – the case where an animal imitates the behaviour
of another of its kind because it sees the result of its comrade's behaviour as
something it would like for itself – is far more difficult than it would at first
appear. Although we may observe two animals performing the same behaviour,
without tight experimental control we just cannot know what might have motivated one animal to perform the same action as another.

In recent years a number of cleverly designed experiments have attempted
to control for the different reasons why two animals might behave in the
same way, and have shed light on the existence and implications of imitation
in animals. These include the 'bidirectional control' procedure described in
Box 2.2.

In order to determine whether the observational learning found in the bidirectional control procedure was true imitation or just social facilitation, Chana
Akins and Tom Zentall (1999) incorporated an extra condition into this procedure in their work with quail. These researchers exposed observer quail to one
of four different types of demonstrator. As in Zentall's earlier work with quail
(Zentall, 1996), half the demonstrators pecked the treadle and the other half

Box 2.2   The bidirectional control procedure

In the bidirectional control procedure, two subjects (rats in the original study) are put into a box containing two compartments separated by a transparent wall (Figure 2.3). The animal on one side of the transparent partition (the 'demonstrator') has a joystick, which it can operate by pushing to the left or the right. Some demonstrators are trained to push the joystick to the left, for which they receive a reward, others are trained to push it to the right to obtain their reward. Once a demonstrator knows what it has to do, a second animal – the observer – is placed in the other half of the box, where it can watch the demonstrator.

When the observer has had a few sessions of watching the demonstrator it is given its own chance in the demonstrator's half of the box. The interesting question here is, does the observer copy what it has seen the demonstrator do? Does it operate the joystick, and if so, does it push it in the same direction as it saw a demonstrator push? Heyes and Dawson (1990) found that rats who observed other rats push the joystick to the left were indeed more likely to push it to the left themselves – and similarly for rats who observed the joystick pushed to the right. This could be evidence of true imitation. However, in a more recent study Heyes and her colleagues (1999) reported that the observer rats, when they were given their chance to operate the joystick, were influenced by the odours or tastes that the demonstrator rats had left on the particular side of the joystick they had touched. This could mean that the imitators were not really watching and learning from what they saw the demonstrators do – they were simply making contact with the side of the joystick that bore the interesting smell or taste.

Tom Zentall and his colleagues at the University of Kentucky developed a version of the bidirectional control procedure for pigeons and Japanese quail that did not seem

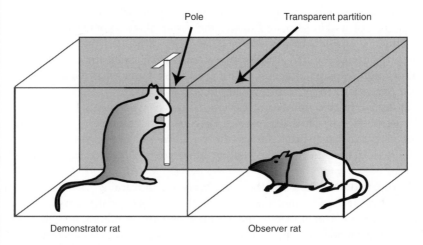

Pole   Transparent partition

Demonstrator rat   Observer rat

Figure 2.3   Heyes and Dawson's equipment for the bidirectional control procedure. The demonstrator rat is pushing the pole on the left while the observer on the right watches (from Heyes and Dawson, 1990)

Box 2.2   (cont'd)

to be subject to the problem of contamination by odour or taste experienced in the rat studies (Zentall, 1996). The birds were presented with a low treadle, which they could operate either by stepping on it or by pecking at it. It was found that pigeons that observed a demonstrator step on the treadle to obtain food were more likely to step on than peck the treadle themselves. Similarly, pigeons that had observed the treadle being pecked at for a food reward were more likely to peck at it themselves when their chance came.

---

stepped on it. In addition, half the demonstrators were seen by the observers to obtain a reward, while the other half had been trained not to expect a reward every time they made an appropriate response and were happy to keep pecking at or stepping on the treadle for five minutes at a time without reward. In summary, an observer quail might watch a demonstrator quail step on the treadle and be fed; step on the treadle without being fed; peck the treadle and be fed; or peck the treadle and not be fed. The crucial question for Akins and Zentall was whether the observer quail would be more likely to copy the behaviour of a demonstrator quail if the observer saw the demonstrator receive a reward. Most interestingly, Akins and Zentall found that observers that watched demonstrators receive food were indeed more likely to make the same kind of response as their demonstrators than was the case with quail that observed demonstrators that were not rewarded for their work. This suggests that, in quail at least, the consequences are important when deciding whether to imitate a comrade's actions. This is the best evidence we have so far of true imitation in animals.

Is that me? Studies on mirror recognition

What do you see when you look in the mirror? Yourself, probably. It was not always so, however. During the first year of life babies do not recognize themselves in mirrors. Only after their first birthday do they start to recognize that the image in the mirror is of themselves. If a mother dabs a spot of rouge on her young child's nose while he is sleeping and then holds a mirror in front of him when he awakes, the child will see the rouge in the mirror and wipe his nose clean. Children younger than about one year show no reaction. People who are born blind but later gain sight, or those who are brought up without access to mirrors, take a little while to recognize themselves in a mirror when they first see their reflection. Several species of our closest relatives – the great apes – can recognize themselves in mirrors. Chimpanzees, after an initial period of reacting to their reflection as if it were another chimpanzee, quickly learn that the mirror shows them themselves and they then go on to use it to inspect areas of their bodies that are not normally easily visible. Interestingly, self-recognition in mirrors has not been observed in chimpanzees younger than four years of age (and, most curiously, appears to decline after the age of eight or so). Orangutans can also recognize themselves in a mirror, and hotly disputed claims and counter claims for this ability have been made for dolphins and a gorilla. Most of the other species tested, including fish, dogs, cats, elephants and parrots, all react to their reflection (if they react at all) as if it were another animal.

An interesting test of mirror self-recognition in animals is the mark test, developed by Gordon Gallup (1997). This is similar to the test for babies and small children described above, where a dot of rouge is applied to a young child's nose while he is sleeping. In Gallup's test the animal is first anesthetized. While it is sleeping its forehead and ear are marked with dots of non-irritating ink. When they awake the animals show no awareness of the ink until they see themselves in a mirror, at which point they may touch the dots on their head, indicating that they have recognized the mirror image as being of themselves. Chimpanzees, orangutans and (possibly) a gorilla have all passed Gallup's mark test, but more than a dozen species of Old and New World monkeys, as well as gibbons, have failed the test.

What are we to make of these mirror-using apes? Gordon Gallup and other supporters of the importance of the mark test argue that it proves that the ape recognizes itself in the mirror, and furthermore that this self-recognition is evidence of a self-concept. This self-concept, they argue, is similar to our human awareness of self, including the ability to see ourselves as others see us, and possibly even an understanding that the self is mortal. This viewpoint has not gone unchallenged, however. Cecilia Heyes (1998) has suggested that these mirror tests do not prove that the animal is recognizing itself – the apes may simply be bored with the mirror and return to grooming themselves (which is what they do most of the time anyway) while keeping a casual eye on the mirror. This might give the impression that the animals are using the mirror to watch themselves as they groom. Heyes argues that we should not just take the word of researchers who claim they can tell what an animal is thinking while it looks in a mirror.

This suggestion seems to be effectively countered by the results of the mark test, which show the animal making a directed response to its own head as a result of something it could only have seen in the mirror. However in controlled studies that have compared the rate at which an ape touches a mark on its forehead with a mirror present with the rate of mark touching when the mirror is absent, the difference between the rates with and without a mirror is not as great as the typical summary of this research implies. It is not the case that chimpanzees *never* touch the mark in the absence of the mirror and then touch it energetically as soon as the mirror is introduced. In one of the few studies to report the frequency with which chimps touched their dye marks, it was reported that on average chimps touched their marks 2.5 times in 30 minutes in the absence of a mirror and only 3.9 times in 30 minutes with a mirror (Povinelli *et al.*, 1993).

The bigger question that these studies raise is: why should we consider the ability to recognize oneself in a mirror as an acid test for self-awareness? Imagine a robot with an eye and the ability to sense its own movements. The robot is shown a mirror. At first it treats the image in the mirror as that of another robot, but gradually it comes to notice the association between the sensation of moving its own limbs (whatever limbs it may have) and the movement of the image in the mirror. In this way it gradually comes to recognize the mirror image as an image of itself. How much self-awareness does this robot need to have in order to recognize itself in the mirror? My guess is that a machine does not need to have any abstract form of self-concept to be able to recognize its own reflection.

On the other hand, imagine that a good friend of yours suffers a stroke. This stroke leaves her intellectually quite unaffected except in one respect – she can no longer recognize herself in a mirror. You have to help her comb her hair and apply lipstick because she is unable to do these things herself, but other than that there are no symptoms of her syndrome. Her mental faculties are unaffected and you have no reason whatever to doubt her sense of self. Although I am not aware of any neurological syndrome that is strictly restricted to the inability to recognize oneself in a mirror, there is a syndrome that causes an inability to recognize faces. This is called prosopagnosia. Severe prosopagnosics are unable to recognize themselves in a mirror, but nobody has suggested that they lack a healthy self-concept. Oliver Sacks describes a prosopagnosic in *The Man who Mistook his Wife for a Hat* (1990). In this fascinating account, Sacks describes a music professor who loses the ability to recognize objects. Unfortunately Sacks does not tell us how his patient, Dr P., reacts to his own face in a mirror. However an earlier report of a case of prosopagnosia caused by a head injury states that: 'In the early convalescent phase he frequently, especially when shaving, questioned whether the face gazing at him was really his own, and even though he knew it could physically be none other, on several occasions grimaced or stuck out his tongue "just to make sure"' (Macreae and Trolle, 1956).

So there exists a neurological syndrome that can lead to failure of mirror self-recognition without any diminution of self-concept. Conversely there is also a syndrome that can lead to disturbed self-concept but does not affect the ability to recognize oneself in a mirror. Autistic people are characterized as severely lacking the ability to see themselves as others see them or to put themselves imaginatively into the situation of others. This lack of self-concept is measured in tests of the understanding of other people's intentions and thoughts. Although autistics' self-concept can be severely limited, their ability to recognize themselves in mirrors is quite normal. Autistic children are able to use mirrors to inspect their bodies and pass the mark test at around the same age as non-autistic children.

Hence there are people who are unable to recognize themselves in mirrors but whose self-concept is unaffected (prosopagnosics), and there are other people who are impaired in their self-concept but are well able to recognize themselves in mirrors (autistic children). Consequently the mirror test cannot be considered a test of an animal's (or human's) self-concept. Insofar as self-recognition in a mirror demonstrates anything, it shows that an animal has what we might call an 'own-body' concept – it is able to differentiate between itself and the rest of the world. Now an own-body concept is something that most animals surely must have. Any animal that knows that when it is fighting it should bite the other animal's limbs and not its own, must have some sense of where its own body ends and the other animal's begins. Heyes (1998) suggests that even to be able to move through the environment without bumping into things implies an own-body concept of this type. Viewed in this way, the interesting question raised by the mirror-recognition experiments is, why are most animals able to recognize their own bodies in normal viewing, but few are able to recognize their own bodies in a mirror? This is a fascinating question, but it will not, I believe, be answered by pondering the deeper nature of a chimpanzee's concept of self. Rather it will be answered by looking at how the different species use vision to identify themselves and others under different circumstances.

An interesting experiment would be to investigate whether different species can recognize themselves in video images. All that would be necessary would be to set up a video camera connected directly to a TV screen, as is done in stores selling video cameras. At first glance the image on the TV screen looks just like a mirror, but closer examination shows that the image is not mirror reversed. When we look at ourselves under these conditions we appear a little unfamiliar because we are much more accustomed to seeing our faces mirror-reversed than the right way round. For most other species however, which do not share our extensive experience with mirrors, this system should make it easier for them to recognize themselves because the image will be the same way round as when they look at parts of their bodies normally. As far as I know this experiment has never been attempted, but it would shed light on the conditions under which animals can recognize themselves.

Do you see what I see?

One way of determining whether people have an understanding of others' minds (a theory of mind) is by observing their ability to reason about the motivations of others. The three everyday examples of behaviour guided by a theory of mind with which this chapter opened all involve putting oneself into the shoes of others and understanding their motivations. What evidence is there that other species can do this?

Consider the following ingenious experiment. A chimpanzee sitting behind a screen sees a laboratory assistant hide food in one of two containers. The assistant then leaves the room and one of two distinctively dressed trainers enters the room. If the chimpanzee points out the location of the food to the 'cooperative' trainer, this trainer will give the hidden food to the chimpanzee. If, however, the chimp points out the location of the food to the 'competitive' trainer, the trainer keeps the food for himself. To get food when the competitive trainer enters the room, the chimpanzee must point out the empty container: under these conditions the competitive trainer receives the empty food container and the chimp receives the other container with the food in it. Chimpanzees tested on this procedure gradually learnt to obtain food in trials with both the cooperative and the competitive trainer (Woodruff and Premack, 1979). This result has been taken as evidence that the chimpanzees had an understanding of the minds of the two trainers. The chimps, it is argued, understood that one trainer was of a cooperative frame of mind, whereas the other was not. There are a couple of problems with this interpretation, however. For one thing, if I imagine myself as a chimp in this experiment, since I have a concept that the trainers have minds and attitudes I think I would figure out almost immediately that I have to be honest to the good guy (the cooperative trainer) and lie to the bad guy (the competitive trainer). I therefore find it puzzling that it took a large number of training trials (120) for the chimpanzees to learn what to do.

In addition the experiment did not depend on the fact that two human trainers equipped with minds were involved. Imagine that instead of a cooperative and a competitive trainer there are two lights in the room, one red and one green. The chimp's task is to point out the food's location when the red light is on, and to point to any other location when the green light is on. Now this is a fairly simple task – one that pigeons could do. Nobody would suggest that the subject in a task like this would need to have a theory of the minds of the red and green lights!

In short, in order to learn to obtain food in this situation the chimps did not need an understanding of the minds of other individuals, all they needed was an ability to learn to do different things to get food, depending on what other stimuli were present in the room. We shall see in Chapter 3 that all the species that have been tested possess the ability to learn which stimuli mean rewards, and to learn what they need to do to obtain rewards. This perhaps simple-sounding talent gives many species an awesome ability to pick up on what is going on in the world. We looked in some detail at one of the most striking cases – Clever Hans – in Chapter 1.

One of the researchers involved in the cooperative-trainer versus competitive-trainer experiment, David Premack, suggested a follow-up experiment to address some of these criticisms. This experiment was put into practice by Daniel Povinelli and his associates (1990). A chimpanzee was shown four cups, one of which hid a piece of food that the chimpanzee was allowed to eat if she could find it. The chimp had not seen which cup the food had been placed in because a screen had been put between her and the containers. To help the chimp make her choice, two trainers pointed to one cup each. One of the trainers was the person who had put the food into one of the cups – consequently he was called the 'knower'. The second trainer (the 'guesser') had not been in the room at that stage. Would the chimp learn to choose the cup that the knower pointed to, and learn that the guesser was not a reliable source of information on where to find the food?

Two of the four chimpanzees tested on this task ultimately learnt to choose the cup pointed to by the knower, and to ignore the cup chosen by the guesser. Again it has been suggested that these chimpanzees operated with an understanding of what was going on in the minds of the two trainers – that they showed evidence of a theory of mind. This experiment, however, is open to the same criticisms as the cooperative-trainer versus competitive-trainer experiment. First, it took the chimpanzees far longer to master this task than seems consistent with the idea that they were applying a knowledge of others' minds (at least 100 trials). Second, it is again possible that the chimps simply learnt to attend to the actions of the knower because that is what consistently led to reward – just as a pigeon can learn to attend to certain colours because they indicate reward. The difference with the knower–guesser experiment was that the factor that determined which trainer could accurately point to the reward was whether he had been in the room when the food cup had been baited – this made the task more difficult but it did not change its structure in principle.

In an attempt to resolve these criticisms, Povinelli and his associates changed the structure of the knower–guesser experiment a little for a final test. This time a third trainer baited one of the cups with food in the presence of the other two trainers – one of whom (the new guesser) had his eyes covered with a bag. The other trainer (the new knower) could clearly see what was going on. The chimp could see who was baiting the cup, who had a bag over his head and who did not, but she could not see which cup was being baited because a screen was placed between her and the cups.

What were the results of this test and what do they mean? In more than 30 test trials of this type, three of the four chimpanzees developed a preference for the cup pointed to by the new knower. Though the learning was quicker than it had been in the original test, the performance was neither immediate nor perfect. The chimps did not spontaneously recognize what to do under the changed conditions. Once again it is perfectly possible that the chimps simply learnt that a person with a bag over his head is a poor predictor of where food is to be found, just as a blue light can be a poor predictor of food to a pigeon.

Later Povinelli became less sure that chimpanzees have a theory of mind. In one very simple but telling experiment, Povinelli and his coworkers offered their chimpanzees a choice between begging for food from a person who could see them and from one who could not. The chimps might be confronted by a person with a blindfold over her eyes, and one with a blindfold over her mouth. Or the person who could not see might have a bucket over her head, her hands over her eyes, or be seated with her back to the chimpanzee. To the experimenters' surprise the chimps were just as likely to ask for food from the person who could not possibly see them as from the person who could see clearly. With enough experience the apes could gradually figure out whom they should ask for food, but they showed no spontaneous understanding that being unable to see would disqualify somebody from providing food (Povinelli and Eddy, 1996; Reaux et al., 1999).

On the other hand a recent study by Brian Hare and his colleagues (2000) indicates that chimpanzees can make use of information about what other chimpanzees can see and can not see. In these experiments pieces of food were placed in such a way that they could be seen by either one or both of two chimpanzees. Before the researchers started the experiments they already knew that one of the chimpanzees was dominant over the other. In competitions over food, the dominant animal was always the one who won the food. In one of the experiments, one piece of food was placed so that both chimpanzees could see it (and each could see that the other could see it), and another piece of food was positioned so that only the subordinate animal could see it. The question of interest was, would the subordinate animal understand that the dominant animal would go for the piece of food that he could see, and leave the subordinate animal in peace with the other piece of food? This was indeed what Hare and his colleagues found. The subordinate chimpanzee, given a choice between a piece of food in sight of the dominant animal and another piece of food hidden from the dominant chimp, preferred the piece that the dominant chimp could not see.

Hare *et al.* suggest that the difference between their results and those of Povinelli and his associates is that in Povinelli's research the animals were expected to cooperate with a human trainer to obtain food. Such cooperation, Hare's group suggests, is a highly unnatural situation for a chimpanzee. It is more usual, they argue, for animals to *compete* for food, and this is why their chimps appeared to understand the implications of what other individuals could see, while Povinelli's chimps had not. Interestingly, in another study by Brian Hare (this time in collaboration with Michael Tomasello, 1999), it was demonstrated that some dogs can understand that a person or another dog is looking at a source of food. In tests on ten dogs, five were able to find hidden food by following the gaze of either a person or a dog. Clearly the question of how much different species understand of the implications of what another individual is looking at is an area ripe for further research.

Conclusions

A number of chimps and a single gorilla have wiped off their faces a mark they could only see in a mirror. Although it is very curious that no other non-human species has passed the so called 'mark test', I think it is quite far-fetched to argue that this is some kind of litmus test for self-awareness, in the way we understand that notion in humans.

Some chimps have been trained to make different responses to obtain food, depending on whether a cooperative or a competitive trainer was in the room, and have also learned which of two people could show them where food was hidden. This learning, however, has been so slow that possession of a theory of mind does not seem to explain how they learnt. It is far more likely that a simple form of associative learning has taken place, of the type to be discussed in the next chapter. Having a theory of mind enables humans, even very young ones, to learn almost instantly who to trust, who to ask for food and who to ignore or avoid. It has been argued that, because they live in social groups, chimpanzees and some other species (such as dogs and dolphins) must have a theory of mind. Furthermore, because possession of a theory of mind is useful in a social context it must have evolved. This argument is not a persuasive one. Just because I might find a four-wheel-drive vehicle useful when I drive in the country, that does not mean that I own one! Even if other species experience the same problems of social living as we do (and we know rather little about how other species manage their social lives), this need not imply that they have evolved the same psychological mechanisms to cope with them as humans have.

The strongest evidence for theory of mind in non-humans comes from a relatively simple situation – that of learning by imitation. The bidirectional control procedure enables us to be sure that at least some form of social learning is going on in an imitative learning experiment; and Akins and Zentall's (1999) finding that Japanese quail need to see their comrade being rewarded before they will imitate what it is doing, is the strongest evidence yet of true imitation, and true imitation is probably the best evidence of theory of mind in non-humans. It is most curious that this evidence should be found not in one of our large-brained close relatives, but in a pea-brained bird. As we shall see in the chapters that follow, birds are always good for surprises in the study of animal cognition. The interesting next step would be to try more species on the test for true imitation that Zentall and his colleagues developed.

FURTHER READING

Dennett, D (1991) *Consciousness Explained* (Boston, MA: Little, Brown). This book contains a very stimulating and wide-ranging discussion of the question of consciousness.

Cheney, D L and Seyfarth, R M (1990) *How Monkeys See the World* (Chicago, Ill.: Chicago University Press). This fascinating book contains varied evidence of imitative behaviour in primates in the wild.

Dawkins, M S (1998) *Through Our Eyes Only? The Search for Animal Consciousness* (Oxford: Oxford University Press). Marian Stamp Dawkins offers a fascinating and highly readable view of the mysteries inherent in trying to access animal consciousness.

Taylor, S T, Mitchell, R W and Boccia, M L (eds) (1994) *Self-Awareness in Animals and Humans* (New York: Cambridge University Press); Snodgrass, J G and Thomson, R L (eds) (1997) The Self Across Psychology: Self-recognition, self-awareness, and the self-concept, in *Annals of the New York Academy of Sciences, 818* (New York: New York Academy of Sciences). There are chapters in these two books that discuss mirror self-recognition in several non-human species, including chimpanzees, orang-utans, dolphins and gorillas, as well as in autistic children.

Heyes, C M and Galef, B G Jr (1996) *Social Learning in Animals: The Roots of Culture* (New York: Academic Press). This book contains many interesting chapters on social learning, including imitation, in several species.

Heyes, C M (1998) Theory of mind in nonhuman primates, *Behavioural and Brain Sciences*, **21**, 101–48. This thought-provoking paper is a highly critical review of the mark test and its interpretation.

Hare, B, Call, J, Agnetta, B and Tomasello, M (2000) Chimpanzees know what conspecifics do and do not see, *Animal Behaviour*, **59**, 771–85. In this paper, Hare *et al.* describe a series of experiments designed to test how much chimpanzees understand about what other chimpanzees can see.

WEBSITES

An interesting debate on animal consciousness between Povinelli, Gallup and others can be found on the Scientific American web site at
http://www.sciam.com/1998/1198intelligence/1198debate.html

Another very stimulating discussion of animal consciousness is on the PBS web site at http://www.pbs.org/wnet/nature/animalmind/consciousness.html

The *Stanford Encyclopedia of Philosophy* entry on animal consciousness, by Colin Allen, is available at http://plato.stanford.edu/entries/consciousness-animal

3

Detecting Cause and Effect

'Tis sufficient to observe, that there is no relation, which produces a stronger connexion in the fancy, and makes one idea more readily recall another, than the relation of cause and effect betwixt their objects. (Hume, 1739/1978)

Animals' ability to recognize causes and effects in the world around them is a simple but at times very powerful mechanism that many animals use extensively to steer themselves through life. The same ability underlies animals' sensitivity to the meaning of signals that indicate when and where significant events will occur. This form of learning is known as 'associative learning' and is one of the best researched topics in animal psychology. Indeed to most academic psychologists, associative learning is all they understand as belonging under the heading 'animal learning'. An interest in associative learning predates even Darwin and stems from the empirical tradition in British philosophy; a tradition enriched by the contributions of David Hume and John Locke in the eighteenth century before being folded into the nascent discipline of psychology in the nineteenth century by Herbert Spencer, William James and others.

Our purpose here in considering associative learning (or 'conditioning' as it is also often called) is to explore the sensitivity of different species to the association of causes and effects in their environment. We will also cover cases where there is no real causation involved, but where one stimulus reliably signals that another is coming up. We shall also look at a little of what is understood about how animals learn about associations in the world around them. In Chapter 6, where memory is discussed, associative learning will be mentioned as a simple form of memory. Chapter 7 looks at the role that associative learning might play in more complex behaviours such as reasoning, and in Chapter 8 we explore the possibility that associative learning underlies some of the abilities that have been termed 'language learning' in several species.

A sensitivity to causes and effects, to warnings, signals, portents, harbingers and the like, can be of use to any animal in almost any environment. There is no point in a tree learning to fear the sound of the chainsaw, but for any species that can move around (and that covers the vast majority of animals) there is usually an advantage in being able to learn about signals and their consequences. The animal that can recognize a rustle in the undergrowth as the approach of either predator or prey is more likely to leave offspring in the next generation than one that cannot. An animal that can learn which flavours are likely to lead to sickness and which to good nutrition will probably lead a longer and healthier life than one that cannot. Similarly, an individual that can learn which of its own actions will enable it to escape from a dangerous situation, how to capture prey or even how to fashion tools is more likely to pass on its genes to future generations. The ubiquity of situations in which a sensitivity to causes and effects in the environment is valuable is at least part of the reason why this ability has been found almost everywhere that animal psychologists have looked for it: from bees and snails through to mankind itself.

Before we go on, it is worth mentioning that I am not talking here about the extent to which different animals *understand* the relation between cause and effect. That's why I have called this chapter '*Detecting* Cause and Effect', rather than '*Understanding* Cause and Effect'. I am only attempting to demonstrate sensitivity to signals and causes – the question of how much an animal understands about them is trickier, and is discussed in other chapters (Chapters 2, 7 and 8). You can no doubt activate a television set by pressing the power button; but do you understand the processes that lead from pressing that button to getting a moving image on the screen? Clearly, understanding is not necessary for successful operation in the world in most cases. Therefore, following Lloyd Morgan's canon (Chapter 1), we shall be careful not to assume that just because animals are sensitive to the relationship of cause and effect between two events in the world around them, they therefore understand what underlies that relationship.

As we shall see, the detection of cause and effect is the success story of the animal kingdom as far as psychological abilities are concerned. While other aspects of animal psychology may be controversial (as with animal language, Chapter 8) or marginal, at least at the present state of our knowledge (such as animal reasoning, Chapter 7), the detection of causation by animals is a very well-established phenomenon. Sensitivity to the relationship between cause and effect was first demonstrated by Ivan Pavlov and Edward Thorndike towards the end of the nineteenth century, and has been replicated in almost every species for which it has been attempted, from bees through to fish and several species of bird and mammal, including of course humans (from infants upwards).

The processes of associative learning (or conditioning) are traditionally split into two classes, and we shall follow that division here. First, there is the question of how an animal learns which signals herald or cause the appearance of things that are important to it, such as food, a sex partner or danger. This process is named Pavlovian conditioning in honour of its discoverer, Ivan Pavlov. (It is also sometimes known as classical, respondent or type I conditioning.) Second, there is the question of how an animal learns which of its own actions cause important things to happen (such as getting food or sex, or avoiding danger). This is known as instrumental conditioning. Pavlovian and instrumental conditioning are the subject of the two main sections of this chapter. Within each section I follow the same pattern. First I outline what exactly is meant by each case of associative learning, then I consider the range of species that have been tested for this ability, and finally I assess a little of what is known about what animals are learning when they show Pavlovian or instrumental conditioning.

Pavlovian conditioning

Outline

Ivan P. Pavlov (Figure 3.1) was originally a physiologist – not a psychologist. In 1904, for his work on the physiology of digestion, he received only the fourth Nobel Prize in medicine ever awarded. The physiology of digestion may seem mundane now, but at the time it was by no means clear how the body turned food into useful nutrients. Pavlov was particularly interested in what fluids were secreted in the body during different stages of the digestion process. This research involved dogs that were strapped into harnesses so that the secretion of bodily fluids could be measured. Pavlov clearly had a great affection for his dogs. Very late in life, when he was asked about experiments he had performed over half a century earlier, he had trouble remembering the names of his students and collaborators, but the names of the dogs were still quite clear to him!

At one stage Pavlov and his assistants were interested in the production of saliva in the mouth. They put a dog in a harness and inserted a tube in its mouth to enable them to measure how much saliva was produced in response to the introduction of pieces of dried dog food. An assistant in a white coat would put food in the dog's mouth, and the dog would salivate. This had been going on for a long time when Pavlov noticed something very strange – the dog would start salivating when a scientist in a white coat entered the room. There was no food in the dog's mouth, but it was salivating. Pavlov labelled the latter secretions 'psychic secretions' – clearly they had something to do with a psycholo-

Figure 3.1   I. P. Pavlov, 1849–1936 (from Pavlov, 1954)

gical stimulus (the scientist in the white coat) rather than the physical stimulus that had previously caused salivation (meat).

The astonishing thing about Pavlov is that he was so taken by this discovery that he turned around his well-established research operation on the physiology of digestion to uncover what was going on with his 'psychic secretions'. He soon discovered that there were four critical components to this situation:

1. A stimulus that already produced a response. In the dog's case this was the dried dog food. Try this yourself: put some dry food into your mouth (it doesn't have to be dog food!) and you will notice the production of saliva. This is usually termed the 'unconditioned stimulus'.

2. The response to that stimulus. In the dog's case (and yours too, if you try it) this was salivation. This response is termed the 'unconditioned response'.

3. Some other stimulus that did not originally produce the unconditioned response. In Pavlov's dogs' case, this was initially the white lab coat, though Pavlov quickly turned to more controllable stimuli, such as the ticking of a metronome or the sound of a tuning fork. (Although tradition says that Pavlov used a bell, it now seems highly unlikely that he ever used one in his experiments: the sound emitted from a bell would have been too variable for Pavlov's taste in tightly controlled experimental conditions.) If you have to queue up for lunch at a counter, you may notice that you salivate as you are waiting: the sights, sounds and smells around you as you wait for your lunch have come to function as 'conditioned stimuli', just as the lab coat did for Pavlov's dogs.

4. Finally, there was the response to the conditioned stimulus. For Pavlov's dogs, this was salivation. For you, as you wait for your lunch, it may be salivation too. This response is known as the 'conditioned response'. (These terms have come down to us from the first English translations of Pavlov's work. Terms that better capture the sense here would be: unconditional stimulus; unconditional response; conditional stimulus and conditional response. These better express the idea that one stimulus-response pair does not depend on any training (is *unconditional*); whereas the other stimulus and response pair is *conditional* on a process of training.)

Before we go on to look at the wide range of species in which Pavlovian conditioning has been demonstrated, let me emphasize a couple of points of procedure. Prior to training the unconditioned stimulus evokes the unconditioned response (being attacked by a predatory eagle [unconditioned stimulus] may cause a small mammal to run for cover [unconditioned response]). The conditioned stimulus (the swooping sound of the eagle) initially has no effect – it is a neutral stimulus. The conditioned stimulus is then repeatedly presented just before the unconditioned stimulus (there is a swooping sound every time the eagle attacks – this is called training), and after a while it is found that there is a response to the conditioned stimulus as well as to the unconditioned stimulus (the small animal runs for cover when it hears the eagle swooping). This response to the conditioned stimulus is called the conditioned response.

In the classic example of salivation by Pavlov's dogs (just as in the example with the eagle and the small mammal), the conditioned response (salivation) appeared to be the same as the unconditioned response (also salivation) – but this is by no means the general case. What is generally true is that the conditioned response shows that the animal has learnt to expect the unconditioned stimulus – the conditioned stimulus has come to function as a signal heralding the unconditioned stimulus. If the unconditioned stimulus is something good, then the response to the conditioned stimulus is likely to be a preparation for that good thing (salivation for food, sexual arousal for a sexual opportunity and so on). If the unconditioned stimulus is something bad, then the conditioned response is usually some kind of protective response (blinking to protect the eyes, cowering, running away and so on). The key point about Pavlovian conditioning is that it shows that animals learn about stimuli that signal or cause important events in their environment.

Pavlovian conditioning through the animal kingdom

The ability to respond appropriately to a stimulus that is innocuous in itself but signals that something important is going to happen has been demonstrated in an astonishing number of species, ranging from snails and other molluscs through to human beings. In fact, no animal that has been tested thoroughly has been found incapable of this type of learning. Before considering just what it is that animals are learning in these situations, let us take a quick tour through the many examples of Pavlovian conditioning.

One of the smallest animals in which Pavlovian conditioning has been demonstrated is the marine snail, Aplysia (Box 3.1). Similar work has been done on at least two species of mollusc.

In the case of bees, it has been shown that Pavlovian conditioning enables bees to learn about colours that signify the availability of food (which, from a bee's perspective, is why flowers are coloured).

Among fishes, lemon sharks have learnt to blink to a light that heralds a mild electric shock close to the eye (Box 3.2). The shock causes them to blink, and after a little training they blink to the light that precedes (and therefore warns of) the shock. The light comes to function as a conditioned stimulus that warns of the unconditioned stimulus, the mild electric shock. Several studies have been carried out on Pavlovian conditioning in goldfish. In one of these studies the fish were exposed to a neutral stimulus that preceded a mild electric shock. After a series of exposures it became clear that the fish had learnt that the neutral stimulus would be followed by a shock as they produced general body movements in response to the stimulus. Here the neutral stimulus acted as the conditioned stimulus, warning of the unconditioned stimulus – the electric shock.

Siamese fighting fish perceive their own image in a mirror as a threatening intruder and react aggressively (see Chapter 2 for more about animals' reactions to themselves in mirrors). In an experiment in which a red light was lit just before the introduction of a mirror, the fish eventually produced elements of their aggressive display in response to the red light, which had become a conditioned

---

Box 3.1   Conditioning in the marine snail

The marine snail, *Aplysia*, is an animal with very few senses and few behavioural options, so how can one test it for Pavlovian conditioning? One of the most important organs of the *Aplysia* is its gill, which it uses to 'breathe'. Usually, water is drawn in through the mantle, which protects the gill, and expelled through an organ called the siphon (Figure 3.2). Any sufficiently strong shock to the animal's tail causes the mantle to be pulled closed in order to protect the delicate and important gill. Thus the shock to the tail can be considered an unconditioned stimulus that produces gill closure as the unconditioned response. The problem is, what could function as a conditioned stimulus? Eric Kandel and his colleagues (Carew *et al.*, 1983) found that a light touch to the mantle had no effect on its own. But if the animal was touched lightly on the mantle and each mantle touch was rapidly followed by a shock to the tail, then – after some training – the animal started to close the gill flap when just the mantle was touched. In other words it had learnt that the innocuous mantle touch meant that a potentially dangerous tail shock was going to occur, so it took evasive action.

In this simple form of Pavlovian conditioning it may appear that the conditioned response and the unconditioned response were the same (both involved closure of the mantle to protect the gill). Closer examination, however, shows that these responses differed in detail. For one thing the unconditioned response was much more powerful and lasted longer than the response to the conditioned stimulus. For another, the unconditioned response usually included the release of 'ink' (a purple defensive material) – inking has never been reported as a response to the conditioned stimulus.

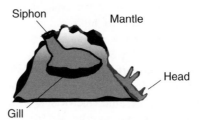

Figure 3.2   Sketch of Aplysia showing siphon, mantle and gill

---

stimulus that warned of the threatening intruder – the unconditioned stimulus. (See Box 3.3 for another example of Pavlovian conditioning in fish.)

A few studies have demonstrated Pavlovian conditioning in amphibia. Leopard frogs blink in response to a touch to the eye, but not to a light touch on the nostril. After several pairings of a nostril touch followed by an eye touch, the frogs came to blink in response to the light touch on the nostril that signalled

---

Box 3.2   Electric shock

Mention of electric shock in animal research conjures up frightening images: the electric chair; horror movie scenes of electrodes and dials marked '250 Volts'. The reality is that electric shock is often used in animal studies because it is the most controllable and therefore the most humane form of mildly unpleasant stimulus. There is value in finding out whether animals can learn about signals that herald unpleasant events. For example several studies have looked at whether animals can learn about stimuli that give warning of the need to blink. In order to do this it is necessary to find a stimulus that prompts the animal to blink. This is sometimes effected through a little hammer set up to tap the animal's head close to the eye. The problem with this is that if the apparatus were to come out of alignment it could hit the animal in the eye and injure it. A blink can also be produced with a puff of air to the eye, but over time the animal's eye dries out and there is an increased risk of infection. The most humane method is to apply a mild electric shock to the cheek, close to the eye. The experimenter starts with a very low current, so low that no blink is produced, and gradually increases it until it is just enough to reliably produce an eye blink. Exactly the same method can be used on human beings, and people describe the sensation as a mild tingle, nothing like the vicious zapping in horror movies.

---

the light touch to the eye. A similar approach was taken in a study on toads. A light touch to the head region, which would not normally produce a blink, came to do so after it had been paired repeatedly with a light touch closer to the eye.

Among reptiles, Bengal monitor lizards learnt that a flickering light indicated the arrival of food and came to attack the light with bites or pecks. Collared lizards changed their breathing, pulse and leg movements in response to a sound and light that together preceded an electric shock. Red-eared turtles learnt to pull in their heads at the onset of a light that warned of a hammer tap on their shell. Garter snakes learnt that eating worms treated with a toxin would be followed by a feeling of sickness and were reluctant to attack worms or other pieces of food that had been dipped in worm juice.

Some studies on Pavlovian conditioning have been performed on birds, especially pigeons. Trained responses include blinking, swallowing, changes in heart rate and respiration, and pecking an illuminated plastic disc. These were responses to stimuli that heralded food, water and shock.

Most of the animals in which Pavlovian conditioning has been studied are mammals. Standard laboratory species such as rats, mice and rabbits have been studied extensively, as have household pets such as cats and (of course) dogs. Farm animals have been conditioned, as have several species of non-human primate (as well as humans). Even those forgotten mammalian cousins, the marsupials, have been tested and found capable of Pavlovian conditioning.

Box 3.3 Pavlovian conditioning in male blue gouramis

Male blue gouramis (a freshwater tropical fish) have difficult lives. In order to impress the females of their species they must hold and protect a good nest site – one that offers protection from predators as well as good fresh water for the optimal development of eggs and young. This involves forcibly repelling other male blue gouramis that may be after the same spot. But it is no use defending their territory so aggressively that female blue gouramis are afraid to approach. Researchers studying these fish have determined that males who hold better-quality nest sites are more likely to mate with females than are males who do not possess a territory. But it has also been found that the territory-holding males react aggressively to all visitors, even egg-bearing females. On occasion, females are attacked to the point that they leave the male's territory without mating with him.

Karen Hollis and her colleagues (1997) have determined that male blue gourami fish are able to learn, through Pavlovian conditioning, that they should not attack a female fish. First the male fish were exposed to a 10-second presentation of a white light (conditioned stimulus). This was immediately followed by a five-minute exposure to a female fish (unconditioned stimulus). Over the course of 18 days of training it was found that the light signal caused the male fish to engage in more and more mating displays, and that the frequency of their aggression towards the female fish was far less than that of a control group of fish that did not experience the Pavlovian conditioning (conditioned response). At the end of the experiment the group of conditioned male fish had mated far more with the females than had the control group of fish. The proof of the effectiveness of Pavlovian conditioning is that each conditioned male fish had a total of over 1000 offspring by the end of the experiment, while on average the control group of male fish had sired fewer than 50 each.

One caveat about Pavlovian conditioning should be mentioned here. Just because an exquisite sensitivity to cause and effect is present in all the animals that have been studied, that does not mean they can learn about all situations with equal ease. For example in the early years of the twentieth century a debate developed in Germany over whether or not bees have colour vision. One researcher tested whether bees could learn different colours as signals of the opportunity to escape from a box and concluded that they do not have colour vision. Other researchers tested bees' ability to recognize different colours as cues for food and concluded that bees have excellent colour vision – including ultraviolet, which we cannot see. The answer to this riddle is that both were right: bees can learn colours as signals of the location of food and the way into the hive; but they cannot learn about colours as signals of a way to escape. (Subsequent studies have shown that bees are particularly attentive to the colours they see in the three seconds before landing on a food source, and that, after just three visits, a bee may remember a colour for the rest of its life.) Animals come equipped by evolution to learn about some cause and effect relationships better than others.

One example, standard in introductory psychology courses, concerns learning about the relationship between flavour sickness. People, like most animals, are very well able to learn to avoid flavours that are associated with sickness. If the flavour is unfamiliar when it first makes the person (or animal) sick, the aversion may last a lifetime. On the other hand, people and other animals have great difficulty learning that a light or sound is going to make them sick. It makes perfect sense – from birth we are prepared by evolution to learn that flavours can warn of consequent sickness, but we are unprepared to learn that a sight or sound could be warning us about the threat of sickness, even though we can learn many other things about sights and sounds.

This selectivity of Pavlovian conditioning does not weaken its effectiveness. On the contrary, by preparing animals to learn to associate some things with their consequences more readily than others, evolution has provided a preliminary focusing of associative learning abilities that is highly efficient. The evolutionary preparedness to learn certain associations rather than others spares animals from getting caught up in 'red herring' associations that are unlikely to be of much use in their daily lives. Next time you wake up feeling unwell, imagine how pointless it would be if you asked yourself, 'I wonder whether this is to do with the decor in the restaurant last night?' rather than 'I wonder if it was something I ate last night?'

What is learned in Pavlovian conditioning?

I have already said that I am not suggesting that animals learn about causes and effects in Pavlovian conditioning because they understand the relationship between the signal (the conditioned stimulus) and the thing it signifies (the unconditioned stimulus), but how much knowledge do they have of the relationship between the signal and the thing signified? Pavlov himself and other early theorists believed that animals learnt about the relationship between the conditioned and the unconditioned stimulus solely because they were close together in time and space. This closeness is known as contiguity. Pavlovian conditioning, it was believed, depended solely on contiguity. Certainly contiguity is important: if the conditioned and unconditioned stimuli are not fairly close together no learning will take place. Just how close depends on the exact situation. In eye blink conditioning, the unconditioned stimulus must usually occur within about half a second of the conditioned stimulus. In taste aversion learning on the other hand (where an animal learns that a novel flavour leads to sickness) the interval between the conditioned stimulus and the unconditioned stimulus can be as much as 24 hours. But is contiguity alone enough? In 1967 Robert Rescorla reported an ingenious experiment, which demonstrated that contiguity alone cannot fully account for Pavlovian conditioning (Box 3.4).

Box 3.4   Rescorla's truly random control experiment

To test the importance of contiguity in Pavlovian conditioning, Robert Rescorla (1967) developed the truly random control procedure. One group of rats experienced conditioned stimuli that were followed by unconditioned stimuli in the normal way. Every so often a conditioned stimulus (light) was followed immediately by an unconditioned stimulus (a mild electric shock to the feet) (see the left-hand panel in Figure 3.3). A second group of rats experienced the same number of conditioned stimuli and the same number of unconditioned stimuli with the same average spacing between them, but their order was jumbled up. No longer were the conditioned stimuli followed immediately and regularly by unconditioned stimuli, instead the conditioned and unconditioned stimuli could come at any time (see the right-hand panel in Figure 3.3). Thus in the first group there was an orderly predictive relationship between the conditioned and the unconditioned stimuli, but in the second group there was not. Rescorla found that only the first group developed conditioned responses – the group that was exposed to jumbled conditioned and unconditioned stimuli did not. This result proves that contiguity alone is not sufficient for Pavlovian conditioning to occur; there must also be a regular predictive relationship between the conditioned and unconditioned stimuli – this relationship is called a contingency.

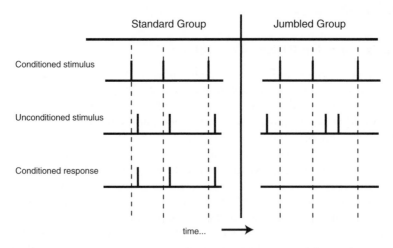

Figure 3.3   The standard (left) and jumbled (right) groups from Rescorla's truly random control experiment

---

Hence Rescorla showed the necessity of a contingency between the conditioned and unconditioned stimuli (a contingency between two items means that one necessarily follows from the other). Quite soon after Rescorla's experiment, other researchers began to ask whether the presence of a contingency might be

Group	Phase 1	Phase 2	Phase 3
Experimental	Training: buzzer → shock	Training: light + buzzer → shock	Light test: no conditioning
Control	No training	Training: light + buzzer → shock	Light test: conditioned fear

Figure 3.4   Design of Kamin's blocking experiment

enough to guarantee that Pavlovian conditioning would take place. Leon Kamin (1968) developed a very ingenious experiment to test this. As outlined in Figure 3.4, he took two groups of rats. The first group (following Kamin we'll call them the experimental group) was trained through Pavlovian conditioning to expect an electric shock every time a buzzer sounded. During this time the second group (the control group) was given no training. Next Kamin trained both groups of rats by means of a buzzer and a light that together signalled an electric shock. The question Kamin was interested in was, what would the two groups of rats have learned about the light? In order to ascertain this, both groups were given a final test with just the light stimulus – would they have learned that the light predicted shock? The control group, which had not had any experience of the buzzer on its own, had obviously learnt that the light indicated that an electric shock would follow – they stopped what they were doing when they saw the light and waited for the shock. The really interesting result was the case of the experimental group – the group that in the first phase had experienced the buzzer on its own, followed by the shock. The experimental group failed to show any fear of the light – they had not become conditioned to it. For both groups there was a perfectly good contingency between the light and the shock – every time the light came on it was followed by the shock. For the experimental group, however, the light was redundant; it only doubled up what they already knew from attending to the buzzer. Kamin concluded that contingency was not enough for Pavlovian conditioning to take place.

Much contemporary research on Pavlovian conditioning is dedicated to finding out what, in addition to contingency and contiguity, is necessary for conditioning to occur. Some researchers believe that the unconditioned stimulus must be 'surprising' for learning to occur; others emphasize that the subject must attend to the conditioned stimulus. Within these camps there are arguments about what makes a stimulus 'surprising' or 'attended to' and so on. For our purposes, what is interesting here is that although animals may not understand cause and effect in a deep way (just as I don't understand in any deep way the relationship between pressing the keys on a keyboard and seeing my words appear on the screen in front of me), they are not just responding to the fact that the conditioned and unconditioned stimuli tend to be close together (contiguity), or that one tends reliably to follow the other (contingency). Learning in Pavlovian conditioning may not be deep, but it is not as superficial as was first supposed.

However it is achieved, Pavlovian conditioning is an evolved mechanism that enables animals to be sensitive to environmental signals that are important to their lives.

Instrumental conditioning

Outline

One part of learning about causes and effects is the case where both the signal and the thing signified are events in the outside world – this is the case with which Pavlovian conditioning is concerned. The other side of the coin is the situation where an animal's own behaviour is the cause of an event in the environment – this is known as instrumental conditioning. Instrumental conditioning (also known as operant or type II conditioning) is so called because the animal's behaviour is instrumental to obtaining some outcome: the cat that pounces on a dove feeding on the ground, the chimp that signs 'gimme' to obtain a toy or food, myself as I turn on the kettle to make a cup of coffee.

Instrumental conditioning was first described by Edward Thorndike at the end of the nineteenth century (Thorndike, 1911). For his doctoral thesis, Thorndike studied the behaviour of many animals. In those days the facilities for animal research in psychology departments were very limited, so Thorndike kept his cats, dogs and a monkey in his lodgings. History has not recorded what his landlady thought of this Columbia graduate student who kept a menagerie in his apartment! Although Thorndike experimented on many species, it is his studies on cats that have become the best known. Thorndike built simple cages out of orange crates. He called these cages 'puzzle boxes' (Figure 3.5). Each puzzle box could be opened from the inside with some kind of latch mechanism. In one box, for example, the latch could be opened by pushing against a vertical pole. Thorndike put cats in the boxes one at a time and observed how long it took each one to learn to operate the latch mechanism. At first Thorndike observed that a cat would just flail around in a fairly directionless

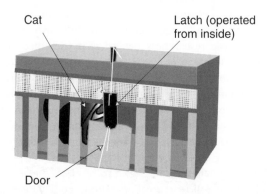

Cat

Latch (operated from inside)

Door

Figure 3.5   An example of one of Thorndike's puzzle boxes

manner until ultimately operating the latch by chance. With each return to the box, however, the cat needed a little less time to operate the latch successfully. Ultimately the cat operated the latch as soon as it entered the box and gained its freedom immediately. Thorndike recorded that he saw no evidence of insight or intelligence in his cats, just blind trial and error learning. Nonetheless the cats were showing sensitivity to a cause and effect relationship between their own behaviour and events in the outside world – the hallmark of instrumental conditioning.

Instrumental conditioning through the animal kingdom

Instrumental conditioning has been tested in almost as wide a range of species as Pavlovian conditioning.

Just as bees have been successfully conditioned using Pavlovian methods, so they have proven to be useful subjects in instrumental learning experiments. The dance language of bees (discussed in Chapter 8) is just one example of a behaviour that has been shown to be modified through instrumental learning.

Amphibia have not been easy to condition instrumentally, probably because our understanding of how to motivate them is very poor. Although adult frogs and toads have proven to be particularly recalcitrant subjects, their larvae have been more cooperative. In a study that combined aspects of Pavlovian and instrumental learning, tadpoles learnt to move away from a light in order to avoid a shock.

Among lizards, in another study combining aspects of Pavlovian and instrumental conditioning, two species of anoles learnt to escape an electric shock by running to another part of an apparatus. Similar results were obtained with collared lizards and desert iguanas.

Fish species that have successfully tested for instrumental learning include goldfish, koi carp and queen triggerfish. In one study, hungry queen triggerfish were trained to press a small plastic rod that was connected to an automatic feeder that dropped food into their tank. Typically these fish needed only about five rewards to learn what they were required to do.

As with Pavlovian conditioning, several species of bird have been popular in tests of instrumental conditioning. Again, pigeons are the most commonly used, but doves, chickens, gulls and even quail have been tested successfully. In a typical instrumental learning experiment with birds, a subject is put in a specially built experimental chamber known as an operant chamber or Skinner box. This box contains at least one plastic key for the bird to peck, and a food hopper to deliver rewards of food grains. The birds are trained to peck at the key in order to obtain rewards according to some programme or schedule, usually controlled by a computer. Figure 3.6 shows a pigeon in a typical operant chamber.

A wide range of mammalian species have been tested for instrumental conditioning, including a couple of marsupials, rodents such as rats and mice, rabbits, cats, dogs, raccoons, skunks, ferrets, minks, some farm animals, several primates

Figure 3.6 Pigeon in an operant chamber

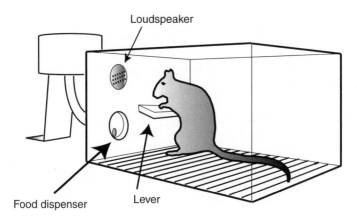

Figure 3.7 Rat in an operant chamber

and many others. A typical operant chamber in which a small mammal can be tested is shown in Figure 3.7. This is a similar box to that used with birds, but instead of a pecking key it contains a lever that the animal can press with its forepaws or snout. The food delivery apparatus is modified to deliver a food item that is attractive to the animal being trained.

A simple instrumental learning experiment with rats might involve making a food reward dependent on pressing the lever in the operant chamber. Similar tests can be done on appropriately scaled equipment for most species. Mazes are another popular piece of apparatus for studying instrumental learning in rodents. These usually have a simple T, Y or star-shape. Figure 3.8 shows a couple of alter-

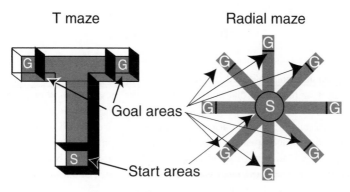

Figure 3.8   T and radial mazes

natives. The animal's task is to learn where to run in order to receive a reward. For example, in a T or Y maze only one arm of the maze may be consistently baited – the left arm perhaps. In the star-shaped maze (usually known as a 'radial maze') all the arms are baited, and the animal has to collect food from the bottom of each arm without re-entering an arm it has already visited. Rats can easily cope with eight arms in this way.

Box 3.5   The ping-pong pigeons

The complexity of behaviour that can be acquired through instrumental conditioning can be quite dramatic. We have already considered one example in Chapter 1 – that of Clever Hans, the horse who appeared to have the intelligence (and knowledge) of a 14-year-old child but was just paying close attention to the body movements of people around him. The most famous proponent of instrumental conditioning in modern times, B. F. Skinner, developed several startling demonstrations of the effectiveness of instrumental conditioning in training animals. One of these was his ping-pong experiment (Skinner, 1962). Pairs of pigeons were taught by means of instrumental conditioning to peck a ping-pong ball back and forth in a form of table tennis. The apparatus Skinner used is shown in Figure 3.9. The playing table had rails around the edges to prevent the ball falling off, and at each end there was a return trough. If the bird defending a shot failed to peck the ball back to its opponent, the ball would land in this trough and roll into a mechanism that triggered a food reward for the opposing pigeon. In this way each bird was rewarded if it succeeded in pecking the ball past its opponent. After training, Skinner reports, the birds were able to maintain rallies of up to six returns, each time pecking the ball back to their opponent.

Box 3.5   (cont'd)

Training started with each bird individually. First the bird was rewarded just for pecking a table tennis ball fixed to the edge of the playing table. Once the bird was reliably pecking the ball in one position the ball was moved to another place, until the pigeon was eventually willing to peck it wherever it might be found. The next stage was to train the bird to peck the ball when it was free to roll around. The final stage before introducing each pigeon to its opponent in the game was to reward the bird only if it succeeded in pecking the ball so that it hit a bar placed across the playing table. Finally the birds were introduced to each other and rewarded for scoring points past each other.

Figure 3.9   Two pigeons playing ping-pong (from Skinner, 1962. © The Society for the Experimental Analysis of Behavior, 1962)

Instrumental conditioning is not just for animals – a large part of learning in human beings is also characterized as behaviour controlled by its consequences. This is how we learn as babies to cry to get attention, as children to study in order to get good grades at school, and as parents to praise and scold our children in order to maintain a comfortable family life.

To reiterate a point made in the discussion on Pavlovian conditioning: the fact that a very wide range of species show some evidence of instrumental conditioning does not mean they will show instrumental conditioning under all circumstances. Take for example the pigeon, probably the single most popular experimental species in instrumental conditioning. Pigeons have been trained to peck, not peck, hop, not hop, swallow, fly and a range of other things in order to get food, water or shelter or avoid noxious stimuli such as an electric shock. And yet they have never been house-trained. As a bird, the pigeon is supremely indifferent to where it leaves its faeces.

What is learnt in instrumental conditioning?

As with Pavlovian conditioning, the first explanation proposed for instrumental conditioning was that animals pick up the fact that their behaviour is causing something to happen just because the behaviour is very close in time and space to the outcome it produces. We saw when discussing Pavlovian conditioning that this closeness together in space and time is called contiguity. Contiguity certainly is important – many species are unable to learn in an instrumental conditioning experiment if too long an interval separates their action from its consequence. 'Too long' in this context often means as little as a second. For many animals an interval of just a couple of seconds between performing an action and experiencing the consequences of that action is long enough to ensure they will not learn the relationship between what they do and its consequence.

The view that contiguity between behaviour and reward was the key element in animals' learning about instrumental conditioning led to an interesting controversy. Skinner (1948/1972) performed an experiment in which hungry pigeons caged individually were given food at regular intervals (every 15 seconds). They did not have to do anything to get this food. Skinner left the pigeons alone for a while and then came back to see what had happened. What Skinner claimed to find was that each pigeon was doing something different in the moment just before food was delivered:

> One bird was conditioned to turn counterclockwise about the cage, making two or three turns between [rewards]. Another repeatedly thrust its head into one of the upper corners of the cage. A third developed a 'tossing' response, as if placing its head beneath an invisible bar and lifting it repeatedly. (Skinner, 1948/1972)

Skinner argued that the following development had taken place. At first each pigeon had been quietly minding its own business, preening, walking around or whatever. Then, unexpectedly, food was delivered. The closeness together in time (contiguity) between the action the pigeon had been performing and the delivery of food led to the pigeon acting as if it had been rewarded for that action, and therefore repeating this action more and more. In other words Skinner was arguing that contiguity alone was a complete explanation of how animals learn about instrumental conditioning.

This account stood until 1971 when John Staddon and Virginia Simmelhag repeated Skinner's experiment, but this time with much more detailed recording of what the pigeons were actually doing. Staddon and Simmelhag did not find the pigeons engaged in different, more or less randomly chosen behaviours after a period of regular food deliveries. Rather, just before each food delivery all the pigeons tended to do the same thing – peck at the food magazine. In other words the pigeons had learnt to expect food at regular intervals and therefore, each time food came around, performed actions that were appropriate to trying to get the food (we shall look at animals' sensitivity to time in more detail in Chapter 5). Certainly, contiguity is important in instrumental conditioning, just as it is in Pavlovian conditioning, but is not the whole story. Animals do not learn what the consequences of their actions are just on the basis of what happens immediately after they perform some action – another factor is necessary.

Part of that something else is contingency – the reliable dependence of one event on another. If a pigeon, or any other animal, is going to learn that something it has done has had a particular consequence on the world around it, then the consequence must reliably follow the action – a behaviour–consequence contingency must exist. The simplest experimental demonstrations of this fact are those in which a reward is not delivered for every appropriate response. This breaks up the contingency between behaviour and its consequence and makes it more difficult for an animal to learn about the outcome of its actions. The contingency between behaviour and consequence can also be disturbed by giving an animal 'free' rewards – rewards that do not depend on the performance of any particular action (this is rather similar to the jumbled condition in Rescorla's truly random control condition – see Box 3.4). Under this condition animals are much less likely to continue performing the intended response. Contingency, however, is once again not the whole story. Much contemporary research in instrumental conditioning is aimed at understanding just how animals come to learn about the relationship between their actions and the consequences of those actions.

Conclusions

The relationship between cause and effect is a fundamental feature of the world around us, as is the value of being able to recognize signals for what they predict about consequences. For any organism that can act on its world, and that covers most animals, the ability to learn about the consequences of its actions must be important and advantageous. Similarly, for any organism that can perceive events in the world around it, the ability to pick up on relationships between those events must be adaptive. The mouse that can hear the sound of the swooping barn owl and run for cover; the dog that comes to understand the word 'walkies'; the sea snail that can learn which gentle touch is a harbinger of a more painful shock and react accordingly – all of these and myriads more are plausible examples of the ability to detect cause and effect (or signal–signifier) relationships being highly advantageous. The range of situations in which the ability to respond to these relationships is very useful is matched by the range of species that have been shown to be capable of picking up on these relationships. Examples are most common among birds and mammals, but this probably reflects the preference of the scientists working in this field. Those that have chosen to work with bees, fish or marsupials, for example, have also been successful in demonstrating both Pavlovian and instrumental forms of conditioning (Box 3.6).

Most of the research on how animals learn to detect cause and effect relationships has centred on a handful of species that are easy to house in the laboratory, especially rats and pigeons. These studies have found that for both

Box 3.6   Sybille's breakfast – a case study in Pavlovian and instrumental conditioning

In the real world outside the laboratory it is often difficult to distinguish between Pavlovian and instrumental conditioning. The habits of animals are often not noticed until they have become well established and we therefore fail to see the process of learning as it happens. With a knowledgeable eye for Pavlovian and instrumental conditioning, however, it is often possible to at least make an informed guess about what is going on.

Take our cat Sybille for example. Sybille is given her breakfast every morning at about 7 am. She sleeps inside but, unless it is raining, she is fed outside. Like all healthy cats, Sybille takes a very serious interest in meal times and does everything in her power to encourage us to remember her needs: she also pays careful attention to any signs that may predict when food is on its way.

The first thing we notice is that she has some sense of the time at which breakfast is likely to be delivered – this sensitivity of animals to the time of day is a form of Pavlovian conditioning and is covered in more detail in Chapter 5. For all the animals that have been studied the time of day can function as a conditioned stimulus that they use to predict the occurrence of important events – unconditioned stimuli. Sybille's way of conveying that she knows it is breakfast time is to attempt to wake us up. This she does by jumping on the dressing table and upsetting bottles and other breakable items. Pavlovian conditioning guides her awareness of the time of day (conditioned stimulus – time of day; conditioned response – waking and jumping on dressing table; unconditioned stimulus – us waking up and getting her breakfast; unconditioned response – eating breakfast), but instrumental conditioning keeps her jumping onto the dressing table and making a racket (instrumental behaviour – making a nuisance of herself; outcome – we wake up). Now that we are awake, the next stage is to get our attention on to her and her needs. This she does by meowing energetically near the bedroom door. Her meows must be an instrumental response, rewarded by our finally getting out of bed. This is the cue for her to run to the back door and meow even stronger – these behaviours might be Pavlovian (conditioned stimulus – someone getting out of bed) or instrumental (rewarded by breakfast). Only controlled experimentation could tell if they were one or the other or a mixture of both. Finally the back door is opened and food is provided.

Pavlovian and instrumental forms of conditioning, contiguity (closeness together in space and time) and contingency (reliable dependency of one event on another) are important, but they are not the whole story. Now it is quite possible that other things may be important in the many species that have not been studied in such detail, but it seems unlikely. On purely logical grounds, contiguity and contingency are the most likely clues to understanding the relationship between cause and effect or the signal and the thing signified. Animals certainly differ in what cause and effect relationships they are prepared to learn about, but if they can learn about something it is likely that they all do so in much the same way.

Before we leave Pavlovian and instrumental conditioning, two more points are worth mentioning. The first is that the exquisite sensitivity to cause and effect (and signal–signifier) relationships that we can observe in many species (and assume to be present in the others) offers a mechanism for surprisingly complex learning under certain circumstances. We saw in Chapter 1 how Hans the horse appeared to be able to perform arithmetical problems but was actually attending to the very slight signs made by the people around him. In a very ingenious way, Hans was detecting causal relationships between their body movements, his foot stomps and the reward he would receive. I think I would find it easier to learn arithmetic than to learn to attend to signals people were making that were so subtle they didn't even realize they were making them themselves! We shall discuss in Chapter 7 how, under certain conditions, animals' reasoning ability may be derived from their sensitivity to cause and effect relationships, as manifested in Pavlovian and instrumental conditioning. Many of the claims about animal language that we review in Chapter 8 are also reducible to associative learning of these types. In short, the ability to detect the relationship between cause and effect is an immensely powerful tool that at least some species are able to exploit to reach astonishing levels of behavioural complexity.

FURTHER READING

Boakes, R A (1984) *From Darwin to Behaviourism: Psychology and the Minds of Animals* (Cambridge: Cambridge University Press). Boakes offers a fascinating history of the early years of research on animal learning, including associative learning's philosophical routes. It also contains many interesting images.

Domjan, M (1998) *The Principles of Learning and Behavior*, 4th edn (Pacific Grove, CA: Brooks/Cole). This introductory textbook on learning includes a very clear and up-to-date exposition of Pavlovian and instrumental conditioning and also discusses how much animals understand in conditioning experiments.

Macphail, E M (1982) *Brain and Intelligence in Vertebrates* (Oxford: Oxford University Press). This slightly earlier book reviews learning in many species, including amphibia, fish and reptiles.

Wynne, C D L and McLean, I G (1999) The comparative psychology of marsupials, *Australian Journal of Psychology*, **51**, 111–16. This paper offers a recent review of learning in marsupials.

Skinner, B F (1972) *Cumulative Record*, 3rd edn (New York: Appleton Century Crofts). Several of Skinner's classic experiments, including the ping-pong pigeons and the original superstition experiment, are described in this collection of papers.

WEBSITES

The *Encyclopaedia Britannica's* entry for animal learning can be found at http://www.britannica.com/bcom/eb/article/1/0,5716,109611+1,00.html

To get something of the feel of what it is like training a rat in an instrumental conditioning task, try http://psychology.wadsworth.com/sniffy/

4
Other Ways of Seeing the World – I: Physical Dimensions

Here we may glimpse the worlds of the lowly dwellers of the meadow. To do so, we must first blow, in fancy, a soap bubble around each creature to represent its own world, filled with the perceptions which it alone knows. When we ourselves then step into one of these bubbles, the familiar meadow is transformed. Many of its colorful features disappear; others no longer belong together but appear in new relationships. A new world comes into being. Through the bubble we see the world of the burrowing worm, of the butterfly, or of the field mouse; the world as it appears to the animals themselves, not as it appears to us. (Jakob von Uexküll, 1934/1957)

The world that we see around us seems complete – we are not aware of anything missing from the world we perceive. And yet physicists tell us that there are many aspects of our environment of which we are unaware. As I look out of my office window I have no sense of the polarization of the sun's light in the sky. I do not experience the magnetic fields that the computer is generating, nor the many sounds of pitch higher than about 18 kHz around me. (One Hertz [Hz] is one vibration per second; 1 kHz is a thousand Hertz.)

The pioneer biologist Jakob von Uexküll was the first to suggest that the world around an animal (the *Umwelt* – its surrounding world or environment) is not the same as its *Innenwelt* – its world as perceived and internalized. This is as true for us as it is for the tick that von Uexküll takes as his example. A female tick sits on a blade of grass waiting for a mammal to come along so that she can pounce on it and get the meal of blood she needs to feed her eggs and complete her life-cycle. But the tick does not recognize a mammal as we might from its size, four-leggedness or furriness. Just one thing tells the tick that a mammal is passing by – the smell of butyric acid. This acid emanates from the skin of all mammals and is therefore a reliable sign of food. Having fallen onto a mammal, the tick searches for a clear patch of skin through which to burrow to reach her blood meal. At this stage it is warmth alone that tells the tick she is heading in the right direction. So for the tick, the rich world surrounding her is reduced to just a couple of signs: butyric acid, which denotes a mammal, and warmth, which denotes blood beneath the skin. As von Uexküll puts it, 'the very poverty of this world guarantees the unfailing certainty of her actions, and security is more important than wealth'.

Every species, not just simple ones, has a unique perceptual world that has evolved out of the demands of the life it leads. These perceptual worlds are astonishingly varied – as varied as the niches their possessors inhabit. There are birds that see ultraviolet; insects that see infrared; many animals that see the polarization of sunlight; bats that hear sounds three octaves higher in pitch than the highest we can hear, and use sonar to 'see' the flapping of an insect's wings. But in the interest of gaining some depth of understanding, rather than just scratching the surface in many places, I have chosen to emphasize the sensory world of one species – the pigeon. Pigeons have been more extensively studied than any other species, they are to be found in a wide variety of countries, and they have a surprisingly rich perceptual world.

First we discuss vision, then smell, hearing, magnetic sense, electrical sense and finally air pressure perception. Perception, however, is not a tool kit of odd pieces, but an integrated package working as the handmaiden of action – action that is directed towards solving the problems of life that an animal faces. So in the final section we place perception into the context of a specific set of problems that many animals have – the problems inherent in navigation.

Vision

> If the eye were not sunlike,
> It could never see the sun.
> (Goethe)

We do not see all of the world we look at: our view of the world is limited by our eyes' and brain's ability to perceive what is around us. What we see as light, physicists understand to be electromagnetic radiation. Our eyes permit us to see only a small part of the electromagnetic spectrum, wavelengths from about 420 nanometres (violet – Figure 4.1) to about 700 nanometres (red). (One nanometre is one billionth of a metre.) Light from the sun includes wavelengths that are both shorter and longer than those we can see. Longer ones are called infrared – these are responsible for the warming effect of sunlight (still longer wavelengths are radio waves). Shorter wavelengths are ultraviolet – these cause skin cancer. Other species can see into both the infrared and ultraviolet parts of the spectrum. In addition our eyes do not directly report the wavelengths of light that impact on them. Rather we have just three types of colour receptor, each tuned to a different wavelength. That is why two colours mixed together look like a single colour rather than a mixture. A mixture of red and green may stimulate two of our colour receptors in just the same way as the colour yellow, which lies between red and green in the colour spectrum (Figure 4.1), and consequently we see the mixture as the intermediate colour. Red and green do not *become* yellow – they only *seem* yellow. A physicist with a sensitive instrument would be able to distinguish a mixture of red and green from 'real' yellow. Some species have more of these colour receptors than we do and therefore can tell the difference between mixtures of colours and pure colours that to us are indistinguishable. Fish and reptiles, for example, appear to have four colour receptors, birds have as many as six.

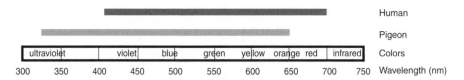

Figure 4.1   Diagram of the electromagnetic spectrum showing the human and pigeon zones of sensitivity

The sun's light has another dimension that is invisible to us – polarity (although under special conditions some people can see a faint coloured pattern, the orientation of which depends on the polarization of the light). Electromagnetic radiation can be thought of as waves passing through space. These waves can oscillate predominately horizontally, vertically or any angle in between. This is their polarity. The only time most of us have any awareness of the polarity of light is when wearing polarized sunglasses. Light reflected from water or glass tends to be horizontally polarized, and so by blocking light polarized in this direction only, polarized sunglasses block the glare caused by reflection. Other species, however, are able to detect the polarization of sunlight. This can be useful in orientation because the polarization of sunlight changes according to the sun's position in the sky. Over 90 species of invertebrate, particularly arthropods (insects, spiders, crustaceans and so on) have been shown to be sensitive to the polarization of sunlight, as have fish and some species of bird.

Since the polarization of sunlight changes with the position of the sun it can be used as a compass. To do this it is not necessary to see the sun itself – any patch of blue sky will suffice. This makes polarization a powerful aid to orientation even on largely overcast days. We shall consider orientation and navigation in the last section of this chapter.

Box 4.1   Investigating the perceptual world of animals

The methods of conditioning outlined in Chapter 3 offer powerful tools to reveal the perceived world of other species.

One flexible procedure is called the 'Go/Nogo' discrimination. This was used by Monika Remy and Jacky Emmerton (1989) to investigate which wavelengths of light pigeons could see in different parts of their eyes. Thirsty birds were trained to mandibulate (open and close their beaks) in return for water only if a light was on. The light came on for 30 seconds and then went off for the same period of time. This pattern of light on followed by light off was repeated 20 times. If the pigeons mandibulated in the dark then they received no water and the period of time they had to wait until the light came back on again was extended by 10 seconds. Pigeons easily learnt to discriminate between the two conditions and within a couple of

Box 4.1 (cont'd)

days of testing were consistently moving their beaks only when the light was on. Obviously, this discrimination between light on and light off can only be learnt if a pigeon can see the light that is being shone on it. If the light is of a wavelength to which the pigeon's eye is not sensitive, then the bird must fail the task. By testing their pigeons with light of different wavelengths, Remy and Emmerton were able to prove that the pigeon's eye is sensitive to ultraviolet.

Another popular procedure is the concurrent operant discrimination. In this situation the subject is given a choice of two (or more) possible responses. For example Juan Delius and his colleagues (1976) gave hungry pigeons a choice of four plastic keys to peck to obtain food. As shown in Figure 4.2, the four pecking keys were arranged at 90° intervals around the box. In the roof of the box was a light fixed with a polarizing filter so that the only light visible to the pigeon was polarized across one or other pair of pecking keys. In order to obtain a food reward the pigeon had to peck one of the two keys that were lined up with the polarization of the light – pecking the other keys produced no food reward. The polarization of the light was changed randomly from trial to trial. The pigeons learnt the correct procedure in about 15 to 20 days of training, showing that they were sensitive to the polarization of the light.

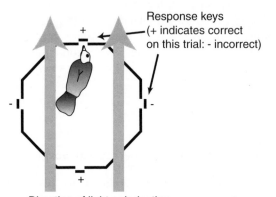

Figure 4.2 The apparatus used by Delius and his colleagues to assess pigeons' sensitivity to the polarization of light. The arrows indicate the direction of polarization of light during the current trial. This was changed randomly from trial to trial (from Delius *et al.*, 1976)

The pigeon's eye view of the world – a case study in animal vision

The human eye is a pretty wonderful instrument, but there is another well-studied eye that has capabilities beyond our own – the eye of the pigeon.

First of all, the arrangement of the two eyes of the pigeon is quite different from in humans. While we see most of our visual fields in stereo (our binocular visual field – the area we see with both eyes – is about 120° out of a total field of view of 200°); pigeons' eyes only coincide in what they see for about 35°, but they have a much larger total visual field – around 340°. They use this small stereo part of their visual field only when considering things close up – when feeding for example. But the large area off to each side that pigeons see with just one eye (the lateral field) means that they can see almost all the way round them (McFadden and Reymond, 1985).

Pigeons can also see into the ultraviolet domain. When looking into the distance (as they do when flying), pigeons use the large, non-overlapping, lateral fields of their eyes. It is these lateral fields that have been shown to be sensitive to ultraviolet light.

When it comes to visual acuity, pigeons are able to bring into focus a seed of about 0.3 millimetres lying at a distance of 50 centimetres. This is only about half as good as the human case (and only one tenth of what a predator bird such as a hawk or eagle can achieve), but it is excellent compared with many other species.

When looking upward and to the sides with their large lateral fields, pigeons have normal or long-sighted vision. When attending to the ground with the frontal field of the eye, however, there is good evidence that pigeons are shortsighted. This combination of shortsightedness in the frontal field and normal or slightly long-sighted vision in the lateral fields means that the eye of the pigeon is perfectly graded for the bird to see both the ground it is standing on and the sky above it, in focus at exactly the same time (Bloch and Martinoya, 1982; Fitzke *et al.*, 1985). Figure 4.3 gives some idea of what the world looks like to a pigeon.

There is also evidence that the pigeon eye can perceive the polarization of light. As discussed in Box 4.1, pigeons can be trained to peck on a key lined up with the direction of polarization of light – even when that polarization changes from moment to moment in a quite artificial manner. In the real world the polarization of sunlight changes as the sun moves across the sky from dawn to dusk. Because all areas of blue sky are polarized, pigeons can use polarization to figure out the position of the sun even when it is not visible, so long as there is sunlight somewhere in the sky. This is useful on largely (though not completely) overcast days and at dusk. We discuss below the sun compass – the Boy Scout's trick of using the position of the sun and the time of day to calculate compass bearings. Awareness of the polarization of sunlight makes it possible for pigeons to use the sun compass even when the sun itself is not visible.

We humans are trichromats – that is, we have three kinds of colour receptor. In essence we have one receptor sensitive to orange-red light (a peak receptivity of around 654 nanometres – see Figure 4.1), one sensitive to blue-green (534

Figure 4.3   Pigeon's eye view. This image is a composite of many photographs pasted together to indicate how the visual world appears to a pigeon. At one and the same time the pigeon can clearly see the grains on the ground in front of it, the distant horizon and most of what is going on behind it without having to change the focus of its eyes

nanometres) and another sensitive to violet-blue (420 nanometres). We can perceive all the hues in between these values because coloured light stimulates more than one of these receptors. A wavelength of around 600 nanometres, which we perceive as an orange light, for example, stimulates both the green and the red receptor. This is why a mixture of green and red can appear indistinguishable from orange – the mixture stimulates the green and red receptors to the same extent as does the 'true' orange light. If we had more than just these three colour receptors then we wouldn't necessarily be fooled by mixtures of primary colours in this way.

The retina of the pigeon contains at least six different kinds of colour receptor. This is partly why they can see the ultraviolet range, and it also means that colour mixtures do not so easily confuse them. Using a Go/Nogo method (see Box 4.1) Adrián Palacios and Francisco Varela (1992) were able to show that there was no mixture of 470 nanometres (blue) and 560 nanometres (yellow) that pigeons would accept as being identical to light of 520 nanometres (green).

Patterns and pictures

It is all very well looking at the specific ability of the pigeon's eye to perceive different aspects of light, but that still leaves open the question of what a pigeon can see when it looks at something.

Several studies have shown that pigeons can perceive three-dimensional objects, and that they can recognize photographs and other two-dimensional images as being the same as the three-dimensional objects they represent. In an interesting study, Cheri Reid and Marcia Spetch (1998) were able to ascertain the kinds of information about three-dimensional depth that pigeons could

Figure 4.4   Examples of the stimuli used by Reid and Spetch (1998). In each pair of objects the image on the left is a three-dimensional representation, the other is either an altered 3-D image (top and middle) or a two-dimensional object (bottom)

extract from two-dimensional images. Pigeons were shown a large number of pairs of computer-generated images of three-dimensional objects. Some of these images are shown in Figure 4.4. For each pair of images, one represented a three-dimensional object with appropriate shading and perspective information (larger at the front than at the back), while the other was a two-dimensional shape – either a shape with appropriate shading but no perspective information, or a shape with the correct perspective but no shading. Using a concurrent discrimination technique (see Box 4.1) Reid and Spetch were able to show that pigeons use both perspective and shading information to recognize the three dimensionality of two-dimensional images. This suggests that three-dimensional objects look similar to pigeons as they do to us.

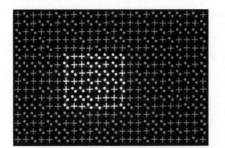 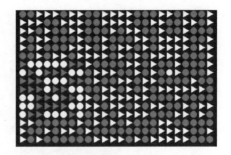

Figure 4.5 Two of the representative displays used by Robert Cook. In the left-hand panel there is a square area that clearly jumps out from the background, while the equivalent area in the right-hand panel is very difficult to spot (courtesy of R. Cook)

As well as the shading and perspective of static objects, we can also detect the movement of a distant object from the way it appears to get larger as it approaches, or smaller as it moves away. You can get this same impression by staring into a rotating spiral. An inward rotating spiral appears to recede away from you, an outward rotating spiral looms towards you. In an ingenious study Carlos Martinoya and Juan Delius (1990) investigated whether pigeons are also prone to this illusion. Using a concurrent discrimination procedure (see Box 4.1) and precision, computer-drawn spirals with windings of several different degrees of tightness spun at different speeds, Martinoya and Delius were able to establish that pigeons can discriminate between apparently approaching and apparently retreating visual patterns.

Robert Cook (1992) has also investigated whether pigeons perceive patterns in a similar way as humans do. One striking aspect of our perception of the visual world is the way in which certain features tend to jump out from their background. In Figure 4.5, for example, the figure on the left clearly shows a square area of different colour that stands out from the background. The figure on the right contains a similar square area but it is very difficult to spot. This is because the square area in the left-hand panel is made up of elements that differ in colour from those in the background, while the square area in the right-hand panel is made up of elements of a different combination of form and colour from the background items (the background elements are light triangles and dark circles, while the square area is composed of dark triangles and light circles). Just like people, pigeons find it more difficult to find the special square area in the right-hand panel than that in the left-hand panel.

How can we tell if the world looks similar to pigeons as it does to us? One thing to look for is whether pigeons confuse similar items. Donald and Patricia Blough (1997) trained pigeons to discriminate between the various letters of the alphabet, and then investigated which ones the pigeons found easy to discriminate between and which were more difficult. They found that the pigeons' difficulties lay mainly with the same letters that people are most likely to confuse, such as A versus R and B versus P.

One indication that the visual world of pigeons may differ from our own comes from an interesting study by Juan Delius and Valerie Hollard (1987). Objects in the world around us present themselves at many different angles. A chair with its back to you is visually very different from the same chair with the seat towards you – and yet both are recognized as the same object: a chair. Delius and Hollard demonstrated that pigeons could also recognize rotated objects as being the same item, no matter what the angle of rotation. The difference from the human case lies in the length of time it takes to make the recognition decision. When humans are asked to identify whether two items that look similar are really the same or different, they take longer to make this decision the further round one object has been rotated relative to the other. In pigeons, on the other hand, the time taken to make the recognition decision does not depend on the angle of rotation. Perhaps the pigeon's avian lifestyle has led to the development of a different system for recognizing objects. It is possible that the view of a flying animal more often contains rotated objects, and therefore pigeons recognize rotated forms more quickly. Whatever the fate of this theory (and a more recent study with a different procedure suggests that pigeons' recognition decision *is* influenced by the angle of rotation of a stimulus – see Hamm *et al.*, 1997), the pigeon has provided many hints of a quite different perceptual world from our own.

Smell

Smell is not usually a particularly salient aspect of our perceptual experience, but for other species it can be very important indeed. Their strong sense of smell enables animals to pick up low concentrations of chemicals in the atmosphere. This ability is useful for finding food (either other animals in the case of predators, or vegetable matter for herbivores), or to avoid becoming food (by smelling the approach of a predator). But smell can also function as a simple form of communication, as when one member of a species releases a chemical that influences the behaviour of other members of that species. Later in this chapter we consider the evidence that pigeons use smell in the process of homing from distant release sites. There is also evidence that other species of bird use smell to find their nests when young. Eduardo Mínguez (1997) studied British storm-petrel chicks at their nesting sites on the island of Benidorm. Mínguez moved young chicks a little way from their nests, blocked their nostrils and then observed whether they were able to find their way back. With blocked nostrils, none of the chicks could find its nest, whereas with their nostrils unblocked they all found their way home.

Many insects use chemicals, known as pheromones, as a simple means of communication. Male currant clearwings, for example, are attracted to the pheromone emitted by females of their species, as are male American cockroaches and many other insect species. Pheromones with a variety of functions have been identified in the fruit fly. These range from those that act to attract other fruit flies to those that cause a fruit fly that senses them to jump. Bumblebees construct scent trails from nest entrance to nest core. Termites also follow scent trails.

Digger wasps recognize prey using chemical cues picked up on their antennae. Several species of fish use pheromones to attract sex partners in a similar manner to that of insects.

Mammals of many species are able to recognize specific individuals on the basis of their smell. Turkish hamsters, for example, are able to detect even the subtle odour differences between brothers (Heth *et al.*, 1999). Giant pandas have also been shown to be capable of discriminating between the odours of different individuals in their species. In one experimental study, both male and female giant pandas were able to discriminate between different male giant panda urine odours, but neither sex could reliably discriminate between different female urine odours (Swaisgood *et al.*, 1999).

Female house mice kept in seminatural enclosures prefer the odour of adult male mice to that of juvenile male mice, and they also prefer the odour of male mice captured within 20 metres of their own nests to the odour of more distant males. When they are at their most sexually receptive, female mice prefer the odour of dominant male mice, but at other times in their sexual cycle they exhibit no such preference (Mossman and Drickamer, 1996).

Pregnancy in female bank voles can be aborted if the females are exposed early in the pregnancy to the pheromones from a male bank vole that is not the father. Malgorzata Kruczek (1998) has demonstrated that during this vulnerable early phase of pregnancy female bank voles prefer the odour of their sex partner to that of another male bank vole. Later in the pregnancy this preference wanes, but it returns during lactation.

Not only do predator mammals find their prey by smell, but also prey mammals avoid areas on the basis of predator smell. Hedgehogs prefer to forage at sites contaminated with the scent of animals that do not prey on them (such as chipmunks) than at sites smelling of predator (badger) (Ward *et al.*, 1997). Water voles avoid cages containing the odour of predators (American mink and brown rat), but show no aversion to cages with a novel control odour (sheep) (Barreto and MacDonald, 1999). Interestingly the voles in these experiments had never encountered American mink before, so their response was largely innate. Mice show a stronger reaction to the odour of cat faeces when the cats have been feeding on mice than when they have been fed a vegetarian diet (Berton *et al.*, 1998).

It used to be believed that birds were almost without any sense of smell. However research from the 1960s onwards has definitively shown that this earlier view was false. It seems likely that all birds have some sense of smell, and some – particularly ground-nesting, water-associated birds – have especially large olfactory bulbs in their brains, suggesting a major role for smell in their lives. Despite this suggestive evidence there are few species of bird whose sense of smell has been studied to any great degree. The olfactory sense of one species that has been studied in some detail – the pigeon – is discussed later in this chapter (under 'Navigation').

Another species whose sense of smell has been investigated is the domestic fowl. Individually housed chicks prefer the smell of wood shavings that have served as their own bedding to that of clean wood shavings or those soiled by another chick.

They also prefer the smell of orange oil if they have been brought up with that smell in their home cages, but not if they have not experienced the scent of orange early in life. Male and female seven-day-old chicks avoided a cloth that had been rubbed over a cat, but not a cloth treated with water or disinfectant. Rather strangely, however, older chicks did not show this aversion. Similar results were obtained with a cloth stained with blood. In general, chickens show a preference for familiar odours over novel ones (Jones and Roper, 1997).

Hearing

Many animals use sound to detect predators or prey, and some (including birds, humans and many other mammals) also communicate with sound. Most animals that use sound to find objects in the world around them rely on the sounds that others make – either intentionally or despite their best efforts to remain silent. A few, however, such as some bats and dolphins, orient themselves by listening for the return echo from sounds they produce themselves especially for that purpose.

Humans and birds that are specialized for locating prey with sound, such as owls and harriers, can locate the position of a sound source to within 2° of arc (that is, 2° out of a total of 360°). Barn owls have been found capable of estimating the distance between themselves and a simulated mouse target with an error of about 10 per cent. It is possible to locate the source of a sound because the signal that reaches each of the two ears differs slightly according to where the sound originated. The further apart the ears are, the easier it is to locate the position of a sound. Smaller birds should therefore have more difficulty identifying the location of a sound because their ears are closer together. However Brian Nelson and Philip Stoddard (1998) have found that, in their natural habitat, eastern towhees, a North American passerine (perching bird), are able to estimate distance with an error of just 7 per cent, and direction with an error of about 9°. The success of these birds, whose ears are only about 1 cm apart, may have been because the experimenters played to male towhees the calls of other male towhees. Since these birds are highly territorial, locating the calls of other members of their species is extremely important to them.

Sound is the product of waves of pressure travelling through the air. Human hearing covers a range of around 100 Hz to nearly 20 kHz. Several species of rodent (including chinchilla, fox squirrel, gerbil, guinea pig and kangaroo rat) have good low-frequency hearing (below 150 Hz). Bats, which echolocate (Box 4.2) using clicks generated either with the tongue or in the throat, have the ability to hear much higher frequencies than other animals. Egyptian fruit bats, which make their echolocating clicks with the tongue, can hear sounds of up to 64 kHz (around two octaves higher than the highest for humans). Bats that use clicks made in the throat for echolocation, such as the big and little brown bats, the Indian false vampire bat, the fish-catching bat and the greater horseshoe bat, can hear sounds of up to 100 kHz – about three octaves higher than the highest tones audible to humans. Dolphins of several echolocating species can also hear sounds of up to 100 kHz.

Box 4.2   Bat echolocation

For centuries the ability of bats to fly in complete darkness without bashing into things, and even to catch flying insects on the wing, was a deep mystery. Back in the eighteenth century, experiments with blinded and deafened bats had suggested that hearing, and not vision, was the critical sense that bats were using. However in the absence of any sounds audible to the human ear, and due to the difficulty of imagining how the sense of hearing could be of any use in navigation, the bat's ability to fly in the dark remained a mystery.

Only in 1941, with the publication of a series of simple but elegant experiments by Donald Griffin and Robert Galambos, did it become clear that bats were producing ultrasound (sounds of a higher pitch than humans can hear) and listening to the echoes in order to perceive the world around them. Griffin and Galambos temporarily covered the ears, mouth or eyes of several species of bat and set them the task of flying through a room containing several vertical wires. Whereas bats with their eyes covered were unperturbed, bats with their ears or mouths covered were reluctant to fly at all, and if forced to fly were quite unable to fly around the wires in the room. Using (for the time) high tech recording devices, Griffin and Galambos were able to determine that the bats were emitting ultrasonic vocalizations while flying.

While blindfolded people can reliably tell if they are in a large or small room, or outdoors, on the basis of the quality of the echoes of footsteps and other noises, further studies with ultrasonic recording devices soon made clear that bats' abilities go way beyond anything a human can do. In the late 1950s Griffin and his associates demonstrated that bats could locate, track and capture flying moths, small flies and mosquitoes using their sonar system. Bats emit ultrasonic 'chirps' lasting about 15 milliseconds when searching, which changes to a continuous 'buzz' when attacking or avoiding an obstacle. But the evolutionary arms race of predator and prey is rarely a one-sided battle, and in 1961 Kenneth Roeder and Asher Treat demonstrated that the noctuid moth, a species regularly preyed upon by North American bats, had a specialized tympanic organ for the detection of bat ultrasound.

Subsequent research in Europe and North America on several species of bat indicates that they typically echolocate their prey within two metres. They accurately correct the tone of the sounds they emit to allow for the distortion of the sounds caused by their own movement through the environment.

The echolocating ability of at least some species of bat is so finely tuned that the bats can perceive the texture of a surface or a change in the wing beat of a moth. James Simmons and his colleagues (1998) report that big brown bats can detect a difference of just 0.3 millimetres between two surfaces. Anne Grossetête and Cynthia Moss (1998) report that the same species of bat can also discriminate between an artificial moth wing beating 50 and 41 times per second.

Box 4.2   (cont'd)

What is becoming clear from the more recent work on bat echolocation is that the phenomenon has been misnamed: we are not dealing simply with a system of location, but also of perception. Echoperception enables bats to 'see' the world – not just to avoid obstacles but also to perceive the position, shape and texture of objects, 'see' the beating wings of an insect and presumably the wing flaps of other bats. Though the nature of their night-time world is hard for us to imagine, it must be a very rich sensory world indeed, not at all like the blank darkness that we perceive.

But as our understanding of the echoworld of the bat has developed, so too has our awareness of the ability of their prey to avoid capture. Shortly after it was discovered that moths could hear bat echo signals, it was also found that these moths emit ultrasound clicks of their own. James Fullard and his colleagues (1994) have demonstrated that the moths refrain from making their own clicks until the bat has shifted from its searching phase to the terminal attack phase. The clicks the moth then emits interfere with the bat's ultrasounds, reflecting them off the moth and sufficiently confusing the attacking bat to cause it to abort its attack.

Several species of dolphin have also been shown, using similar methods to those used with bats, to be capable of echolocation. The sensitivity of the dolphins studied thus far does not quite match that of bats, but Atlantic bottlenose dolphins have been found to be capable of identifying differences in the thickness of objects of about three millimetres, and they can determine the distance of an object from themselves with an accuracy of around one centimetre at a distance of one metre (Au, 1997).

Magnetic sensitivity

The suggestion that some species are sensitive to magnetic fields is a very controversial one. The various opinions on the question of whether pigeons use sensitivity to the earth's magnetic field to find their way home are discussed below in the section on navigation. Though the possession of magnetic sensitivity has been suggested for many species, there are few in which sensitivity to magnetic fields is beyond dispute. The waggle dance of the bee, for example, whereby bees communicate to hive mates the direction and distance from the hive of sources of food (see Chapter 8), may be disrupted by magnetic fields. Bees have also been trained in experiments to choose food placed on top of a magnet in preference to a less rich (but otherwise identical looking) food source not placed on a magnet (Walker and Bitterman, 1985).

Migrating fish (see Box 4.3 below) may also depend on magnetic fields to aid navigation, as may rats and other rodents. Magnetic material has even been found in the bodies of monarch butterflies, though whether it enables them to use magnetic fields to navigate remains an open question.

Electrical sense

Several species of fish, some amphibians and even a few mammals, such as the platypus and star-nosed mole, are sensitive to electric fields. Weak electric fields are generated by the muscles in an animal's body and vary as the animal moves. Consequently a sensitivity to electric fields can help a predator animal find its prey in situations where other senses are not much help, such as fish that catch crayfish lurking in silty river beds.

While most animals are content to use the energy already in the world around them to find things, a few produce signals of their own, whose echo tells them about the state of the world. Echolocating bats have already been mentioned (Box 4.2). Although we may not make much use of echoes – especially not in the very high-frequency range utilized by bats – we have all heard echoes at some time, so the notion is not completely alien to us. Stranger to imagine, however, is what the world must feel like to those animals that perceive the world by 'listening' for the electric echo produced by the reflection of electric fields they have produced themselves.

Weakly electric African fish are nocturnal animals from South America and Africa. They produce weak electric fields using an organ in the tail and possess sensor organs under the skin along both sides of the body. By attending to the electric field reflected back onto their bodies from the objects around them, they are able to form an impression of what surrounds them in the dark water. These fish are confronted with a special problem if they want to find out how far away an object is. For the senses most commonly used to find distance information (hearing and vision), animals have a pair of receptors separated by some distance. The animal can estimate how far away an object is from the difference in signal strength received by these two receptors (ears or eyes). The weakly electric African fish cannot do this however, because the electric field reflected off an object will only fall on one side of the fish. Furthermore the size of the reflected electric field cannot be used as a cue to find distance, because a nearby large object will reflect a similar sized electric field to a distant small object (electric reflections, like shadows, become larger the further away the object is).

Gerhard von der Emde and his colleagues (1998) have shown not only that these fish are capable of estimating distances, but also how they do so. Figure 4.6 shows one of these fish. What changes as the object moves closer, apart from the size of the electric reflection, is the sharpness of the edges of the reflection. A closer object has a sharper edged electric reflection than a more distant object. Von

Figure 4.6   Weakly electric African fish (photograph courtesy of G. von der Emde)

der Emde *et al.* tricked the electric fish with objects that were situated the same distance from the fish but differed in the sharpness of their electric reflections, and were thereby able to confirm that the edge sharpness of the reflected electric field was the critical factor that enabled the fish to determine distance.

Sensitivity to air pressure

One species – the pigeon again – has been shown to be sensitive to changes in air pressure (Kreithen and Keeton, 1974). These changes are equivalent to a difference in altitude of just 10 metres (about 33 feet). As well as providing altitude information to a flying animal, air pressure also changes with the weather (which is what is shown by barometers) and could therefore indicate to a migratory animal when the season has come to migrate.

Navigation

So many wonderful perceptual abilities – but what are they good for? It is unlikely that evolution would have equipped animals with these abilities without there being some need for them. And there is one very major problem that faces many animals that demands finely honed perceptual abilities – the problem of navigation.

Humans are almost incapable of navigation. Of course we can find our way to the corner shop and back, but real navigation – finding our way across an ocean or a desert – is something we have only been able to do reliably in the last few hundred years through the development of increasingly complex pieces of technology. Without these devices, when stuck on a boat on an ocean without a radio, compass or global positioning system device we are almost completely helpless.

Pigeons, on the other hand, are fully capable of finding their way home from places they have never visited before and that lie up to 1800 kilometres (1300 miles) from home. Careful tests have shown that pigeons can find their way home even if they are kept in visual, magnetic and olfactory isolation on the outward journey, with continuous rotation of their cages so that they cannot keep track of the direction in which they are being taken.

Although bees do not fly the distances that pigeons can cover, their ability to find their way back to the same patch of nectar-bearing flowers is no less dramatic on its own scale than that of homing pigeons over longer distances. To the skill of homing, bees add the ability to communicate the direction and distance of nectar sites to their hive mates (see Chapter 8).

Pigeon homing

The sun compass

Well-trained boy scouts find north by pointing 12 o'clock on their watch at the sun: south is half way between the hour hand and the 12 (or north in the southern hemisphere). This trick, known as the sun compass, works because the sun progresses from east to west via south (north in the southern hemisphere) during the course of each day. So if you know what time it is and where the sun is, you can figure out compass directions.

In a series of ingenious experiments, pigeons have been shown to be able to use the boy scouts' trick of considering the position of the sun and the time of day to find north, or any other direction they need. Pigeons, like most animals, have a clear sense of the time of day (see Chapter 5), which they combine with the position of the sun to find any bearing. This was demonstrated by training birds in an enclosed box. They could only receive a reward by pecking on a plastic key lined up in a certain compass direction. First the birds were trained to peck onto the plastic key placed in the east corner of the box with normal sunlight coming into the box. It was found that they could learn this without difficulty. Next the birds were trained with sunlight coming into the box as normal, but then tested under conditions where the light appeared to come from a different direction because mirrors had been used to shift the apparent light source. It was found that if the sunlight was reflected by 90° in one direction then the pigeons would peck on the key in the north corner of the box – with 90° reflection in the other direction the pigeons pecked on the south key (Schmidt-Koenig et al., 1991). This experiment demonstrates that pigeons use the source of the sun's rays to identify compass directions.

As we saw earlier in this chapter, pigeons are also sensitive to the polarization of sunlight. This means that they can find the sun's position by means of the polarization of sunlight in any patch of clear sky, and they can utilize the sun compass even on partially overcast days, or at dusk after the sun has dipped below the horizon. But do pigeons actually use the sun compass to find their way home when they are displaced hundreds of kilometres from their home loft? To see if this was the case, Schmidt-Koenig et al. first confused the pigeons about the time of day. A pigeon's sense of the time of day comes from the sunrise and sunset entraining its circadian clock (see Chapter 5). To confuse the birds about the time of day the lights in their home aviary were switched on and switched off six hours earlier than usual (for other birds the lights were turned on and off six hours later than usual). When they were released to fly home from a distant site birds that had been exposed to the days that had started and ended six hours earlier than normal flew off in a direction that was 90° off the correct compass direction – in other words they made exactly the same error that a boy scout would if he had been given a watch that was six hours off the correct time.

More recent studies have indicated that experienced pigeons are not thrown off course by clock shifts as much as they ought to be. Furthermore homing pigeons can home successfully on completely overcast days when no blue sky is visible. Both these facts indicate that the sun compass cannot be the only navigation aid for homing pigeons.

Magnetic compass

Every boy scout true to his creed ('Be prepared!') will carry with him a proper magnetic compass whenever he is out and about. A magnetic compass works because there is a magnetic field around the whole planet that can be thought of as an ordinary bar magnet, with north close to the north pole and south close to the south pole. There is much controversy about whether pigeons are sensitive enough to the earth's magnetic field to be able to use it when finding their way home.

Indirect evidence that pigeons might be using the earth's magnetic field to help them navigate comes from the observation that birds are slower to reach home when there is high sunspot activity – sunspots interfere with the earth's magnetic field. Magnetic storms also disrupt pigeon homing, or at least according to some studies. In an extensive series of studies conducted over several years at two sites in North America, William Keeton and his colleagues (see Wiltschko and Wiltschko, 1996) found that the homing direction of a group of pigeons varied according to the amount of background magnetic activity. A more direct way of testing the hypothesis that pigeons can navigate by the earth's magnetic field is to strap a small magnet onto a pigeon's head – this should create an additional, larger magnetic field that makes magnetic navigation impossible. Keeton's group tried this and found a small shift in the pigeons' homing bearings (3° to the left). The small magnitude of this divergence is a little strange, since the field created by placing a magnet on the pigeon's head should have been large compared with the earth's natural magnetic field. Subsequent studies have failed to replicate this result, and another study in North America found that magnets attached to pigeons' heads caused a navigational shift in the opposite direction. However European studies have found course variations that lie in the same direction as Keeton's original results.

Hence the evidence for a magnetic compass in pigeons is mixed. It is quite possible that different pigeons in different places may rely on magnetic information to different degrees. Charles Walcott (1991), for example, reports that areas of magnetic anomaly on the earth's surface confused the homing bearing of one group of pigeons, but not of another group. There may have been strain differences between different groups of pigeons, or these birds may have relied on different cues depending on the kind of terrain they normally flew over.

Odour maps

Despite the above, no compass system, sun-based or magnetic, can explain how a pigeon, having been transported 600 kilometres (400 miles) in the back of a truck to a place it has never visited before, can find the correct bearing to fly home. For a compass – any kind of compass – to be of use, you need to have at least a rough idea of where you are relative to where you are trying to go. The biggest unsolved riddle in pigeon navigation is how these birds choose the right direction home from places they have never visited before.

Many European researchers are convinced that pigeons use their sense of smell to find their way home from distant release sites. These scientists propose that even locked up in their cages, pigeons are exposed to different odours depending on which way the wind is blowing. Consequently when inexperienced pigeons are trucked out to an unfamiliar site and released, they can figure out which direc-

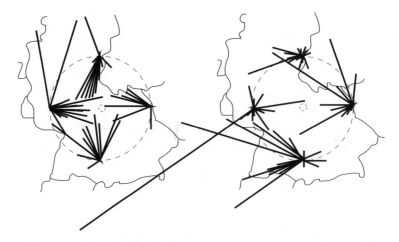

Figure 4.7   Homing of anosmic pigeons. Inexperienced homing pigeons released at sites about 180 kilometres from their home loft at least headed for home in approximately the right direction (left-hand panel), even if they were not always totally successful in getting home. Pigeons deprived of their sense of smell, however (right-hand panel), headed off in random directions. The central dot is the home loft (Würzburg), and the borders of the then West Germany are shown (from Wallraff, 1980)

tion they have come from on the basis of the smells they have passed through on their trip to the release site. This suggestion is supported by an experiment in which one group of pigeons was raised in cages open to the outside air while another was raised in an air-conditioned unit that excluded all odours from the outside world. When these two groups of pigeons, which had been driven to the same location, were subsequently released, only those pigeons brought up in cages open to the air were able to find their way home. Similarly pigeons that were raised normally but had their nostrils blocked before being taken out and released, had difficulty finding the correct direction home (see Able, 1996; Wiltschko, 1996).

Figure 4.7 compares the homing success of a group of anosmic pigeons (birds that had had their nostrils blocked so they could not smell anything) and a normal control group of pigeons. All were transported around 180 kilometres from their home loft to sites they had never visited before, and then released. Whereas the majority of the control birds found their way home fairly directly, very few of the anosmic birds homed successfully (Wallraff, 1990).

Another experiment suggesting a role for smell in pigeon homing involved driving two groups of pigeons along different routes to the same release site. Presumably, along these different routes the two groups passed through regions with different smells (Figure 4.8). After their release the two groups followed different flight paths back to their home loft – each group of pigeons headed more in the direction in which they had been brought (Baker, 1980).

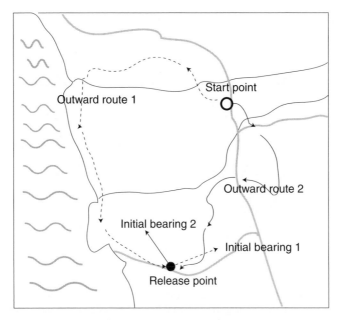

Figure 4.8   Pigeons taken out on two different routes return by two different paths (from Baker, 1980)

Paolo Ioalé and his colleagues (1990) carried out a more direct test of the odour hypothesis. These researchers kept a group of pigeons in an aviary where fans blew air containing an odorous chemical (benzaldehyde) across the pigeons (left side of figure 4.9). This smelly artificial wind was directed from the north. Later the pigeons were taken to a distant site, benzaldehyde was painted onto their nostrils and they were released. All of these pigeons headed off in a southerly direction – the opposite direction from which the benzaldehyde had come in their home cages (right side of figure 4.9). This makes sense in terms of an odour map. If one smell predominates in winds from the north, and birds are released with that smell on their nostrils, then they may reasonably conclude that since the smell is at high levels of intensity they must be north of their home cage, and should therefore head south in order to return home.

For each of the possible navigational strategies considered here – sun compass, magnetic compass and odour maps – contradictory studies exist. In particular, older and more experienced birds continue to navigate successfully under exper- imental conditions where the manipulation of one or other navigational system should throw them off course. The obvious answer to this apparent paradox is that with increasing experience homing pigeons learn to integrate navigational information from more than one source, and that if one type of information is unreliable the other types are given a heavier weighting when choosing a course home.

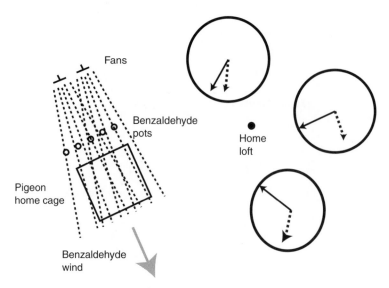

Figure 4.9   Experimental pigeons kept in a home aviary (left-hand diagram) through which the odour of benzaldehyde is blown by fans. The three circles indicate the release bearings of birds from three different sites. The solid dot between the three circles indicates the direction of the home aviary from each of these three release sites. For the control birds (those not previously exposed to benzaldehyde: solid lines), the home bearings were accurate from all three release sites. The experimental birds, however (dashed lines), all headed in a southerly direction (from Wallraff, 1990)

Box 4.3   Migration

A surprisingly wide range of species undertake a major migration at some point in their lives. The numerous species of bird that make an annual move from their winter to their summer homes are but the best-known examples of a very large contingent. Spiny lobsters migrate down the coast of islands in the Bahamas every autumn. Locust swarms migrate many thousands of kilometres (though they never retrace their steps). Monarch butterflies in the new world migrate over 3000 kilometres southwards in the autumn and return north in the spring. About 120 species of fish migrate between fresh water and the sea, including eels and several species of salmon. European eel larvae migrate on a three-year journey from their hatching grounds in the Sargasso Sea in the North Atlantic to their adult homes in Europe or Africa. Salmon spawn in autumn and winter in freshwater lakes or streams and the young later head out into the ocean. In approximately three years the now mature offspring themselves return to the same spawning grounds to breed. Amphibians such as newts, salamanders, frogs and toads are reported to migrate relatively short distances (a few kilometres) to and from breeding ponds in spring. Turtles are the record holders among migrating reptiles. The green turtle covers a round trip

Box 4.3   (cont'd)

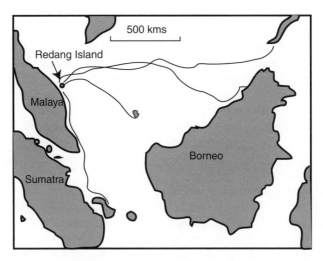

500 kms

Redang Island

Malaya

Borneo

Sumatra

Figure 4.10   Migration path of green turtles tracked by satellite from Redang Island in West Malaysia (from Papi and Luschi, 1996)

of nearly 2000 kilometres between its breeding grounds on Ascension Island (in the middle of the South Atlantic) and the Brazilian coast. Individual green turtles return to breed on the exact same beach every three years. Quite how they achieve this largely remains a mystery, although it seems very likely that sensitivity to magnetic fields plays an important role. It is possible that turtles are sensitive not just to the direction of the earth's magnetic field, as a compass is, but also to the strength of the earth's magnetic field. This would provide them with extra positional information.

Among mammals, the record for the longest migration also goes to an aquatic family – the whales. Whales such as the grey whale migrate each year between their warmer breeding grounds and a cooler summer feeding area. Several species of large land-based mammals are quite accomplished migrators too, such as elks, gnus, moose, caribou and zebras, which move annually between feeding grounds that differ in their productivity at different times of the year. The caribou of Canada, for example, spend summers in the more northern areas where they can feed on the leaves of low branches, but move about 500 kilometres south in the winter to feed on lichens and grasses.

Many of the perceptual and navigational abilities of the homing pigeon, such as use of a sun compass, sensitivity to the polarization of sunlight, magnetic sense and odour guidance, have been demonstrated in several migrating species. In addition some species that migrate at night make use of the stars to navigate, as ancient mariners did. Sylviid warblers and indigo bunting have been tested under planetarium domes. These experiments demonstrated that star patterns alone were sufficient to enable these night-migrating species to find their migratory direction. When the stars in the planetarium were turned off, the birds were confused as to which direction they should head (Emlen, 1970).

Bees foraging

The brain of the bee is only about one cubic millimetre in size – about the size of a single grain of sand. And yet the cognitive feats of bees, which fly up to two kilometres (over a mile) from the hive to forage on flowers before finding the correct way home, are certainly not trivial. As we shall see in Chapter 8, once back at the hive they can also communicate the location and distance of the feeding site to their hive mates.

The first trick that bees have in their navigational toolbox is the sun compass, already discussed above. Just like boy scouts and pigeons, bees are able to use the position of the sun, combined with a knowledge of the time of day, to estimate the points of the compass.

The next strategy available to foraging bees is an awareness of how far they have travelled – this is known as 'dead reckoning'. Dead reckoning means keeping track of how far one has travelled and in what directions. The bee knows how far it has travelled, not from the amount of energy it has expended in flying, nor from the sensation of air moving past it, but on the basis of the visual images moving past its eyes. This was demonstrated in experiments in wind tunnels in which bees were not confused by different head and tail winds that changed the amount of energy they had to expend in flying and the sensation of air moving past them. However the bees were confused about the distance they had to fly if the patterning on the walls of the wind tunnel was changed so that it looked as though they had covered more ground than they really had (Srinivasan *et al.*, 1996).

But dead reckoning, even aided by a sun compass, is an inexact business. Small errors at the beginning of a journey become progressively larger as the trip continues, and reversing the process to fly home means that errors might have become dangerously large by the time the hive should have been reached. For more accurate navigation, bees also have the ability to use land-marks they see along the route. Exactly how they do this is the subject of some controversy.

It is clear that bees flying to and from the hive use landmarks such as rows of trees, hills or other salient features to find their way. It seems that as they fly out they commit scenes to memory, which they then use to guide themselves on future trips. This has been demonstrated by experiments in which bees were captured and then released in the vicinity of landmarks that were in sight of the hive or the foraging site. Experiments using a landmark that could be moved by the experimenters (a car) pointed to a similar conclusion (Menzel *et al.*, 1996).

A claim that bees use landmarks in a far more complex way was made by James Gould (1986). Gould proposed that bees not only recognize landmarks when they are heading to or from a foraging site, but also that the bees' representations of landmarks are integrated into a proper map. A map is something much more than just a set of landmarks with information about which way you should head as you pass by them. I can find my way to an unfamiliar spot if I am given such information as 'turn right at the lights by the vet', 'head straight past the football field' and so on. However if I get lost, or want to approach this unfamiliar spot from a different direction, then this route-sketch method is completely ineffective. If I have a proper map, on the other hand, I should be able to find my way even if I take a wrong turning, and I can find my way no matter which direction I am coming from. A map is a far superior instrument to a route sketch, but it is also far more complex – is it really possible for one to be constructed and stored in the sand-grain sized brain of the bee?

The most direct way to test if a person or a bee really has a mental map or is just relying on landmarks is to let them travel some way along their route and then capture them and remove them to another place, before releasing them to see if they can figure out which way to go. This is just what Gould did with his bees, and he found that after being captured and displaced by the experimenters the bees were able to correct their course for their goal when released – he therefore reasoned that they were using mental maps. For several years other researchers attempted to replicate Gould's results, but without success. However the explanation for Gould's success and the other researchers' failure to demonstrate mental maps in bees now seems to have been found.

Imagine you are travelling in a car using a route sketch to find your way somewhere, but that you are displaced from your route and have to find your way back. In general you will be completely lost. However if your route sketch includes things such as 'head for the mountains' or 'keep the cliffs on your left', you may well be able to find your way even after quite a large displacement. It seems that this was the situation for Gould's displaced bees – they were still able to see some relevant landmarks from their displaced position. A better test of whether bees have mental maps involves displacing them to a position where landmarks are definitely not visible. In a test of this type, shown in Figure 4.11, the displaced bees were definitely unable to find their way (see also Dyer, 1996).

There is still much to be learnt about just how the sand-grain brain of the bee integrates sun compass, dead reckoning and landmark information flexibly and reliably enough to find its way to and from sources of food (and communicate this information to its hive mates), but it seems that constructing a proper mental map is not one of their abilities.

Conclusions

Taken as a grab bag of almost magical abilities, the perceptual worlds of animals are like something out of science fiction. But we can be sure that what we are considering here are solutions to various problems that have come up during evolution. Colour vision, for example, is what enables humans and birds to differentiate ripe berries from unripe ones – food from poison. The hearing of bats, specialized to pick up very high frequencies, is essential to their echolocation system. Finely tuned hearing is also central to the evolutionary arms race between

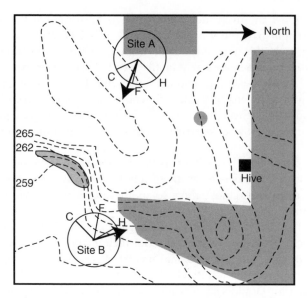

Figure 4.11 Evidence that bees do not have a proper cognitive map. Shaded areas are trees; open areas are grass. Contour lines show elevation in metres. Circles show the release bearings of bees that were heading from the hive towards a feeder placed at the other site when they were captured. From each release site bees might fly towards the hive (shown as H in the circle diagram); the feeding site (F); or the compass direction they were heading in when caught (C). From site A, bees could see the landmarks that had been visible from their original foraging flight and so corrected their paths successfully and flew predominantly in the direction of the feeder they had originally been heading for. From site B, however, the landmarks of their original foraging route were not visible, and so they were unable to correct for the displacement that they had been exposed to, and when released they headed predominantly homewards (H) (from Dyer, 1991)

predator and prey: predators use their ears to find prey, and prey use theirs to catch sound of the predators first.

Often, though, we can see the solution – the perceptual ability – but can only hazard a guess at the nature of the problem it is solving. Why, for example, do pigeons have six colour receptor channels and the ability to see ultraviolet? Francisco Varela and his colleagues (1993), when considering the question of why pigeons (and other birds) can see ultraviolet, turned the question on its head: 'the question is not "Why do many animals see ultraviolet?" but rather "Why is it that most mammals do not?"' Ultraviolet light shows up more of the pattern in the coats of animals, in flowers and in blue sky than we can see. Varela *et al.* suggest that the reason why mammals lack ultraviolet sensitivity is not that they lack a use for such vision, but that a long evolutionary history of nocturnal habits has limited the functionality of the mammalian eye in daylight. Thus evolution not only solves problems but, because of its historical nature, it is also constrained in how it can go about solving them.

FURTHER READING

Schiller, C H (ed. and trans.) (1957) *Instinctive behavior:The development of a modern concept* (New York: International Universities Press). This volume contains an English translation of Jakob von Uexküll's (1934) *Streifzüge durch die Umwelten von Tieren und Menschen* ('A stroll through the world of animals and men'), from which the quote and example at the start of this chapter were taken.

Zeigler, H P and Bischof, H-J (eds) (1993) *Vision, Brain, and Behavior in Birds* (Cambridge, MA: MIT Press). Many aspects of bird vision are reviewed in this wide-ranging book.

Wiese, K, Gribakin, F G, Popov, A V and Renninger, G (eds) (1993) *Sensory Systems of Arthropods* (Basel: Birkhäuser Verlag). In this volume smell and other sensory systems in arthropods are reviewed.

The best recent source on animal navigation (including migration and homing) is a special issue of the *Journal of Experimental Biology* dedicated to this topic (vol. 199, part 1, 1996, also available on the web at http://www.biologists.com/JEB/). Many of the examples in this chapter were drawn from that source.

Berthold, P (1991) *Orientation in Birds* (Basel: Birkhäuser Verlag). This book contains many excellent chapters on pigeon homing.

Gould, J L and Gould, C G (1988) *The Honey Bee* (New York: Scientific American Library). This entertainingly written book contains a wealth of information on honeybee perception and navigation.

WEBSITES

This excellent site describes the perceptual world of the shark
http://www.pbs.org/wgbh/nova/sharks/hotsciencesharks/

The following site makes a serious attempt to show the world through the eyes of a bee http://cvs.anu.edu.au/andy/beye/beyehome.html

A good site on weakly electric fish is
http://www.bbb.caltech.edu/ElectricFish/index.html

5
Other Ways of Seeing the World – II: Abstract Dimensions

'What sort of insects do you rejoice in, where *you* come from?' the Gnat inquired.

'I don't *rejoice* in insects at all,' Alice explained, 'because I'm rather afraid of them – at least the large kinds. But I can tell you the names of some of them.'

'Of course they answer to their names?' the Gnat remarked carelessly.

'I never knew them do it.'

'What's the use of their having names,' the Gnat said, 'if they won't answer to them?'

'No use to *them*,' said Alice; 'but it's useful to the people who name them, I suppose. If not, why do things have names at all?'

'I can't say,' the Gnat replied. (Lewis Carroll, *Through the Looking Glass*, 1871)

The way the world appears to an animal is not just a question of the animal's perceptual abilities – what it can hear, see, smell or sense in any other way. There is also the question of how the pieces of experience can be put together to organize the relationship between raw perceptual experience and what is going on in the world. It is this more abstract level of conceptual perception that is the subject of this chapter.

Research on the ability of animals to form concepts is, with a few worthy exceptions, the product of just the last few decades. Consequently it is not surprising that most of the research carried out so far has taken human conceptual abilities as its starting point. While there is a danger here of failing to take an appropriately species-centred point of view, experimental tasks used in human psychology, particularly those designed by developmental psychologists, have certainly proven useful.

We start this chapter with a discussion of a very simple extension from direct perceptual experience – the question of object permanence. Can an animal understand that a hidden object continues to exist even when it is out of sight? This apparently simple concept does not appear to be clear to most of the species that have been tested. A handful of not very closely related species (dogs, chimpanzees and gorillas) can solve even the most difficult object permanence tasks, while others such as birds and cats fail consistently.

This leads us to a consideration of some other, to us very simple, concepts such as recognizing what is 'same' and what is 'different'. These matters are so deeply engrained in us that it is surprising to find that it has proven very difficult to demonstrate that any animal species can learn to discriminate between objects on the basis of whether they are the same as or different from each other. An even more basic conceptual distinction is to recognize that all trees have something in common that distinguishes them from non-trees. Fish, people and chairs are further examples of these perceptual concepts. Although this is one of the older branches of research in animal concept formation, there is still controversy over whether other species form perceptual concepts in the same way as we do.

The study of the concept of time in animals is probably the oldest area of study in animal concept formation. Many species have been shown to have a strong sense of the time of day, as well as the ability to learn about shorter and variable intervals between important events.

Finally, in this chapter we consider the evidence for animals' sense of number. Although the study of animals' numerical ability got off to a bad start in the nineteenth century with Clever Hans – the horse who fooled everybody into thinking that he could perform advanced mathematical calculations (see Chapter 1) – more recent studies have uncovered some important evidence of basic numerical ability in a range of species.

Research on animals' conceptual abilities is still at an early stage, but there is already evidence of both commonality and diversity across species. Some abstract dimensions of experience, such as time, seem to be appreciated by a very wide range of species and, as far as we can tell, in very similar ways. On the other hand a concept as simple as object permanence – the idea that a hidden object continues to exist – has proven far harder to demonstrate in any non-human species. It is to the concept of object permanence that we turn first.

Object permanence

If I take a chocolate in one hand, pass my hand behind a box, stop for a moment and then bring my hand out and show you that it is empty, where would you expect to find the chocolate? Most likely, behind the box. You saw everything that happened: if the chocolate is not in my hand then it must be behind the box. Your ability to reason in this way is known as 'object permanence' – you have a concept that objects continue to exist even when they disappear from sight. Object permanence was recognized by the famous child psychologist Jean Piaget. Small children below about 12 to 18 months of age, Piaget (1952) found, do not yet appreciate that objects that disappear from view continue to exist.

Testing for object permanence is straightforward. One test is simply to make a desired object disappear from view and see whether the subject searches for the object in the spot where it was previously placed – just like the example above with the chocolate behind the box. A task of this type is known as 'visible displacement'. There is no 'trick' – everything that happens to the object is clearly visible to the subject (adult human, child or animal). Somewhat more complex is the 'invisible displacement' task. In this case a desired object is first placed in a container, which is then taken behind a screen, out of the subject's sight, and the object is removed from the container. Finally, the empty container is shown to the subject, who is then free to search for the desired object. An individual

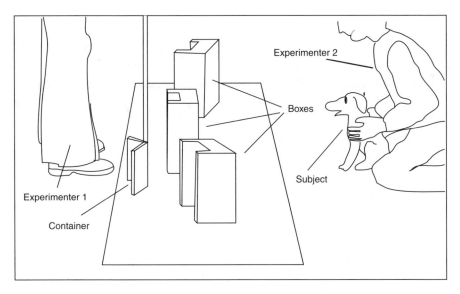

Figure 5.1   Gagnon and Doré's testing arena for dogs. Experimenter 2 holds the dog while experimenter 1 moves the desired object (Gagnon and Doré, 1994)

capable of object permanence will recognize that if the object is no longer in the container, then it must have been removed while it was behind the screen. Consequently this subject will search for the object behind the screen. Children can solve the simpler task, the visible displacement, at around 12 months of age. Only children above about 18 months are able to solve invisible displacement problems (see also Box 5.1 below).

Figure 5.1 shows a typical arrangement for studying object permanence in animals. In their study of the development of object permanence in puppies, Sylvain Gagnon and François Doré (1994) allowed a puppy to watch as an experimenter placed a favourite toy behind one of the three boxes. Once the object was hidden the puppy was released and allowed to search for the toy. The puppy was scored as being successful at this visible displacement task if it went straight to the box where the toy was hidden. Gagnon and Doré found that puppies started to master this test at around seven weeks of age.

For an invisible displacement test, in full view of the puppy the experimenters placed the toy into a small opaque container. The container with the toy was then placed behind one of the boxes shown in Figure 5.1. While out of sight behind the box the toy was removed from the container. Next, the now empty container was removed from behind the box and shown to the puppy so that it could see that the container was empty. Where would the puppy search for the missing toy? Very few of even the oldest puppies showed any sign of searching for the toy behind the box where it had been left. After several tests some of the dogs did search in the right spot, but it seems likely that this was just trial and error learning. With repeated testing using the same target box, the dogs simply learned to go to that box to get their toy. There was no evidence that they understood the sequence of events that had led to the toy ending up in that box and not another. Gagnon and Doré found adult dogs to be successful at the invisible displacement task, but the ability only developed after about one year of age.

The visible displacement task has been tested with a wide range of species, all of which have solved the task and found the hidden object. These include great apes (chimpanzees, orangutans and gorillas), monkeys (cebus monkeys, crab-eating macaques, Japanese macaques, rhesus macaques and squirrel monkeys), other mammals (cats, dogs and hamsters) and birds (chickens, doves and parrots). Far fewer species have proved successful at the invisible displacement task. The only uncontroversial examples of success at the invisible displacement task are two species of great ape (chimpanzees and gorillas) and adult dogs. Some researchers believe they have successfully demonstrated invisible displacement performances in monkeys, parrots and cats, but others dispute their results. The apparent success with invisible displacement by these species could have been due to the kind of trial and error learning described above for Gagnon and Doré's puppies, to cueing by the experimenters or to problems with experimental design.

Sonia Goulet and her colleagues (1994, 1996) studied the factors that lead to apparent success at invisible displacement tasks in cats. They found that the cats in the study were more successful at finding a hidden toy if they were prevented from looking for it until 20 seconds had elapsed since the placing of the toy. Why should these cats have been *more* successful if they were forced to wait 20 seconds before making their response? Surely with time their memory of where the toy had been placed should have decayed – not improved (see Chapter 6 for more on animal memory)? Indeed cats' memory does decay, and this is precisely why they do better after 20 seconds than if they are free to make a response immediately. The cat's memory of where the toy is fails to take account of the toy's invisible displacement, and is therefore incorrect. After 20 seconds, the cat has forgotten where it last saw the toy and therefore makes fewer incorrect choices. In Goulet *et al.*'s study, by making fewer incorrect choices there was an inevitable, but purely coincidental, increase in the incidence of cats searching behind the box where the toy had indeed been hidden.

Just why should so many species be capable of solving visible displacement tasks, and so few succeed at invisible displacements? The suggestion has been put forward that visible displacement tasks reflect more ecologically meaningful problems than invisible displacements. Visible displacement is the sort of thing any predator animal has to put up with. A hunted prey animal disappears behind a rock. Clearly there is an adaptive advantage to be had from looking behind the rock. Conversely it has been suggested that invisible displacements do not correspond to any problem that an animal would confront in its daily life. But consider again the predator searching for prey. The prey slips behind a stone and then, unseen by the predator, leaves that stone for the next stone. Our predator goes up to the first stone and fails to find its prey. In the design of invisible displacement experiments this would be counted as an error. To be scored as successful, the subject must *not* look behind the first stone where the prey

Box 5.1   How to test your dog or cat for object permanence

While much contemporary animal cognition research is carried out on rats and pigeons – excellent lab species, but not common pets – considerable research on object permanence has been performed on dogs and cats. Since this research requires no special equipment and is completely harmless, there is no reason why you should not test your own dog or cat for object permanence. In my experience there is considerable variation between individual dogs and cats, making the results of these tests by no means a foregone conclusion.

You will need a human assistant, three boxes (cardboard grocery boxes are excellent), your subject's favourite toy (it's probably worth washing it!) and a container large enough for the toy (an empty yogurt or ice cream container will do nicely).

First catch your dog or cat, and make sure that he or she is in an alert but not too boisterous mood. Just before a regular meal is a better time than just after; and it is wise to maintain a sober demeanour so as not to overexcite your animal.

While your assistant holds the cat or dog arrange the three boxes about 20 centimetres apart in a semicircle about one metre from your animal. Lay them on one side so that the open edge faces towards you and away from the animal (Figure 5.1).

To ensure that your dog or cat's motivation and general sensory abilities are up to the task, show him the toy and let him go. Check that he can find the toy by sight alone (many older dogs and cats have poor eyesight, in which case the experiment is impossible for them). Once he has found the toy, praise him and let him enjoy it for a moment. If it seems necessary to maintain motivation you might want to give him a small treat.

Assuming that your dog or cat has passed this preliminary test, start the visible displacement task. One of you (experimenter 2 in Figure 5.1) should hold your subject while the other (experimenter 1) visibly places the toy in one of the three boxes. Place it deep inside so that it can only be seen by going right inside the box. While you are doing this maintain eye contact with the other experimenter – don't follow the toy with your eyes as your animal might follow your eyes instead of the toy. Now experimenter 2, let your subject go and see where he searches for the toy. If he heads straight for the box containing the toy, score that as a successful trial. If the first box he searches out is any other, score that as a failure. Try this a few times, selecting a different box each time.

If your dog or cat succeeds at the visible displacement test it is time to try invisible displacement. To do this, set up the boxes and subject as at the beginning of the visible displacement experiment (Figure 5.1). Place the toy inside the yogurt carton (or other container) in full view of your subject. Now move the container with the toy behind one of the boxes and quietly empty the container into the box. Move the now empty container back out from behind the box and show your

---

Box 5.1   (cont'd)

subject that it is empty (turn the container to face your subject). Finally – experimenter 2, let your dog or cat loose to see where he searches for the object. A success is only scored if he heads straight for the box containing the toy. It does not count as a success if your subject gradually improves over several trials with the toy hidden behind the same box – he could be learning by trial and error always to go to that one box. If you perform multiple trials, you must use a different box each time.

If your dog or cat is successful at the invisible displacement test you might like to try a better-controlled version of the task. Instead of reaching in and removing the toy from the container, set up a container that makes it possible for the toy to be removed without any movement by the experimenter that is visible to the subject. Figure 5.1 shows a V-shaped container on a pole. With this set-up Gagnon and Doré were able to release the toy from the container simply by twisting the pole to which the container was attached – an operation that could not be seen by the animal under test. You could construct a V-shaped container of your own out of cardboard.

With this very simple testing arrangement the controversies in the literature can be addressed in your own backyard. Is it the case for example, as Goulet et al. have claimed, that success at the invisible displacement test improves if a delay is imposed before the animal is released to fetch the toy? Or does your dog or cat perform better if he is already moving towards the toy at the point when it disappears?

---

animal disappeared. It would typically make sense for a predator first to search in the last place where the prey had been seen for sure, before widening the search to places to which it may have moved. This makes the task a rather unrealistic one compared with the demands of life beyond the realms of psychological experiments.

An invisible displacement task has many components to it. To be successful the subject must understand that an object can be carried by another object (the toy is carried inside a container). The subject must also appreciate that the object can be removed from the container without any obvious intervention. Since the object in these tests is inanimate there is no strong reason why the subject should appreciate that it can leave the container without any visible intervention. Then, on being shown the empty container, the subject must remember where the container has been. This form of memory may be difficult for many subjects because they are given no cue to indicate that they are going to have to remember where the container had gone.

Given the many cognitive demands made by the invisible displacement task, it is perhaps not surprising that most of the species tested have failed. As so often in the study of animal cognition, these failures raise many more questions than they answer. For example would a cat be more successful at the task if the hidden object were animate (a mouse, say)? Would subjects be more successful if they were given some kind of cue to encourage memorization of the pattern of movement of the container? While it is refreshing to see species other than the standard rats and pigeons being tested, it would be valuable to assess object permanence in the more commonly studied species. With rats and pigeons we have far more knowledge of their abilities in the domains of memory and attention (see Chapter 6). Armed with this knowledge, interpretation of success and failure at invisible displacement tasks might be easier.

Concept learning

What is a concept? For our purposes a concept is an abstract or perceptual category: it is a grouping together of items that share common features or functionality. The concept of a chair, for example, groups together as equivalent a great many objects that differ in any number of ways, but share a certain functionality – they can all be sat on. The concept of fish groups together all those animals that live in water, have a backbone, gills and various other qualities that biologists have determined qualify them as fish. Some simple concepts, such as triangles, may be defined by certain common features that all triangles share (three straight lines intersecting at three angles). With natural concepts such as chairs and fish, however, the boundaries of the category may be much fuzzier. There is probably no single feature common to all chairs. Concepts such as this can be called perceptual concepts because they group together some objects and differentiate them from others on the basis of certain properties that are available to our senses. Some other concepts, however, have nothing to do with individual objects at all, but say something about the relationship between objects. Consider the concept 'same'. How do we know what counts as the same as what? This may sound like a very trivial question, but it turns out to be by no means a straightforward issue. For humans, for example, notions of same and different vary between different cultures. Where English speakers consider objects on one side of them to be in the same position, no matter where they are standing, native speakers of Guugu-Yimithirr (a language of the native peoples of north-eastern Australia) only consider objects placed at the same point of the compass to be in the same position, irrespective of where they are standing and whether the object is on their left or right.

Research on concept learning in animals is still very much in its infancy, but some exciting discoveries have already been made.

Same–different

Evidence that any animal species can learn to identify objects as being the same or different has been a long time coming. Anthony Wright and his colleagues (1988) trained pigeons to identify pairs of pictures presented on a computer screen as either the same or different. The apparatus used in this study is shown in Figure 5.2. Each trial started with the presentation of a stimulus that the

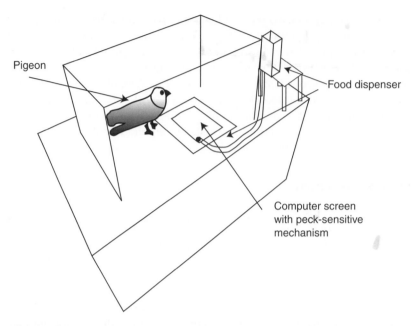

Figure 5.2 The apparatus used by Wright and his colleagues to study pigeons' comprehension of the same–different concept. The pigeon pecked onto a horizontally mounted computer screen and correct responses were rewarded with food grains dropped onto the screen from food hoppers mounted on top of the testing chamber (from Wright *et al.*, 1988)

pigeon had to peck a couple of times (this is known as the 'sample' stimulus). As soon as it had done this, two comparison stimuli were placed next to the original stimulus. One of the comparison stimuli was the same as the original stimulus, the other was different. The pigeon's task was to peck the comparison stimulus that was identical to the original stimulus (known as the 'matching' stimulus). One group of pigeons was trained with just two sample stimuli: these pigeons mastered the problem in little more than two weeks. A second group of pigeons was trained with 152 sample stimuli that were presented only once each in each daily training session. These subjects required 18 months to master the same task.

The critical question in concept learning, however, is not just whether the subjects can learn to respond to the correct stimuli during training, but whether they have abstracted the conceptual rule under investigation. To test whether the two groups of pigeons had abstracted the same–different concept, Wright *et al.* presented each group of pigeons with a completely new set of stimuli they had never seen before. The question now was whether the pigeons would apply the same–different rule to these new stimuli. It was found that the pigeons that had been trained with just two stimuli, although they had learnt quickly, had not abstracted any kind of rule – they were completely stumped by the novel stimuli. The pigeons that had been trained with 152 stimuli, on the other hand, although they had learnt very slowly, were much better able to categorize the novel stimuli as either the same or different. This indicates that they had learnt an abstract rule.

Successful tests of the same–different concept have been conducted with rhesus monkeys, chimpanzees, California sea lions and a dolphin.

Stimulus equivalence

A more extended notion of 'sameness' is the recognition that some things, although they are not the same as each other, may share certain properties that make them equivalent. A picture of an apple comes to have the same significance for a child as the spoken word 'apple', and later as the written word. An apple is a red or green spherical object that can be eaten: the word 'apple' – spoken or written – has none of these qualities, and yet it functions in some of the same ways as the object it names. This ability of objects to substitute for each other under certain conditions is known as 'stimulus equivalence' and is an important prerequisite for symbolic thought. Peter Urcioli, Thomas Zentall and their colleagues conducted an extensive study of whether and to what extent pigeons could learn about stimulus equivalence (Urcioli *et al.*, 1989). In their training method a single stimulus (the sample stimulus) is presented alone, followed by two simultaneously presented comparison stimuli. Depending on which sample stimulus is presented, response to one or other of the comparison stimuli is rewarded. Thus a pigeon may be trained to respond to a circle stimulus after presentation of a red sample, but it must respond to a dot stimulus after presentation of a green sample. This is the original phase 1 training. In phase 2 the pigeon is trained to expect new comparison stimuli to go with some of the familiar sample stimuli. In the example shown in Figure 5.3, the pigeon learns that

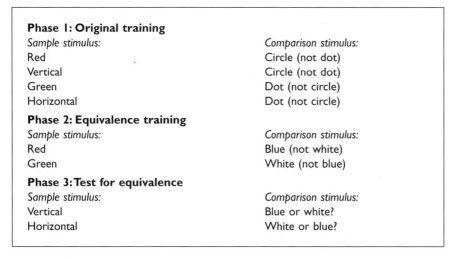

Phase 1: Original training

Sample stimulus:	Comparison stimulus:
Red	Circle (not dot)
Vertical	Circle (not dot)
Green	Dot (not circle)
Horizontal	Dot (not circle)

Phase 2: Equivalence training

Sample stimulus:	Comparison stimulus:
Red	Blue (not white)
Green	White (not blue)

Phase 3: Test for equivalence

Sample stimulus:	Comparison stimulus:
Vertical	Blue or white?
Horizontal	White or blue?

Figure 5.3   Design of Urcioli *et al.'s* (1989) stimulus equivalence experiment

the red sample goes with a blue comparison stimulus and the green sample goes with a white comparison stimulus. The question of interest now is, what will the pigeon make of the vertical and horizontal sample stimuli when it is given blue and white comparison stimuli? Will it recognize that because red and vertical (and green and horizontal) stimuli had similar consequences in the original training, and red and green now have new consequences, that those new consequences will also apply to the vertical and horizontal stimuli, or will it simply be confused when it is given sample stimuli followed by comparison stimuli that it has not been trained to expect? Urcioli *et al.* (1989) found that pigeons tended to choose the blue comparison after the vertical sample, and the white comparison after the horizontal sample. This suggests that the pigeons treated the red and vertical (and green and horizontal) stimuli as equivalent because they had had the same consequences in the first phase of training.

Perceptual concepts

Nearly thirty years ago Richard Herrnstein and his colleagues (1976) performed a simple but very interesting experiment on pigeons. These pigeons were presented with photographs – many hundreds of them – one at a time. Some of the photographs contained images of people, in others there were no people present. If the photograph contained a person, the pigeon could earn a food reward by pecking at it: if there was no person present the pigeon had to withhold its responses or the delay to the next rewarded picture would be lengthened (the Go/Nogo method, see Box 4.1). Even though the photographs were very varied the pigeons gradually mastered the distinction. In subsequent experiments Herrnstein *et al.* explored pigeons' ability to categorize photographs containing trees, bodies of water or even a specific person. Thousands of pictures were used in these experiments (making memorization of individual pictures highly unlikely), but the pigeons learnt to discriminate between them and achieved considerable success when a novel example from the category was presented to them for the first time.

These early demonstrations of perceptual conception in pigeons inspired a number of imitations. Pigeons have been found capable of discriminating between the locations used in pictures. They can form concepts of cats, fish, flowers, oak leaves, other pigeons, cars and chairs, and correctly generalize examples of concepts they have never seen before. In a study by Shigeru Watanabe and his colleagues (1995), pigeons were even able to discriminate between paintings by Monet and Picasso. The pigeons also correctly identified novel paintings by these two artists. In the first study of the categorization of schools of art by a non-human subject, paintings by Cezanne and Renoir were spontaneously categorized as belonging to the Monet school, while paintings by Braque and Matisse were categorized as belonging to the Picasso school.

Several of these studies compared pigeons' success at categorizing stimuli grouped according to concepts that arise naturally in human language (for example chair, fish and so on), compared with groups of stimuli formed according to no specific rule – just a random conglomeration of items. This kind of comparison serves two functions. First, it ensures that the pigeons are not just memorizing all the stimuli and learning what to do to obtain a reward when they come along – in other words it acts as a control for rote learning (pigeons have a prodigious capacity for rote learning – see Chapter 6). The second and more interesting function of these so-called 'pseudo-category' tasks is that they test the hypothesis that conceptualization requires language. It has been argued that we need the word 'tree' in order to conceptualize trees successfully. The fact, however, that pigeons more successfully discriminate between pictures containing trees and those not containing trees than they do between two random groups of pictures suggests that they have also formed a concept of a tree. Since pigeons do not have language, this implies that there is something about the visual image of trees that enables them to be conceptualized as a group of similar objects even without the need for the linguistic term 'tree'.

Although very little research has been conducted on perceptual conception in species other than pigeons, it has been shown that monkeys are able to demonstrate the concept of a person through the use of person and non-person photographs and methods broadly similar to those employed with pigeons. Monkeys have successfully classified pictures of other monkeys and people (Schrier *et al.*, 1984). Likewise blue jays can classify pictures of cryptic moths and leaves damaged by cryptic caterpillars (Real *et al.*, 1984).

But how do we know that these animals are really learning *concepts* and not just noticing features that photographs and slides (positive and negative) have in common? We know (see Chapter 6) that many animals, particularly pigeons, have an astonishing ability to memorize many hundreds of slides. In addition it has been known since the early days of psychological study on animals that they can *generalize*. Generalization is the ability, having been trained to respond to one stimulus, to respond similarly to other stimuli that are similar in some way. Certainly Herrnstein and the other researchers who performed the original studies on conceptualization in pigeons included a 'pseudo-concept' control – where half the slides were randomly positive and the other half negative. The pigeons were unsuccessful in this task, suggesting that there was something about the sorting of slides into those containing the concept in question and those without it that made the slides easier to learn for the pigeons. This control procedure, however, and the pigeons' failure to master it, does not guarantee that when the pigeons do learn to differentiate between person and non-person slides (to take just one example) that what they have learnt is really the concept of a person, as we understand it.

It must be admitted that even among psychologists who study concept learning in human beings there is no consensus about what it is that makes a concept a concept. There are, however, results from animal research that strongly suggest that, whatever a concept may be to a human being, pigeons and monkeys are not learning concepts in the same way.

Michael D'Amato and Paul van Sant (1988) trained *Cebus apella* monkeys to discriminate between slides containing people and slides that did not. The monkeys quickly learnt to do this. Then the monkeys were presented with novel slides they had never seen before and which either contained people or similar scenes with no people in them. Here also the monkeys spontaneously classified the majority of slides correctly. So far, so good – clear evidence that the monkeys had not just learnt the particular slides they had been trained with, but had also abstracted a person concept from the slides that they then successfully applied to pictures they had never seen before. Or had they? D'Amato and van Sant did not end their analysis with the observation that the monkeys had successfully transferred their learning to novel slides – rather they went on to look carefully at the kinds of error the monkeys had made. Although largely successful with the novel slides, the monkeys had made some very puzzling mistakes. For example one of the person slides that the monkeys had failed to recognize as a picture of a human being had been a head and shoulders portrait, which to another human would have been a classic image of a person. One of the slides that the monkeys had incorrectly classified as containing a human had actually been a shot of a jackal carrying a dead flamingo in its mouth; both jackal and its prey were also reflected in the water beneath them. What person in their right mind could possibly confuse a jackal with a flamingo in its mouth with another human being?

The explanation of both these mistakes is the same: the monkeys had generalized on the basis of the particular features contained in the slides they had been trained with, rather than learning the more abstract concept that the experimenters had intended. The head and shoulders portrait of the person had lacked the head-torso-arms-legs body shape that had been common among the images that the monkeys had been trained with, and consequently they had rejected it as not similar enough to the positive image they were looking for. Similarly, during the training period the only slides that had contained flashes of red happened to be those of people. Three of the training slides had contained people wearing a piece of red clothing, whereas none of the non-person slides had contained the colour red. Consequently when the jackal with prey slide had come along during testing and it had contained the colour red, the monkeys had classified it as a person slide. Richard Herrnstein and Peter de Villiers (1980) drew similar conclusions from a detailed analysis of the errors pigeons made when categorizing slides of fish, such as those shown in Figure 5.4.

The above findings may suggest that non-human species learn to categorize images by relying more on particular features of images than humans do. This, however, is to overlook the fact that in humans perceptual categorization takes a very long time to develop. Young children commonly make misclassifications, such as calling all four-legged animals sheep for many years (to the amusement of those around them). The fine distinctions of adulthood take a long time to develop. Although experiments on perceptual categorization among non-humans use hundreds of images and may involve a year or more of training, that is very little compared with the child's continuous exposure to an unlimited set of perceptual experiences. A child's experience involves real three-dimensional objects viewed from many angles, not just the flat images used in animal studies. The richness of the three-dimensional world may discourage learning based on individual features and encourage a more holistic view. Perhaps future experiments on animal conceptualization may find ways to capture more of the real world

A

B

Figure 5.4   Examples of stimuli readily classified by pigeons as fish (A), and pictures commonly misclassified (B) in Herrnstein and de Villiers's experiment (courtesy of P. de Villiers)

experience of learning about concepts, and answer the question of whether animals are really able to generalize from individual features when they learn perceptual concepts.

Although the range of species that have been studied for their conceptual abilities is not large, Evelyn Hanggi (1999) has recently reported on the categorization ability of horses. Two horses were trained to select a black circle stimulus

Box 5.2 Can pigeons learn prototypes?

One explanation of how humans learn perceptual concepts is that they do so by recognizing a prototype of the concept under consideration. A prototype is the perfect example of a concept. For example in one study people had to classify cartoon drawings into one of two categories. In one category of cartoon, the faces had small foreheads, short noses and closely spaced eyes. In the other category the faces had larger foreheads, longer noses and more widely spaced eyes. Once the subjects had passed this test they were introduced to new cartoons. The novel test cartoons that were most successfully classified represented the average of all the training cartoons in each category. The average cartoons were the easiest to categorize, it is argued, because they were representative of the prototype of each class of cartoon.

Lorenzo von Fersen and Stephen Lea (1990) trained pigeons to discriminate between sets of photographs of outdoor scenes in order to see if the pigeons did this by forming prototypes. These photographs differed from each other in five ways. First, they were of two different scenes (a pub in a town, or a university building). Second, they were photographed under two different weather conditions (sunny or cloudy). Third, the photos were taken at two different camera distances (near or far). Fourth, there were two different camera orientations (horizontal or oblique). And fifth, there were two different camera heights (ground level or 20 metres above the ground). Two sample images from this study are shown in Figure 5.5. For each of these five dimensions, one value was arbitrarily designated as positive. If an image had three or more positive qualities, then pecks at that photograph were rewarded with food. If an image had three or more negative qualities, then pecks at it were not rewarded (the Go/Nogo method, see Box 4.1). The image with positive values for all five qualities was taken as the positive prototype, and the image with all five negative

A   B

Figure 5.5   Two sample images from the experiment by Fersen and Lea. The image on the left shows a university building, photographed from street level on an overcast day with the camera at an oblique angle. The right-hand image shows the opposite conditions. It is a photograph of a pub, taken on a sunny day from 20 metres above the ground and with the camera held level (courtesy of S. E. G. Lea)

Box 5.2 (cont'd)

qualities was deemed the negative prototype. Fersen and Lea found that their pigeons responded fastest to the positive prototype. This result cannot, however, be seen as strong evidence that the pigeons had formed a prototype to solve the discrimination problem – they may simply have been responding on the basis of the features individually. The positive prototype image may have been responded to fastest just because it contained more of the features that were individually associated with reward.

A stronger demonstration that pigeons form prototypes comes from an experiment by Aydan Aydin and John Pearce (1994). These investigators also showed images to pigeons that contained features whose discrimination would be followed by reward or non-reward. In this case the images consisted of three bars of different colours and patterns placed together on a computer screen. There were six different types of bar altogether, which for simplicity were designated as A, B, C, D, E and F. Bars A, B and C were positive; bars D, E and F were negative. In any given trial the pigeons saw three bars and these were always either two positive and one negative (response to these patterns was followed by a food reward), or one positive and two negative (no reward). Once the pigeons had mastered this discrimination exercise they were tested on a pattern of wholly positive bars (A, B and C) and a pattern of wholly negative bars (D, E and F), which had never been presented during the training period. These patterns could be considered as the prototypes of the concepts the pigeons had learnt during training, and sure enough they responded at a higher rate to the positive prototype, and a lower rate to the negative prototype than their response rates for any of the patterns they had been trained with. This suggests they had conceptualized the prototype during training, even though they had never seen it.

Aydin and Pearce go on to suggest, however, that prototype extraction, in humans as well as animals, can be explained with simple learning rules and the laws of generalization. In essence their argument is that the positive prototype, even though it had never been seen during training, contained more of the elements associated with reward than did any of the training patterns.

with a contrasting centre in preference to a solid black circle . Once this had been mastered, the horses were trained on additional but similar stimuli – selection of a contrasting-centred stimulus always being rewarded. (One of Hanggi's horses is shown making a choice in Figure 5.6.) By the end of their exposure to a series of 15 pairs of stimuli, the horses were making very few errors when presented with a novel pair of items, indicating that they had abstracted the concept of always choosing the stimulus with the contrasting centre.

Hank Davis and his colleagues (1997) carried out an interesting series of studies on whether different species can recognize individual people. In one study they found that rats, given just one ten-minute opportunity to interact with a

Figure 5.6   One of Hanggi's horses choosing between a filled and an open sun-like stimulus (courtesy of E. Hanggi)

specific human being, would later choose that person when given a choice between two different people seated at a table. In subsequent studies Davis *et al.* found a similar ability to discriminate between individual people in chickens, rabbits, sheep, cows, seals, llama and even penguins.

Research on perceptual conception in a number of species indicates that the ability to categorize objects – even quite abstract objects such as paintings by different artists – is widespread among mammals and birds. The evidence from more detailed studies of just how animals achieve these feats of conceptual learning suggests that the mechanisms may be relatively simple forms of associative learning and generalization. Complex behaviour can often arise as the outcome of relatively simple underlying principles.

Time

Learning about the time of day

Most animals and many plants show typical daily rhythms of activity. Bean seedlings open out their leaves each morning to catch the sun, and close them again in the evening. Likewise many flowers open during the day and close at night. Many animals are more active during the day than at night, but many others are more active during the night than the day: hamsters, rats and cockroaches, for example, all engage in more movement during the night. Some animals, such as fiddler crabs and some lizards, change their body colour from day to night. Sparrows, like most birds, are more active during the day than at night, for the simple reason that they would probably bump into things if they tried to fly in the dark. Bees can learn that certain sources of food are available at certain hours of the day and not at others. Humans have these circadian (approximately day-length) rhythms too – as anyone who has flown more than a couple of time zones can attest.

As the experience of jet lag suggests, we and other species do not simply become active because the sun has risen. There is an internal component to circadian cycles of activity. Experiments have been performed in which animals were left in an environment that did not change in terms of light or in any other way over a 24-hour period. Despite the lack of external stimulation, the animals developed a pattern of waking and sleeping, activity and inactivity, flying and not flying, or whatever other behaviour was being measured, that approximated the 24-hour cycle of the normal day. Sparrows left in the dark, for example, developed a spontaneous rhythm of hopping and not hopping that was repeated approximately every 24 hours.

Although jet lag shows us that our pattern of waking and sleeping has an endogenous component, the fact that jet lag ultimately passes and we become accustomed to the day and night cycle of the time zone we have moved to shows that circadian rhythms are entrainable. Factors that can entrain the natural daily rhythm of an animal's activity are given the German name *Zeitgeber* – literally 'time-giver'. Although the natural daily rhythm has a 24-hour cycle, many animals will entrain to shorter or longer periods of time given the right *Zeitgeber*. Light is a very important *Zeitgeber*. Other signals that animals use to set their circadian rhythm include temperature (it is usually cooler at night than during the day); social factors (two sparrows in adjacent cages entrain each other to the same circadian rhythm); and feeding (delivery of food at regular times can entrain the circadian rhythm even when other *Zeitgeber* are absent). With suitable entrainment, many animals can adapt to cycles of activity of less than 24 hours (in some cases as short as 16 hours, but most animals cannot adapt to cycles of less than 20 or 22 hours). The upper limit in plants as well as animals is around 28 to 30 hours, although entrainment to such extreme values requires bright light.

The circadian clock is also very accurate. Bees and rats, to take two random examples, can regulate their daily activity patterns with an error of between five and ten minutes. This represents an accuracy of over 99 per cent.

The importance of circadian rhythms is not just that they ensure that an animal's activity is suited to the environment in which it lives, though that is certainly important, but also an internal sense of the time of day is extremely useful to animals that have to navigate. As we saw in Chapter 4, pigeons, bees and other animals that navigate combine their sense of time of day with the position of the sun in order to establish their bearings. It is not known how many species use this trick, but its presence in two such unrelated species suggests it may be quite widespread.

Learning about short time intervals

The ability to gauge accurately the time of day – circadian timing – is without doubt highly useful to animals. It enables them to structure effectively their patterns of activity throughout the day, as well as providing the basis for the sun compass. Circadian timing, however, has two limitations. The first is that it is restricted to periods of approximately 24 hours. Many of the things that happen in this world at regular intervals are not restricted to a period of approximately one day. The arrival of predators, prey and other important events may reoccur at intervals of seconds, minutes or hours. The second drawback with circadian timing is that it can only be used to place events within a daily cycle – animals are not able to use the circadian clock to judge arbitrary time intervals.

Long-tailed hermit hummingbirds feed on nectar-bearing flowers in the Costa Rican jungle, where their feeding habits have been studied by Frank Gill (1988). Male hummingbirds need a great deal of energizing food to survive, but foraging time is scarce as male hummingbirds spend as much time as possible trying to impress female hummingbirds. Every moment that the male hummingbird is away looking for nectar is a possible mating opportunity lost. To add to the difficulty of the male hummingbird's situation, flowers are not always full of nectar. After the nectar has been removed, different flowers refill at different rates. The longer the hummingbird waits before going off on a foraging trip, the greater the probability that the flowers he last visited will have refilled with nectar, but there is also an increased risk that another bird will have made off with that nectar. Consequently the hummingbird is confronted with a difficult timing problem. He needs to time his nectar foraging trips so that the interval between his visits to the flowers coincides as closely as possible with the length of time it takes each flower to refill. Any shorter and he will fail to pick up the maximum amount of nectar from each flower; any longer and there is a risk that another bird will get there first.

Gill (ibid.) set up some artificial flowers that he could fill with nectar whenever he wanted in order to test how well hummingbirds are able to time their flower visits. Just as his field observations had suggested, Gill found that when he refilled the flowers with artificial nectar ten minutes after the birds' last visit, the birds adjusted the interval between their visits to a little longer than the ten-minute refill time. How soon a hummingbird returned to a flower also depended on whether the bird had exclusive use of that flower, or whether other birds were feeding from the same nectar source.

But sensitivity to time intervals is not an obscure ability of a handful of species that have special timing problems to deal with. One of the most direct ways of ascertaining any animal's sensitivity to time intervals is simply to give it food at regular intervals – say once every two minutes. The first couple of times the animal receives the food it may be surprised, but it will very quickly come to expect the food at the two-minute point and will demonstrate this expectation by approaching the feeder about half way through the interval. Other species-specific food-directed behaviours may also develop. A pigeon may peck any food-like detail in the environment; a rat might gnaw on something near the feeder; a cat may meow and rub itself against a suitable object. Each of these behavioural patterns occurs at characteristic points in the interval, and they indicate that the animal has an ability to time the interval, and that this ability is quickly entrained.

An experiment that is only slightly more involved than this requires a rat or pigeon (though many other species have been used) to make at least one response on a lever (for rats) or a pecking key (for pigeons) after a set interval has elapsed. In order to obtain food a response is required *after* the interval has elapsed, but hungry pigeons and rats (and other species) start making their lever or key responses well before the interval is up. Typically, responding starts after about one third of the interval has elapsed, and then gradually increases in rate so that the animal is responding very quickly as the interval reaches its end and the reward becomes available. In this situation, known as a fixed interval schedule, the fact that the pigeon or rat will start responding earlier if the interval is shortened, or later if the interval is lengthened, is further evidence of these animals' sensitivity to time intervals.

A simple modification to the fixed interval procedure provides further insight into the way in which these animals assess time intervals. Now, instead of food being provided at the end of each interval, occasional intervals do not end with food. Instead they run for three or four times the normal length. Under this condition it has been found that, with training, the response rate peaks at around the time the food would normally be delivered. For this reason, this modified fixed interval procedure is known as the 'peak interval' procedure. The fact that the response rate peaks at the time when food would normally be delivered suggests that the animals tested have an expectation of when the food will arrive. Figure 5.7 shows a typical pattern of response from a peak interval experiment with rats.

The fixed interval and peak interval procedures are examples of situations where an animal's sense of time becomes apparent in the patterns that develop in its own behaviour. The rats used to compile the data for Figure 5.7 revealed their awareness that food would normally be delivered after 40 seconds by producing their highest response rate at the 40-second point. In another type of procedure, animals are presented with stimuli of different durations and indicate their perception of these durations by responding to different alternatives.

Rats can be trained to make a response on one lever after a short stimulus (a tone of two seconds' duration, say) and on a different lever after a longer stimulus (a tone of eight seconds). The same task can be given to pigeons, using pecking keys rather than levers. In experiments like these, standard laboratory species such as rats and pigeons readily show an ability to discriminate between stimuli of different durations. If they are given stimuli similar in duration to the original training stimuli they indicate that they recognize this similarity by making the response they have been trained to make to the original duration stimulus. Thus for a pigeon trained to respond on one key (we shall call this the 'short' key) after a two-second stimulus and another (the 'long' key) after an eight-second stimulus, a novel three-second stimulus will produce a response on the short key, and a novel seven-second stimulus will produce a response on the long key.

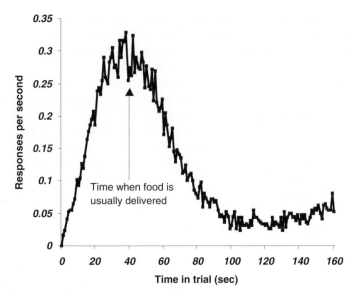

Figure 5.7   This graph shows the average rate of lever pressing for a group of rats accustomed to receiving a food reward every 40 seconds. In this trial the interval between food was 160 seconds, but it can be seen that the rats' rate of lever pressing peaked at around 40 seconds – the time when food would normally be delivered (data provided by E. Ludvig)

Box 5.3   How do animals time short intervals?

For many years the dominant explanation of how animals time short intervals has been based on a sort of internal clock theory. According to 'scalar timing' theory, proposed by Russell Church (1978), timing in animals is controlled by something akin to a ticking clock. When an event happens that the animal wishes to time, the ticks of the clock are counted into a short-term memory store. The animal knows that the correct time has elapsed when the number of ticks in the short-term memory matches the number of ticks stored (on the basis of previous experience) in the long-term memory.

Although this theory can account for many of the results obtained from fixed interval and peak interval procedures as well as the duration comparison task, it has been criticized in recent years by John Staddon and his collaborators. Staddon has proposed an alternative theory that does away with the idea that animals have a digital clock (Staddon and Higa, 1999). In Staddon and Higa's theory, timed behaviour is controlled by a steadily decaying memory of salient events. For example on a fixed interval schedule (where, as described above, food is given for the first

---

Box 5.3   (cont'd)

response made after an interval of time has elapsed), each food reward sets up a memory trace that gradually decays in the interval until the next food reward is delivered. Animals, it is proposed, can learn to associate a particular level of this memory trace with an action. Once the memory trace decays below that memorized level the subject starts to make responses.

What this theory implies is that if the food reward is made larger, then the memory trace will start off larger. If the memory trace starts at a high level, then it will take longer to decay to the critical level at which responding commences. Consequently larger food rewards will lead to delayed responses in fixed interval experiments. Conversely the replacement of a food reward with a neutral stimulus of equal duration (for example a light) should lead to a shorter response delay in such experiments. Both of these findings were published many years ago (Staddon, 1970), but they were largely ignored because they did not fit the dominant theory of animal timing.

Although interval timing is far more flexible than circadian timing, that flexibility does come at a cost. When events of approximately daily frequency can be timed with an accuracy of around 99.5 per cent, the accuracy of interval timing decreases with the length of the interval being timed. Consequently, though an interval of seconds or a few minutes can be timed quite effectively, the error in timing an interval of several hours in this way is catastrophic. In a simple but interesting experiment, David Eckerman (1999) compared the ability of pigeons to time intervals from 12 to 48 hours. Just as would be expected in interval timing, accuracy was generally proportional to the duration of the interval – longer intervals were less accurately timed than shorter ones. However at intervals of 24 hours, and also 12 and 48 hours (simple multiples or sub-divisions of 24 hours), an anomaly appeared – the pigeons' timing was much more accurate than with slightly shorter or longer intervals. This must have been because the pigeons switched to their circadian timing ability, which, though less flexible, is far more accurate.

Numbers

What does it mean to have a sense of number? At its simplest, it can just mean being aware that ten items are more than five items. This is known as relative number judgment, which differs from the (presumably simpler) judgment of quantity, by virtue of it being the total number of items that is critical in making the judgment – not their total amount. Twenty ants are larger in number than two elephants, despite being much smaller in terms of quantity. The next level of complexity in the appreciation of numbers is the recognition that all quantities of the same number have something in common. This is called absolute number judgment: what it is that three cars have in common with three plums. Counting implies more than just a relative and an absolute sense of number. To count implies at least using certain number names in a consistent order to 'tag' groups of items, and recognizing that the name of the last item in a counted group is the name for the number of items in the whole group. Counting can also mean using arithmetical operations.

Relative number judgments: more or less

As we saw in Chapter 1, the study of animal cognition started out with a terrible embarrassment in the consideration of animals' numerical perception – the case of Clever Hans. This inhibited research on animals' ability to judge number for close on a century. During this period, however, there were a couple of exceptional individuals who maintained an active interest in the subject. One of these was Otto Koehler. Koehler, together with his students and colleagues, studied the numerical ability of several species of bird. Jackdaws, crows, budgerigars, ravens, magpies and pigeons were favoured subjects in experiments where the subject had to choose between containers with different numbers of grains glued to their lids. If the bird chose incorrectly no food reward was forthcoming from the container, and if necessary the bird was shooed away verbally, by hand or, in recalcitrant cases, with something akin to a fly swatter. Koehler and his coworkers were able to demonstrate that pigeons could learn to choose the container with the smaller or the larger number of grains glued to its lid. The pigeons found it easier to choose when the alternatives presented to them were further apart in number (for example seven versus four) than when they were consecutive (such as five versus four).

There was a problem with these early studies however, of which Koehler was fully aware. How could he be sure that the pigeons and other subjects were attending to the *number* of grains when they made their choice? They could have been making their choice on the basis of some other, perhaps simpler, aspect of the containers' grain-covered lids. For one thing, when there were fewer grains on a lid, less of the lid would have been covered over – hence there might have been confusion between number and the area of the lid that was covered. Though Koehler did try to control for this problem in one experiment by using lumps of plasticine instead of grains, the equipment available in his day did not permit wide-ranging control of the problem. Another problem with the early studies was that, with such small numbers of grains, the birds may have recognized the characteristic visual patterns that small numbers of items typically make. One item is always just a point; two items form a line; three items typically form a triangle; four items a quadrilateral. With larger numbers this becomes less of an issue, but with small numbers it is a considerable problem, particularly when modern knowledge about the number of visual patterns that animals are able to learn by rote is taken into account (see Chapter 6).

Jacky Emmerton adapted Koehler's experiment using modern methods to control for the alternative ways that birds might be choosing between fewer or more items, apart from the control by number of items that we are interested in

(Emmerton *et al.*, 1997; Emmerton, 1998). Emmerton's subjects were pigeons, trained in a Skinner box (see Figure 3.6) to respond to slides containing different numbers of dots. During their initial training the pigeons were rewarded for pecking on one response key if six or seven ('many') dots appeared on a slide, and rewarded for pecking a different response key if one or two ('few') dots appeared. Emmerton's results suggested that the pigeons had abstracted a concept of number because the birds, after their initial training had taught them to discriminate between six or seven dots and one or two, performed correctly when given choices between three, four or five dots. Unlike Koehler, Emmerton was able to test that it really was the number of dots that was influencing the pigeons' choices, and not some other factor, by systematically varying other dimensions of the stimuli that might have been important to the pigeons, and observing whether these variations had an impact. The factors Emmerton considered included the shape of the dots, their size, brightness and how closely packed together they were. Emmerton's results show clearly that pigeons are capable of learning the abstract concept of relative number – that is, they can discriminate between 'fewer' and 'more', at least for numbers up to seven. Similar results have been obtained with monkeys and – using sounds instead of images – rats.

Absolute number

As well as understanding that seven is more than five, using the concept of number effectively also means understanding that every group of five items has something in common. This quality – which, say, a certain number of ants share with the same number of elephants – is known as 'absolute number'. Otto Koehler and his students were the first to investigate absolute number in animals. A raven called Jakob was trained to choose a pot with five spots on its lid from among five pots with different numbers of dots on their lids. Jakob succeeded at this task even though the area on the lids that the different numbers of dots occupied varied 50-fold.

More recently Hank Davis (1984) and various colleagues conducted detailed studies of several species' ability to comprehend absolute number. In one experiment a raccoon named Rocky learned to pick out a clear plastic cube containing three objects (grapes or small metal balls) from a set of plastic cubes containing from one to five items. Only the cube containing three items could be opened. Rocky's rewards for a correct choice included being able to eat the grapes or wash the metal balls. In addition Rocky was given a social reward in the form of hugs from a researcher (Figure 5.8).

Davis and his colleagues carried out several other experiments on absolute number using the more familiar rat subjects. In an experiment reminiscent of Monty Python's holy hand-grenade ('The number thou shalt count shall be three'), Hank Davis and Melody Albert (1986) demonstrated that rats could learn to make a response only after three bursts of white noise, not two or four. These bursts of noise were of random duration, so the rats could not solve the task on the basis of their ability to judge time intervals. In a follow-up experi-

Figure 5.8   The left-hand photo shows Rocky the raccoon selecting the transparent cube containing an object in an early phase of training. In the right-hand photo Rocky is receiving social reinforcement (courtesy of H. Davis)

ment Davis and his colleagues (1989) considered whether rats could distinguish between three touches to their whiskers and two or four. In this experiment, the timing of the whisker touches was also randomized so that the rats had to distinguish the number of touches, and not their timing. Other studies showed that rats could learn to restrict their feeding to a fixed number of food items even if the type of food was changed after the original training. Different groups of rats were designated as three-eaters, four-eaters or five-eaters. If they ate the correct number of items they were praised verbally and given an extra food item. If, however, they tried to eat too many items they were punished with a loud 'no' and a frightening hand clap (Davis and Bradford, 1991).

Studies with a quite different design support the hypothesis that rats can distinguish absolute numbers. Hank Davis and Sheree Bradford (1986) trained rats to take food from the third of six tunnels. All the tunnels contained food (so odour cues were controlled), but all except the third tunnel had their doors jammed so that the rat could not enter and eat the food within. The exact positions of the tunnels could be moved around so that positional cues were controlled for. Figure 5.9 shows part of the apparatus and a rat choosing the correct tunnel. With training the rats would go directly to the third tunnel, ignoring the others on their way.

Research by other investigators has shown that rats and pigeons can be trained to make a specific number of responses on a response lever. Accuracy is only high for fairly small numbers (below ten – Mechner, 1958), but some evidence of

Figure 5.9   One of Davis and Bradford's rats selecting the correct tunnel
(courtesy of H. Davis)

perception of the number of responses made has been demonstrated with
numbers up to 50 (Rilling and McDiarmid, 1965).

Counting

Though some would use the term 'counting' to refer to any ability to perceive
numbers, there is really much more to counting than just the relative and absolute
number competencies we have considered so far. In order to count it is not just
necessary to recognize that five items are more than four items (relative number).
It is not even enough to recognize that every group of five items has something
in common with every other group of five items (absolute number), whatever
those items may be. Counting also means recognizing at least two further
qualities of numbers:

1. *Tagging*: a certain number's name or tag goes with a certain quantity of items.
   In our language the name 'one' or symbol '1' stands for a single item. 'Two'
   or '2' goes with a pair of items, and so on. These tags must always be applied
   in the same order

2. *Cardinality*: the tag applied to the last item of a set is the name of the number
   of items in that set. Thus if I tag the pens on my desk I call the first one 'one',
   the next one 'two' and the last one 'three'. 'Three' is consequently the correct
   name for the number of pens on my desk.

Although, as we have just seen, there is some evidence that at least a few species
of animal are sensitive to the concept of number, evidence that animals can count
is harder to come by. For one thing, to demonstrate an appreciation of tagging
and cardinality a subject has to be able to produce a range of different responses.
Without a range of different number tags available to it, an animal could never

tell us whether it appreciates that three items deserve the tag 'three', and not 'two' or 'four'.

Some of the strongest evidence of counting comes from an African grey parrot called Alex, trained in a rather original way by Irene Pepperberg (1987, 1994). Box 5.4 outlines the training method used with Alex. Alex was trained to respond verbally in English to questions presented to him verbally by an experimenter. He would be presented with a tray of several objects and asked 'What's this?' or 'How many?' In tests with novel objects Alex was able to identify correctly the number of items in groups of up to six objects with an accuracy of around 80 per cent. Even mixed groups of more than one type of object were not an

---

Box 5.4   How to train a parrot to count

Irene Pepperberg has developed a unique training procedure that takes advantage of the enthusiasm of African grey parrots to imitate human sounds. During training the parrot is encouraged to answer questions put to him by the experimenter using the model–rival technique. In this technique humans demonstrate the required response. A human acts as a model for the parrot by answering the experimenter's questions, and as a rival with the parrot for the experimenter's attention.

During training the experimenter might present a tray of objects to the parrot and the other human, and ask 'What colour?' If the parrot shows no inclination to answer, the second human will give a response and receive praise and a reward from the experimenter if correct. The second human sometimes makes errors, copying the kinds of mistake the parrot might make. Errors are 'punished' with disapproval from the experimenter, who removes the materials, shakes her head and says 'No' emphatically. The parrot's natural desire for attention and the opportunity to play with the objects presented is enough to encourage him to attempt to answer the question himself the next time it is asked. Thus the second human acts both as a model for the parrot to attempt to copy, and as a rival for the rewards the experimenter is offering. Reward for the parrot typically takes the form of an opportunity to play with the objects presented (which ensures he makes a detailed inspection of the objects). To encourage the parrot to keep working even when he is no longer interested in the objects being presented, he is also permitted to ask for and play with a more preferred object after he has answered a question correctly.

To test what the parrot has learnt, a different experimenter is brought in to ask questions. The primary trainer now sits facing away from the parrot and acts solely as an interpreter, repeating to an assistant the words the parrot has said (which can be difficult for an untrained ear to understand).

Using this method, one parrot, Alex, was trained to produce over 100 English words, and he could answer questions about several qualities of the objects presented to him, such as their colour, shape and material, as well as number.

insurmountable problem for Alex, though his accuracy suffered a little. Only small numbers were tested, so Pepperberg took care to ensure that the objects did not fall into characteristic patterns on the tray. Alex was also able to answer questions such as 'How many purple wood?' when presented with a tray containing pieces of purple wood, orange wooden items, pieces of purple chalk and orange chalk all intermixed.

More evidence of what might be construed as counting comes from a chimpanzee, Ai. Ai was trained by Tetsuro Matsuzawa and coworkers to touch numerals on a computer screen in ascending numerical order (Biro and Matsuzawa, 1999; Kawai and Matsuzawa, 2000). Up to five numerals, selected at random from the range zero to nine, appeared simultaneously in randomized positions on the computer screen. Ai first had to touch the lowest numeral, which then disappeared. Then she had to pick the lower of the remaining numerals, and it too disappeared. This process was repeated until Ai touched the only remaining numeral (the highest number in the original set) and she received a small food reward. Ai succeeded at this task even when all the remaining numerals were replaced by white squares after the first numeral had been touched.

Experiments by Elizabeth Brannon and Herb Terrace (2000) on three macaque monkeys shared some of the design features of the research on Ai the chimpanzee. Brannon and Terrace's monkeys touched stimuli that appeared on a computer screen in order of numerosity. In Brannon and Terrace's experiments, however, the stimuli were not numerals (as Ai's had been), but different numbers of objects. These objects could be simple squares or circles of differing size, items selected from clip art software or even objects that differed in size, shape and colour. A sample array is shown in Figure 5.10. The monkeys were well able to select quantities from one to four in ascending or descending order, even though the stimuli used varied greatly throughout training.

Brannon and Terrace point out that it is not particularly difficult to train a monkey to respond to any series of four arbitrary items in a specific order. Their success in training monkeys to select quantities from one to four in certain orders might therefore have had nothing to do with counting, and could just be evidence of an ability to order arbitrary stimuli and responses. In a follow-up experiment to test this possibility, the monkeys were shown groups of two quantities at a time. The correct response involved selecting the groups of items in either ascending or descending order of numerosity depending on which type of training the monkey had undergone in the first experiment. Some of these stimuli involved quantities in the one to four range, which were familiar from earlier training: others contained quantities of five to nine, which the monkeys had not previously experienced. Tests involving novel quantities were not rewarded, and therefore served as a test of whether the monkeys really had abstracted the rules involved in counting objects, or had just learnt certain sequences of responding. All three monkeys performed at a very high level when choosing quantities of one to four, for which they had previously been rewarded. Choice in the five to nine range was less reliable, but exceeded the level of chance for two of the three monkeys – the two who had been trained to select quantities in ascending order. The third monkey, who had been trained to select quantities in descending order,

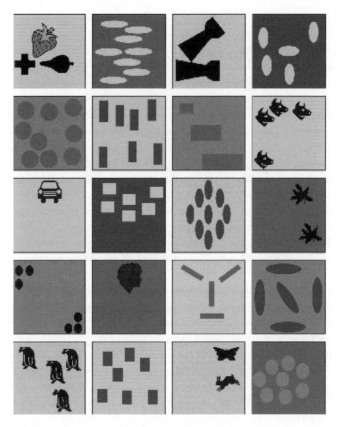

Figure 5.10   Examples of stimuli used by Brannon and Terrace showing different numbers of various kinds of object (the originals were coloured) (courtesy of E. Brannon)

was completely unsuccessful with the new quantities of five to nine. However all three improved in their performance on the novel quantities when a reward for correct choice was introduced.

Numbers are useful to us for more than just counting objects, they can also be used to add and subtract quantities of items. The only suggestion that an animal can use numbers in this way comes from one of Sarah Boysen's chimps, Sheba. Boysen (1992) and her colleagues first trained a group of chimpanzees to select cards with Arabic numerals on them and match them with a number of objects presented on a tray. As shown in Figure 5.11, the chimps were given cards bearing the numbers 1, 2 and 3, and they then had to choose the correct one to go with a tray containing three treats. Once this had been mastered, the task was reversed and the chimpanzees were required to pick the correct tray of items to match an Arabic numeral.

The quickest of these chimps, Sheba, was selected for further training on an arithmetical problem (Boysen and Berntson, 1989). Sheba was trained to make a circuit around three different places in her training environment (Figure 5.12).

Figure 5.11   Sarah Boysen's chimp Sheba selecting the set of items that match the numeral shown on the screen (from Boysen, 1992)

Figure 5.12   The room in which Sheba carried out the adding task. Dots mark the three places where Sheba might find oranges. She then had to pick the card bearing the numeral that corresponded to the total number of oranges she had seen (from Boysen and Berntson, 1989)

In any one trial, two out of three of these places contained oranges. After Sheba had made a circuit of the room, cards bearing the Arabic numerals from zero to four were placed on a wooden platform. Sheba's task was to select the Arabic numeral that matched the total number of oranges she had seen on her trip round the training area. Sheba quickly learnt, for example, that if there was one orange on the tree stump and two more in the plastic bowl, that the numeral she must select was '3'. Sheba's next task was to solve the same problem but now with the oranges replaced by cards with Arabic numerals on them. She was immediately able to transfer what she had learnt with the oranges to the numerals, correctly performing three quarters of the first tests given to her.

Intriguing as this apparent demonstration of addition may be, it needs to be kept in mind that Sheba was only tested with numbers up to four. To make totals of up to four requires very few combinations. A total of zero can only be made by two quantities of zero. Likewise a total of one can only be achieved in one way, by adding zero and one. Two can be constructed in two ways (zero plus two, or one plus one), as can three (zero plus three, or one plus two). Even a total of four can only be constructed in three ways (zero plus four, one plus three, or two plus two). Consequently the five possible totals can be achieved in just nine different ways. It surely would not be difficult for a chimpanzee to learn these nine alternatives by rote memorization.

Consequently, though Boysen's demonstration of Sheba's arithmetical competence is thought provoking, it cannot be considered definitive until further research has been carried out.

Conclusions

In Chapter 4 we saw that the perceptual worlds of other species can be very different from our own. Many animals can see ultraviolet and infrared radiation, which is invisible to us, or hear tones that are too high or too low for us to hear, or perceive electric fields. In the realm of the more abstract aspects of experience that are the subject of this chapter, there does not seem to have been the same uncovering of 'superhuman' abilities in other species. This may be because we cannot conceive of how to look for conceptual skills that we do not have. Nonetheless the experiments reviewed in this chapter have shown that several species share aspects of human conceptual experience. An understanding of the permanency of hidden objects has been shown in adult dogs and some apes. Perhaps it will be found in other species as better means of testing are developed. Various forms of perceptual categorization have been shown in some mammals and birds. Much more widespread evidence is available to demonstrate that animals have both a sense of the time of day and an ability to learn about short, arbitrary time intervals. Some aspects of the sense of number, including the ability to discriminate relative and absolute numbers, have been found in some birds and mammals. Some components of the more advanced aspects of number sense that contribute to the ability we call counting have been demonstrated by non-human primate species, as well as an African grey parrot. That these abilities should be found in such a disparate group of animals suggests that further studies on other species may also produce successful results.

FURTHER READING

Watanabe, S, Lea, S E G and Dittrich, W H (1993) What can we learn from experiments on pigeon concept discrimination?, in H P Zeigler and H-J Bischof (eds), *Vision, Brain and Behavior in Birds* (Cambridge, MA: MIT Press), pp. 351–76; Wasserman, E A (1995) The conceptual abilities of pigeons, *American Scientist*, **83**, 246–55; Cook, R G (2000) The comparative psychology of avian visual cognition, *Current Directions in Psychological Science*, **9**, 83–9.

These three contributions review a range of studies on cognitive processes in pigeon vision.

Zentall, T R (2000) Symbolic representation by pigeons, *Current Directions in Psychological Science*, **9**, 118–22. Zentall summarizes the results of several experiments on stimulus equivalence.

Binkley, S (1990) *The Clockwork Sparrow: Time, Clocks, and Calendars in Biological Organisms* (Englewood Cliffs, NJ: Prentice Hall). In this book Binkley presents a thorough review of research on how animals learn about the time of day.

Domjan, M (1998) *The Principles of Learning and Behavior*, 4th edn (Pacific Grove, CA: Brooks/Cole). This text is one of several sources on basic research on learning about short time intervals.

Koehler, O (1951) The ability of birds to 'count', *Bulletin of Animal Behaviour*, **9**, 41–5. This article is Otto Koehler's only English account of his research.

Davis, H and Perusse, R (1988) Numerical competence in animals: Definitional issues, current evidence, and a new research agenda, *Behavioral and Brain Sciences*, **11**, 561–615. Davis and Perusse offer a wide-ranging review of research (up to 1988) on animals' sense of number.

Boysen, S T (1992) Counting as the chimpanzee sees it, in W K Honig and J G Fetterman (eds), *Cognitive Aspects of Stimulus Control* (Hillsdale, NJ: Lawrence Erlbaum Associates), pp. 367–383. This chapter offers a review of research on the counting ability of chimpanzees.

Hauser, M (2000) What do animals think about numbers?, *American Scientist*, **88**, 144–51. Hauser's article is an interesting survey of recent research on animals' sense of number, written for a wider audience. The text is also available on the web at http://www.amsci.org/amsci/articles/00articles/hauser.html

WEBSITES

This is the first academic text on any aspect of animal cognition to appear on the web. It includes contributions on bird visual cognition by several of the researchers mentioned in this chapter http://www.pigeon.psy.tufts.edu/avc/toc.htm

Irene Pepperberg's research on African grey parrots is surveyed at http://www.alexfoundation.org/index.html

A summary of the above research and a transcript of Alex using number terms are available at http://www.sciam.com/specialissues/1198intelligence/1198pepperberg.html

Evelyn Hanggi's research on horse cognition is summarized at http://members.aol.com/EquiResF/horse.html

Interesting research on how blue jays learn about cryptic moths is summarized at http://abcnews.go.com/sections/science/DailyNews/jays981007.html

6
Remembering

I had a dog who was savage and averse to all strangers, and I purposely tried his memory after an absence of five years and two days. I went near the stable where he lived, and shouted to him in my old manner; he showed no joy, but instantly followed me out walking, and obeyed me, exactly as if I had parted with him only half an hour before. A train of old associations, dormant during five years, had thus been instantaneously awakened in his mind. (Darwin, 1877/1989, p. 74)

Whenever the behaviour of an animal in the present shows the influence of events in the past, memory of some kind must be implicated. Viewed in this way, it is clear that we have already considered many examples of memory. In Chapter 3, when discussing Pavlovian conditioning, for example, we saw many cases of an animal's behaviour being altered by past experience. Even the marine snail, which responds differently to a light touch to its mantle after training with a shock to its tail, can be said to have a memory of tail shocks. The Siamese fighting fish, which produces aggressive displays in response to a red light after the light has been paired with the presentation of a mirror, has a memory of that mirror. Instrumental conditioning also implies simple forms of memory. Take the queen triggerfish that learnt to press a plastic rod in order to obtain a piece of food. She performed this action more frequently as training progressed because she remembered that doing so would help her get food.

In Chapter 4, where navigation was under consideration, the ability of species such as pigeons and bees to 'home' from distant sites implies a memory for where they have come from. Similarly the migratory abilities of many hundreds of animal species imply a long-lasting memory for places. Even locusts, which journey over thousands of kilometres and never return from whence they came, must have some kind of memory of the direction they have come from in order to be able to avoid it in the future.

The ability to act now on the basis of experience in the past – the ability to use memory to guide action – must often bring with it significant biological advantages. Take for example a Hawaiian nectar-feeding honeycreeper, the amakihi, which feeds on mamane flowers. After an amakihi has taken the nectar from a flower it takes the mamane about an hour to refill with nectar. Consequently there is little point in the amakihi returning to that flower for about an hour. An amakihi that can remember which flowers it has collected nectar from and avoid returning to them for a while will have a significant advantage over a bird that wastes its time and energy repeatedly returning to flowers it has recently emptied. And sure enough, these birds have been found to avoid returning to clusters of flowers they have recently visited (Kamil, 1978).

Memory is one of the most intensely studied areas of animal cognition and it will not be possible in this chapter to provide more than a 'taster' of the wide range of research that is going on at present.

First we consider the simplest forms of memory in the simplest organisms – the simplest possible cases of past experience influencing present behaviour. These simple forms of memory are also present in more complex organisms, including ourselves. Other forms of memory, those closer to our everyday understanding of the term, can be considered in many different ways. We shall follow one of the simplest categorizations of memory: short term and long term. Short-term memory refers to a limited capacity store and usually lasts only a short time (perhaps a few minutes). Long-term memory refers to the storage of information that appears almost unlimited both in terms of the amount that can be retained and the length of time it can be remembered.

Simple memories

Around a hundred years ago Herbert Jennings (1906) undertook a study of the behaviour of the 'lower organisms', as he called them. Jennings studied the reactions of the barely visible unicellular animals that congregate in the sludge and slime at the bottom of ponds and other areas of still water. One that particularly attracted Jennings' interest was the *Stentor*, shown in Figure 6.1. *Stentor* usually attach themselves to a firm base and feed by wafting water into their mouths with little hairs called cilia. If something nasty comes along the *Stentor* contracts into its tube to protect itself until the threat passes. Jennings found that the first time the *Stentor* is stimulated with something that disturbs it but does no harm, such as a jet of water, it contracts into its tube, but with subsequent stimulations it

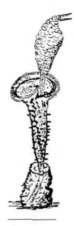

Figure 6.1   A Stentor

grows progressively less perturbed and eventually maintains its normal feeding posture. Here we see behaviour, albeit very simple behaviour, that is modified by experience. The response to later jets of water is not the same as the response to the first jet. This simple change in response with repeated stimulation is called 'habituation', and we shall count this change in the *Stentor*'s behaviour as the simplest form of memory. Habituation is found in all animals. The ability to ignore and sleep through the at first disturbing ticking of an unfamiliar clock is the same response as the *Stentor* shows to repeated stimulation with harmless water.

Pavlovian and instrumental conditioning also imply simple forms of memory. It used to be believed that such memories were only very brief. Take Pavlovian conditioning of the eye-blink reflex for example. In this situation an animal learns to blink to a tone or other initially neutral conditioned stimulus (see Chapter 3) because it is repeatedly paired with a small shock close to the eye that evokes a reflex blink. In this situation the interval between the tone (the conditioned stimulus) and the shock (the unconditioned stimulus) must be very short (around half a second) for conditioning to progress well. Studies of this type led to the belief that the memories instilled in Pavlovian conditioning were always extremely short. Researchers in the 1970s, however, found situations where the interval between the conditioned and unconditioned stimuli can be very much longer.

John Garcia and his colleagues (Garcia and Koelling, 1966) studied how rats learn about foods that cause sickness. In this form of Pavlovian conditioning animals learn that a certain new flavour is later followed by sickness. The conditioned stimulus is the unfamiliar flavour, the unconditioned stimulus is a poison to induce sickness. The unconditioned response to the poison is sickness. With experience a response develops to the novel flavour – that response is to avoid the novel flavour in the future. (Described in the clinical language of Pavlovian conditioning this may sound like a strange scenario, but it is in fact a very common experience. Who has not woken up in the morning feeling sick and with an intense aversion to whatever it was that they ate the night before – especially if exotic food was consumed?) What is interesting about this form of Pavlovian conditioning for our consideration of memory is that the conditioning is still effective with conditioned stimulus–unconditioned stimulus intervals of many hours. This demonstrates that the memories implied in Pavlovian conditioning can be of far longer duration than was originally believed.

In instrumental conditioning it is generally important that the consequence of an animal's behaviour (the 'reinforcement') promptly follows that behaviour. If a delay is imposed between, say, a rat choosing one or other arm of a T maze and obtaining its food reward, then even very short delays will cause the rate of learning to slow dramatically. Early experiments showed that a delay of as little as a second was enough to disrupt the learning of a rat (Grice, 1948). Later research found that the problem with instrumental conditioning experiments using delayed reinforcement is that the animal goes on to engage in a variety of behaviours after the one that has yet to be reinforced. So how is the animal to know which of its behaviours is being reinforced? Subsequent studies have 'marked' the to-be-reinforced behaviour with a neutral stimulus such as a tone or a light (Lieberman *et al.*, 1979). Under these conditions the animal is much better able to identify which of its behaviours is being reinforced and a much longer memory can be demonstrated.

Short-term memory

Short-term memory is, as its name implies, a relatively brief memory store. Though its duration varies in different experiments, a range of seconds or minutes is usual. As well as being of brief duration, short-term memory is also of limited capacity. In humans seven items is about the limit for short-term memory.

Box 6.1   Methods used in short-term memory research

Two methods have become very popular in short-term (and some long-term) memory research because of their great flexibility. These are mazes (of various types) and the 'delayed matching to sample' method.

Mazes of many kinds have been a part of the study of animal cognition since its earliest days as an experimental science. The first maze used in animal research was modelled on the Hampton Court maze in the garden of a royal palace outside London. These early attempts with very complex mazes were not particularly successful, and in modern times simpler mazes have been more popular.

One of the most popular kinds of maze in use today is the radial arm maze, developed by David Olton in the 1970s (see Olton, 1985). Rats are the most common subjects in radial arm mazes, though mice and other rodents are occasionally used, and versions have been developed for use with fish and pigeons. As was shown in Figure 3.8, the radial arm maze consists of a central area with a number of arms running off it. At the end of each arm a small piece of food is hidden in a food cup. The animal's task is to run down each arm and collect the hidden food as efficiently as possible. Normally the food, once taken, is not replaced by the experimenters, so the rat must remember which arms it has been down in order not to waste time and energy returning to arms in which the cup has already been emptied. Different numbers of arms can be attached to the central area, but eight is the number commonly used in memory research. The animal can be detained in the central area by means of small doors operated by remote control by the experimenters. This enables them to test how long the rats can remember which arms they have been down and allows them to modify the apparatus in the middle of a trial (for example by moving arms or other stimuli around) in order to test how the animal remembers where it has been and where it still needs to go.

A highly original form of maze that has grown in popularity since its invention by Richard Morris (1981) is the water maze (see Figure 6.2). This 'maze' is simply a circular vat of water (1.3 metres in diameter). The water is made opaque by the

Box 6.1   (cont'd)

addition of milk powder or white powder paint. Hidden beneath the surface of the water is an escape platform. No food is used to motivate the rat in this maze – the desire to escape from the water-filled vat is motivation enough. Rats are competent but reticent swimmers and are highly motivated to find the hidden platform, which saves them from having to swim any longer. The ingenuity of this maze is that it gets round the problem of motivation (each time a rat is put in the water it can be assumed to be equally motivated to find the hidden platform: in a more orthodox, food-motivated maze an animal may become less motivated as its hunger abates). The water maze also prevents all possibility of the rat finding its way by using local information – for example by scent marking the parts of the maze it has already explored. The maze's internal featurelessness ensures that the rats must be navigating solely on the basis of whatever is visible outside the maze (doors, windows and so on in the laboratory) and their memory for where they have already swum in the maze.

The delayed matching to sample (DMTS, Figure 6.3) task is far simpler than its rather convoluted name might suggest. It is similar to the procedure described in Chapter 5 to demonstrate the development of a concept of 'same'. A subject (this could be a human or a member of a great many other species) is shown a sample stimulus. This stimulus could be a picture, a sound or an object of any kind. The stimulus is then removed and the subject is left in peace for a period of time that is known as the retention interval. At the end of the retention interval the subject is shown two (or more) similar stimuli. One of these is the same as the originally presented sample stimulus – this is the matching stimulus; the other stimuli are distracters. The attraction of the DMTS procedure is that it is simple enough to be used with a wide

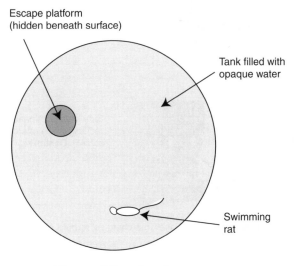

Figure 6.2   A rat in a water maze

Box 6.1 (cont'd)

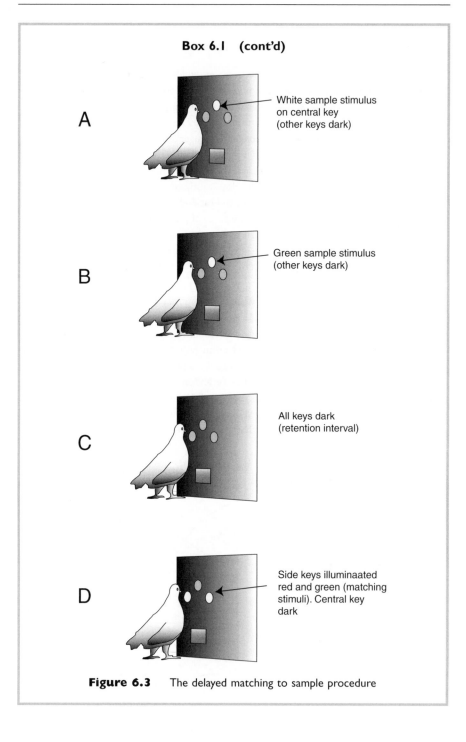

A — White sample stimulus on central key (other keys dark)

B — Green sample stimulus (other keys dark)

C — All keys dark (retention interval)

D — Side keys illuminaated red and green (matching stimuli). Central key dark

Figure 6.3 The delayed matching to sample procedure

Box 6.1 (cont'd)

range of species, thus permitting interspecies comparisons. But it is also flexible enough for almost any type of object to be used as the stimulus. Duration of memory can be ascertained simply by testing retention at longer and longer retention intervals, and other aspects of memory can be examined by judicious manipulation of the distracter stimuli presented in the matching phase of the procedure.

As it is commonly tested with pigeons, DMTS requires a standard operant chamber (see Chapter 3) with three pecking keys in a row. First, the central pecking key is lit up with white light to attract the pigeon's attention. After the pigeon has pecked the white light a couple of times, a sample stimulus is presented on the centre key. This could be the colour green. Usually the pigeon is required to peck this stimulus a couple of times, after which it is turned off. There then follows the retention interval, during which stimuli are not normally presented. After the retention interval the two side keys are illuminated: one the same as the sample stimulus (green), the other a distracter (red, say). The position of these two stimuli is randomized across trials so that the pigeon cannot simply learn always to peck one or other of the side keys. If the pigeon now pecks the matching (green) stimulus, it obtains a food reward. After an interval the central pecking key is lit up with white light again to indicate the start of the next trial.

Capacity

While long-term memory has an almost limitless capacity, short-term memory is a temporary store for just a few items at a time. The capacity of a rat's short-term memory can be readily tested in the radial arm maze by adding more and more arms until the rat starts to make errors. In a standard sized radial maze of eight arms, rats rarely return to an arm they have already visited. Numerous control experiments have demonstrated that rats really do use memory to keep track of which arms they have visited (they do not, for example, scent-mark arms they have already been down). It has also been shown that rats do not simply go around the maze clockwise or anticlockwise – to a human observer their activity seems fairly random. If more than eight arms are used, accuracy starts to decline. Rats can still perform above chance level with 17 or 24 arms, but as the number of arms increases they start to simplify the task by adopting strategies such as always turning to the right when leaving an arm.

Duration

Duration is perhaps a pointless subheading to consider under 'short-term memory', since if it lasts too long it isn't 'short-term' any more! Nonetheless there is value in considering how long animals' memory in these tasks can last.

In one investigation, rats working in the eight-arm radial maze were removed from the maze after making their first four choices and returned to their home cage. After a delay of four minutes to 24 hours they were brought back to the maze to finish their task by collecting the food from arms they had not yet visited. After a gap of up to four hours the rats completed the task without error, but after eight or more hours errors became frequent (Beatty and Shavalia, 1980).

Marcia Spetch and Werner Honig (1988) developed a task similar to the radial arm maze for use with pigeons (see also Spetch, 1990). The birds were tested singly in a room set up with eight possible food sites (Figure 6.4) constructed from modified two-litre milk cartons. A semicircular opening was cut in the side of each milk carton and the tops were removed so that pigeons could see and peck inside the carton. At the bottom of the carton Spetch and Honig placed grit with a couple of seeds on top. The pigeons' task was to fly around the room and collect the seeds from each milk carton as efficiently as possible.

The pigeons' memory was tested in similar conditions to those in which rats had been found capable of remembering for four hours which four arms of the radial maze they had already visited. Spetch and Honig allowed the pigeons to collect food from milk cartons positioned at four out of the eight possible locations shown in Figure 6.4, and then removed them to a holding cage. After periods ranging from two to 120 minutes the birds were allowed back into the room to complete their selection with cartons in all eight possible positions. Only the four food cartons that had not been visited in the initial phase of the experiment now contained food. These pigeons' memory of food location started to

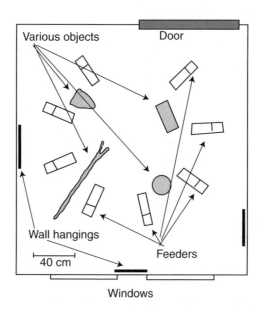

Figure 6.4   A sketch of the layout used by Spetch and Honig to study pigeons' memory for locations in a room (from Spetch and Honig, 1988)

decay after half an hour, was still above chance level after one hour, but was down to chance level after two hours.

The delayed matching to sample procedure does not demonstrate such lengthy short-term memories as the radial maze. For example pigeons trained with different colours as stimuli could only remember which of two matching colours to choose when the delay between presentation of the sample and matching stimuli (the 'retention interval' – see Box 6.1) was less than three seconds – anything longer and there was no evidence of memory. In an heroic effort involving 17 000 training trials, Douglas Grant (1976) found that pigeons were able to remember stimuli over retention intervals of up to one minute. Even monkeys and dolphins have only demonstrated a memory length of a couple of minutes in the delayed matching to sample procedure. Clearly delayed matching to sample is a difficult task for most species.

Serial order effects

A phenomenon that was noticed long ago when humans were attempting to memorize lists of items, was that the items at the beginning and end of lists tended to be better remembered than those in the middle. Better memory for the items at the start of a list is known as 'primacy', and better memory for the last items in a list is called 'recency'. Together these are known as 'serial order effects'. Recency can probably be explained by the fact that nothing comes after the last items in a list; they are the most recently seen, and consequently are least likely to decay in memory or become confused. The existence of primacy is perhaps a little more surprising. Why should the first items in a list be better remembered than items in the middle? The reason probably has to do with the fact that there are no items before the first items that could become confused with them – this places them at an advantage to items in the middle of a list, which can be confused with both earlier and later items.

Evidence of recency has repeatedly been found in non-human subjects tested for their memory of a list of items. Roger Thompson and Louis Herman (1977), for example, played dolphins a sequence of six sounds. At the end of the sequence, the dolphins were presented with a test sound. Sometimes this sound was one of the six that had just been played; other times it was not. The dolphins' accuracy in identifying whether or not the test sound had been included in the sequence would provide an indication of their short-term memory. Their memory was strong for the fourth, fifth and sixth sounds (recency), but very weak for the earlier ones. Similar evidence of strong recency but no primacy has been found among monkeys, pigeons and rats.

Evidence of primacy has proven difficult to find in non-human subjects. However, Johan Bolhuis and Hendrik van Kampen (1988) were able to demonstrate primacy and recency in rats gathering food in a radial arm maze. These rats were trained in an eight-arm maze modified so that the experimenters could control access to the arms by the use of remote-controlled doors in the central area of the maze. First the experimenters opened all the doors so that a rat could freely access all eight arms of the maze. After the rat had run down and collected

---

Box 6.2   Memory in honey-bees

While most research on animal memory has focused on a small group of vertebrate species, some researchers have studied the memory of an invertebrate – the
honey-bee. We saw in Chapter 3 that bees can be conditioned, which implies a
simple form of memory. In addition, in Chapter 4 we discussed how bees can navigate to food sites and find their way home. This implies a memory for the route
they have taken to find food.

Recent research indicates that the memory of the bee extends not just to navigation but also to colour. Michael Brown and his coworkers (1998) trained bees on
delayed matching to sample of colour stimuli. The bees collected sugar solution
from petri dishes placed on top of a horizontally mounted computer monitor. This
monitor was programmed so that different coloured circles could appear directly
beneath the glass dishes. In this way the bees were given sugar solution on one
colour and after a delay presented with a choice of two colours. Sugar solution
was now available on the same colour as it had been originally. It was found that
the bees chose the originally rewarded colour significantly more often than chance
(though still making, it must be conceded, a high rate of errors).

---

the food from five of the arms (which typically took less than two minutes) the
doors were lowered to block off all the arms, and the rat was removed from the
apparatus and taken to its home cage. After delays ranging from 30 seconds to
60 minutes the rat was returned to the central area of the radial arm maze, where
all but two of the arms were blocked off. One of the two open arms was one the
rat had been down before, the other it had not previously entered. The rat's task
was to select the arm it had not already visited – only this arm contained food.
Of course, in order to select the arm it had not already visited the rat had to be
able to remember where it had been. Bolhuis and van Kampen found that the
rats were most successful in recollecting which of the two arms they had not
already been down when the previously visited arm was either one they had visited
at the very beginning of the experiment (primacy), or one they had just visited
(recency). Just as in the human case, Bolhuis and van Kampen found that primacy
was more common when the retention interval (the length of time the rat was
absent from the apparatus) was longer (greater than 16 minutes), and recency
was more common at shorter retention intervals.

Though at first difficult to demonstrate, reliable primacy and recency effects
have been shown in recent years in pigeons, rats and monkeys.

What causes forgetting?

Forgetting is just a failure to remember – right? Well perhaps, but recent research
on animal (and human) memory suggests that there may be more to forgetting
than just not remembering.

It seems very likely that a large part of the phenomenon of forgetting is due not to the decay of some kind of memory trace, but to confusion arising from other things that an animal is trying to remember. This confusion is known as 'interference'. Interference can take two forms. Either information already in the memory store can interfere with new information – this is called 'proactive' interference. Alternatively, new information may interfere with what is already in memory – this is 'retroactive' interference. Primacy and recency effects suggest the existence of proactive and retroactive interference. Items in the middle of a list are not well remembered because they are subject both to proactive and to retroactive interference. They are exposed to proactive interference from the items earlier in the list, and are vulnerable to retroactive interference from the items that come after them. The items at the beginning of the list are better remembered because they are subject only to retroactive interference and not to proactive interference. Conversely the items at the end of the list are better remembered because they are subject only to proactive interference, and there are no items following them that could cause retroactive interference.

It is quite easy to demonstrate the effects of proactive and retroactive interference. Proactive interference in the radial arm maze can be shown simply by requiring a rat to work through the task of finding food in the eight arms of the maze several times in quick succession, instead of just once per day. The first time a rat is tested each day it performs very well. With each successive test on the same day, however, the rat's performance declines, presumably because of proactive interference from the previous trials on the same day.

A simple demonstration of retroactive interference consists of testing an animal on delayed matching to sample but making a change in illumination during the retention interval between the sample and matching stimuli (see for example Grant and Roberts, 1976). Pigeons, dolphins and monkeys have all been found to perform less well under these conditions, presumably because the illumination change interferes retroactively with their memory of the sample stimulus.

Recent studies have shown that the old view that forgetting is the passive decay of information over time is not accurate. Forgetting is better thought of as an active rejection of information no longer relevant to a situation. Adaptive forgetting is crucial to an efficient memory system. Without forgetting, the limited short-term memory capacity would become saturated and unable to absorb any new information.

William Maki and Donna Hegvik (1980) introduced an ingenious modification to the delayed matching to sample procedure for pigeon subjects. Immediately after being shown the sample stimulus the birds were shown an additional stimulus. This could either be the 'remember cue' or the 'forget cue'. In trials where the sample stimulus was followed by the remember cue, the trial proceeded as normal, with a retention interval being followed by two comparison stimuli – the pigeon had to choose the stimulus that matched the sample stimulus, just as in the normal procedure. In trials where the sample stimulus was followed by the forget cue, however, the comparison stimuli were not presented – there was no need to remember the sample stimulus. The question that Maki and Hegvik posed was, are pigeons capable of remembering or forgetting the sample stimulus on command – do they have active control over the memorization process? To test this the researchers occasionally tricked the pigeons by introducing the comparison stimuli in trials that had started with the forget cue. Sure enough, in trials where the pigeons had not been expecting to have to remember the sample stimulus their matching performance was poor.

These results remain controversial and are the subject of ongoing studies attempting to resolve theoretical difficulties. Somewhat clearer evidence for the active nature of memory and forgetting comes from rats in the radial maze. Until now we have assumed that an eight-arm radial maze requires a rat to remember seven arms (the first one is chosen at random; at the second arm the rat must remember to avoid one arm; at the third arm the rat must avoid two arms; by the eighth arm the rat has seven arms it must remember to avoid). On the other hand, if the rat has active control over its memory it could make the task easier by remembering which arms it visited for the first four entries, and then just remember which arms it has not visited for the remaining four. That way it would never have to remember more than four arms at a time. Robert Cook and his coworkers (1983) designed a simple test to see whether rats are able to control their memory in this way. Using a radial arm maze with 12 arms, Cook *et al.* occasionally removed a rat from the maze after its second, fourth, sixth, eighth or tenth choice. If the rat always remembered the arms it had visited (and not the arms it still had to visit), then this interruption should have become harder to deal with the later it came in the rat's exploration of the maze. (During an interruption after just two arms have been visited the rat only has two arms it must remember; during an interruption after its tenth choice it has ten arms to remember.) On the other hand, if the rat starts out by remembering which arms of the maze it has already visited, but halfway through switches to remembering which arms it still needs to visit, then by the time it has made its tenth choice it only has to remember two more empty arms of the maze, and the inconvenience of being removed from the maze should be relatively easy to deal with. On this basis the most difficult interruption would be after six arms have been visited, because here the rat would have to remember either the six arms it has visited, or the six arms it has not yet entered. Sure enough, Cook *et al.* found that the rats made the most errors if they were removed from the maze midway through, and fewer if they were removed towards the beginning or the end of their search through the maze.

Long-term memory

Food-storing birds

Some of the most impressive feats of memory in the animal kingdom are those of food-storing birds. Clark's nutcracker, from the American south-west, stores up to 33 000 pine nuts in around 6000 different sites in the late summer. Over the course of winter and into spring the birds return to recover their caches. The research we shall consider here indicates that they do this largely by remembering for months where they have put the nuts. On a smaller scale, when English marsh tits and North American chickadees find a rich source of food, instead of eating it all at once they take seeds away and store them nearby for consumption over the next few hours or couple of days. They may store over a hundred seeds in this way.

Marsh tits and chickadees

Richard Cowie and his colleagues (1981) gave marsh tits radioactive sunflower seeds (the seeds were only made mildly radioactive – just enough to be found later with a Geiger counter). True to form, the marsh tits took the seeds and stored them in various places. The experimenters then tracked these seeds with their Geiger counter and placed other seeds either close to (within 10 centimetres) or far from (one metre) each of the seeds the birds had stored. It was found that all the seeds added by the experimenters were less likely to be collected later by the marsh tits than the seeds the birds had stored themselves. This suggests that the marsh tits were not just looking for seeds in certain kinds of nook and cranny, but remembered to within 10 centimetres where they had placed seeds earlier.

Field studies can only take us so far in identifying for certain that these birds use memory to find their stores of seeds, and how they do so. In a sequence of experiments John Krebs, David Sherry and Sara Shettleworth investigated the role of memory in food storing by marsh tits and the related North American chickadees. One ingenious experiment that demonstrated definitively that marsh tits rely on memory to find cached seeds made use of the fact that each eye of the bird is connected only to one side of its brain (the side opposite). By covering up one eye with an eye patch while the birds were hiding seeds, and then letting them recover the seeds later with either the same or the other eye covered up, Sherry *et al.* (1981) found that only if the same eye was covered during caching and recovery were the birds able to find the seeds. This indicated that information stored in the bird's brain is crucial to finding the seeds again, and that this information cannot be transferred from one side of the brain to the other.

Sherry (1984) also performed an experiment on black-capped chickadees, the results of which suggest that chickadees use more distant, global cues to find seeds in preference to closer, local cues (Sherry, 1984). Chickadees were tested in a two-metre cubic enclosure (Figure 6.5). This enclosure contained four identical artificial 'trees', into which 32 holes had been drilled for the birds to use as storage places for seeds. These holes were identically placed in each tree, so that for each food storage site in one tree there were three identical sites in other trees, making it difficult for the bird to identify which store was which. The experimenters placed a large coloured shape on each wall of the enclosure (a global cue) and small coloured cards next to each seed storage site (local cues). The birds were given an opportunity to store seeds with both the global and the local cues present. Later they were returned to the enclosure to find their seeds under one of four conditions. The experimenters either left the enclosure as it had been when the birds had stored their seeds (local and global cues present); removed

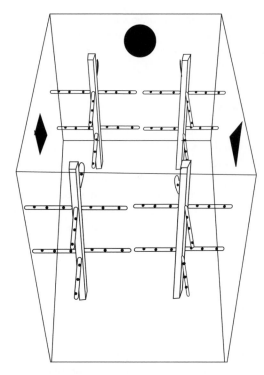

Figure 6.5   The environment in which Sherry and his colleagues studied how birds rely on global cues to remember where they have stored food (from Sherry, 1992)

either the local or the global cues; or they removed both sets of cues. Perhaps surprisingly, the birds were most confused by the removal of the global cues – the large coloured shapes on the walls. The removal of the local cues – the coloured cards next to the food storage sites – had no significant effect on their success in recovering seeds. In a subsequent experiment Sherry and his colleagues (Herz *et al.*, 1994) found that if the global cues were rotated around the box by 90°, 180° or 270°, then the birds also looked for the seeds they had cached in positions 90°, 180° or 270° respectively from where they had originally hidden them.

Nutcrackers

Laboratory studies on nutcrackers and other birds that store seeds for the winter have so far also been restricted to comparatively brief storage times. Stephen Vander Wall (1982) allowed two Clark's nutcrackers to hide food separately in an indoor aviary. Each bird was given an opportunity to store seeds before the other was allowed back in to recover its seeds. A strong indication that the birds were relying on memory and not simply choosing parts of the aviary that looked

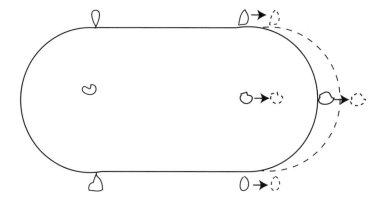

Figure 6.6   The arena used by Vander Wall to test nutcrackers' memory of stored seed positions. All the objects on one side of the aviary were displaced 20 centimetres during the interval between the nutcrackers storing the seeds and their recovery of them (from Vander Wall, 1982)

good for hiding seeds, was that each bird accurately recovered its own seeds without disturbing those which the other bird had hidden. Vander Wall discovered, however, that seed finding was seriously disrupted if significant objects in the aviary (such as logs and rocks) were moved around between the time the birds hid the seeds and when they returned to look for them.

In another experiment by Vander Wall (ibid.), all the objects (except the hidden seeds) on one side of an aviary were displaced 20 centimetres during the interval between the nutcrackers hiding the seeds and their recovery of them (Figure 6.6). When they were allowed back in to try to recover the seeds the birds were spot on in the undisturbed side of the aviary, but missed their caches by 20 centimetres on the side where objects had been moved.

In all the above experiments the possibility exists that the birds are making their task of remembering where they hid seeds easier by always placing the seeds in the same kind of spot each time, rather like making the task of finding your car in a large car park easier by always parking under the largest tree. Alan Kamil and Russell Balda (1990) tested for this possibility by forcing Clark's nutcrackers to hide seeds in spots that the experimenters and not the birds had chosen. They gave the nutcrackers seeds to store in a room that contained 180 sand-filled holes. The experimenters were able to close these holes so that only enough were left open for the number of seeds the birds had to store. Even when the birds were forced to store seeds in holes arbitrarily chosen by the experimenters, they were still successful at finding their seeds 10 to 15 days later.

There is evidence that food-storing birds such as black-capped chickadees and scrub jays use the sun compass to find seeds they have hidden (the sun compass was introduced in Chapter 4). This involves combining information about the time of day with the position of the sun to find compass directions. Since an animal's sense of time of day stems from when it observes sunrise and sunset, tests of use of the sun compass system can be made by keeping the birds in an indoor aviary and turning the lights on earlier or later than normal. In tests where scrub jays were woken up six hours later than normal, it was found that they searched for food in an octagonal aviary 90° clockwise from where they should have – just as the use of a sun compass would predict (Duff *et al.*, 1998).

Pigeons

Russell Balda and Wolfgang Wiltschko (1995) tested pigeons under rather similar conditions to those used to test the food-storing birds mentioned above. Their pigeons were trained to dig up food that had been hidden by the experimenters in one of eight sand-filled plastic cups in a large (five metres in diameter) aviary. The pigeons quickly learnt to dig up the seeds, and having learnt which of the eight cups had been baited, they could easily remember this for ten months. Balda and Wiltschko found no difference in the pigeons' memory whether they were tested hours or up to four days after the original training. Even after ten months no pigeon made more than one false choice (out of eight possibilities) before identifying the correct cup.

Two studies have looked at the long-term memory capacity of pigeons. William Vaughan and Sharon Greene (1984) trained pigeons in Skinner boxes to discriminate between 80 pairs of slides. In one experiment the slides had random shapes ('squiggles') drawn on them; in another the slides were photographs taken around the Cambridge, Massachusetts area. In each experiment the pigeons were trained using a Go/Nogo procedure (see Box 4.1) to respond to one stimulus in each pair (the positive stimulus), and to refrain from responding to the other stimulus. The choice of which stimulus in each pair was positive and which was negative was completely arbitrary. With sufficient training (nearly 1000 daily sessions for the squiggles, about 850 for the photographs) the birds reliably chose the positive stimulus in each pair. They were then given a break for eight months in the case of the squiggles and two years in the case of the photographs before being retested. On retesting they showed a good memory of which were the positive and which were the negative stimuli. The slowness of the initial learning of the distinction between these stimuli may in part be explained by the difficulty of some of the distinctions they were required to learn.

Lorenzo von Fersen and Juan Delius (1989) trained pigeons to discriminate between 100 positive stimuli and 625 negative stimuli using a concurrent discrimination method (see Box 4.1). The stimuli Fersen and Delius presented were black designs on a white background (a sample is shown in Figure 6.7). The birds learnt to discriminate reliably between these objects over 224 sessions. In the subsequent tests, Fersen and Delius replaced either the 100 positive or the 625 negative stimuli with novel items that the pigeons had never seen before. Their excellent performance under these test conditions indicates that they had memorized both the positive and the negative stimuli. In fact the pigeons performed slightly better when the negative stimuli were replaced with novel items, suggesting that they were perhaps discriminating between positive and negative stimuli on the basis of their familiarity.

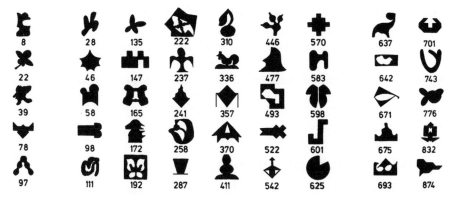

Figure 6.7 A selection of the stimuli used by Fersen and Delius in their study of pigeons' rote memorization ability (from Fersen and Delius, 1989)

After training the pigeons were given a six-month break from the experiment. When they were returned to the experimental environment, unlike Vaughan and Greene's subjects, Fersen and Delius's pigeons did not immediately recognize the objects with which they had been trained earlier. However after a few days' practice with a subset of the stimuli they had previously seen, they were reintroduced to the remaining stimuli (which they had not seen for over six months) and were able to categorize them correctly to a very high degree.

In studies of human long-term memory, people are often just asked whether they recognize an object or scene as one they have seen before (under which condition people have been shown to be capable of recognizing up to 10 000

Box 6.3 Memory despite metamorphosis

Many animals undergo metamorphosis – a complete change of body form – at some stage in their lives. Ralph Miller and Alvin Berk (1977) investigated whether memory is preserved in the African claw-toed frog when it metamorphoses from tadpole into frog. Miller and Berk first trained tadpoles and frogs to avoid one compartment of a two-compartment chamber by delivering a mild electric shock from the floor of one of the compartments. This was readily learnt by both tadpoles and adult frogs. Then they waited 35 days, during which time the tadpoles metamorphosed into frogs and the animals that had already been frogs just grew older. Next all the subjects were tested again to see whether they could remember which compartment was the dangerous one. Miller and Berk found that, despite the great changes the tadpoles had undergone in metamorphosing into frogs over these 35 days, they showed a considerable memory of which side of the chamber was dangerous. Their memory was equivalent to that of the animals that had been adult frogs all along.

pictures). This familiarity measure would seem to be an easier task than discriminating between negative and positive items, as Vaughan and Greene's and Fersen and Delius's pigeons were required to do. It also appears a more ecologically relevant task, as home-bound pigeons often need to differentiate between familiar landmarks and unfamiliar territory. Darwin's account of his dog's long-term memory, quoted at the start of this chapter, is a case of using familiarity to test memory, and it shows a longer-lasting memory than has been demonstrated in any modern experiment.

Implicit and explicit memory

One of the many distinctions drawn in studies of human memory is between implicit and explicit memory processes. Explicit memory is the remembering of things that we can describe in words – memories that we are conscious of. Explicit memory is the kind of memory activated when somebody asks you, 'Do you remember when . . . ?' Not all memory is conscious, however. Many memories manifest themselves even when there is no conscious 'recollection' of the events in question. Motor skills, such as riding a bicycle, fall into this category of implicit memories. Experiments on people whose explicit memory has been impaired through brain damage suggest that many simple patterns of behaviour are remembered without the need for conscious recollection.

When considering animal memory it is very difficult to judge whether we are dealing with explicit or implicit memory. Since there is no way of demonstrating consciousness in animals (see Chapter 2), it has generally been assumed that animal memory must be implicit. We need not necessarily accept this argument, however. Although we cannot demonstrate that an animal is conscious, we can explore whether it can report on its own behaviour – this would seem to be the fairest animal analog of explicit memory. Charles Shimp (1981, 1982) trained pigeons to report on the number or pattern of pecks they had just performed. The pigeons were first trained to peck either quickly or slowly at a central response key. Occasionally, two side keys would light up. A peck on one side key was rewarded if the previous response sequence on the centre key had consisted of fast responses; a peck on the other side key was rewarded if the response sequence had been slow. The pigeons became quite adept at reporting their memory of their response patterns in this manner. In a similar way, the pigeons were trained to report whether they had just made a short or long run of responses.

A more recent experiment by Nicola Clayton and Anthony Dickinson (1998) suggested that scrub jays may have some form of explicit memory. Jays were given the opportunity to learn that 'wax worms' (wax-moth larvae) – a highly preferred food – become unpalatable after a period of several hours. Next the jays were trained to take either wax worms or peanuts (an acceptable but less preferred food) and store them in trays of sand. Clayton and Dickinson found that, given a choice between retrieving cached wax worms or peanuts after just four hours (when the wax worms were still very palatable), the scrub jays would selectively recover the wax worms. Given the same choice after 124 hours (long enough for the wax worms to have decayed and become unpalatable), the jays recovered the peanuts instead. This indicates that the jays were able to recall not just where they had stored food, but also which type of food they had stored and when. This is the kind of rich multidimensional memory that is considered explicit memory in humans.

Conclusions

This chapter has shown that there are many different types of memory. The unicellular *Stentor*, which alters its response to a repeated innocuous stimulus, is obviously far removed from the Clark's nutcracker, which stores thousands of seeds in the autumn to keep it going through the winter. Clearly an animal's lifestyle – its ecological niche – determines the kind of memory it will have. Though this statement is generally true when very different species are being considered, it has proven quite difficult to demonstrate differences in memory between more closely related species. Throughout the 1990s Shettleworth, Krebs and others compared the memorization abilities of food-storing birds (such as the nutcrackers, marsh tits and chickadees considered above) with those of their non-storing relatives, such as jays (which are related to nutcrackers) and titmice (which are related to chickadees and marsh tits). While it has been shown that birds that hoard food rely more on spatial information than do their non-hoarding cousins (non-hoarding species make more use of visual information and patterns), differences in their memorization abilities as such have proven harder to demonstrate. Krebs, Shettleworth and their colleagues have suggested that food-storing birds (marsh tits) are less vulnerable to proactive interference than are non-storing birds (blue tits) (see for example Krebs *et al.*, 1990). However when Robert Hampton *et al.* (1998) compared the memorization abilities of food-storing chickadees with those of dark-eyed juncos (non-storing birds), it was the non-storing juncos that showed less vulnerability to proactive interference.

Comparing the cognitive abilities of different species at more than a superficial level is always fraught with problems. Can we be sure that even closely related species see the world in the same way? If their sensory and attentional abilities are not comparable, then their memories can hardly hope to be. In the case of memory, an additional complexity arises from our lack of knowledge about what any given species needs to remember. It is known that certain species of bird store food and use memory to find their caches later – but what about non-food-storing species of bird? Is it reasonable to assume that they do not have as much to remember? They may indeed remember where and when they have been foraging, where there are predators, where to find mates and avoid rivals – the list is potentially endless.

This may partly explain why laboratory tests have so far failed to find any clear-cut distinction between the memorization abilities of different species of bird. The birds we classify as non-storing may have other substantial memory tasks to deal with in their lives of which we are simply unaware.

FURTHER READING

Honig, W K and Fetterman, J G (eds) (1992) *Cognitive Aspects of Stimulus Control* (Mahwah, NJ: Lawrence Erlbaum). Several chapters of this wide-ranging book are relevant to research on memory in different species.

Sherry, D F and Duff, S J (1996) Behavioural and neural bases of orientation in food-storing birds, *Journal of Experimental Biology*, **199**, 165–72, and Kamil, A C and Roitblat, H L (1985) The ecology of foraging behavior: implications for animal learning and memory, *Annual Review of Psychology*, **36**, 141–69, provide very good reviews of the research on memory in food-storing birds.

WEBSITE

The following site summarizes research by Clayton and Dickinson that suggests scrub jays have some form of explicit memory

http://abcnews.go.com/sections/science/DailyNews/birdmemory980916.html

7
Reasoning

To reason, according to the *Oxford English Dictionary*, is to adapt thought or action to some end. Though the dictionary adds that this intellectual power is usually regarded as characteristic of mankind only, the definition it offers would appear to cover all the forms of behaviour considered in this book. Although almost any form of behaviour directed towards some end could be considered as reasoning, the term is usually reserved for more complex cases of problem solving – cases that appear to demand the drawing of conclusions beyond what is immediately available to the senses. Traditionally, these kinds of problem have been considered to involve some kind of mental calculation, although more recently it has often proved possible to explain behaviour with simpler mechanisms than the complex ones that were originally proposed. As we shall see here, many of the examples of behaviour that appear to demand abstract mental calculation for their solution are in fact solved by applying simple rules of association, such as those considered in Chapter 3. Some would say that if these problems can be solved by simple associative rules then they no longer qualify as 'reasoning'. I think, however, that this is too harsh a position, and I would rather keep these interesting phenomena together – as examples of complex behaviour, however achieved.

Spatial reasoning

Just as the spatial dimension enables many species to reveal memory abilities that are not apparent in other forms of testing (see Chapter 6), so it is with reasoning. Spatial problems enable many species to demonstrate reasoning abilities that are not apparent in other dimensions of experience.

One type of spatial problem that tests the reasoning ability of animals is the detour problem. Given experience with a lengthy route round an obstacle, can an animal deduce the shortest route when the obstacle is absent? The pioneer of animal cognition, Edward Tolman, set rats to explore a rather complex maze, as shown in Figure 7.1 (Tolman and Honzik, 1930). In this maze there were three paths between the starting box (where the rat was placed at the start of a trial) and the goal box (where food could be found). Path 1 was the most direct, path 2 involved a short detour and path 3 required a longer detour. By blocking one or more of these paths at a time, the rats were encouraged to investigate all three

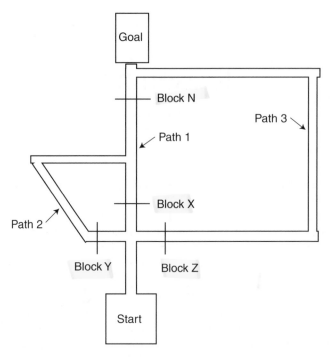

Figure 7.1   A sketch of the maze used by Tolman and Honzik to study detour learning in rats. Blockages could be placed at points X, Y and Z as well as at N (from Tolman and Honzik, 1930)

paths. Tolman and his colleagues found that the rats would first explore the most direct route, path 1. Only if they found that path blocked would they explore path 2; and only if that was also blocked would they head down the longest path, path 3.

In another of Tolman's original experiments (Tolman *et al.*, 1946), rats were required to explore the maze shown in the left-hand panel of Figure 7.2. In this maze there was only one path from the starting area to the goal box, but this path was rather lengthy and twisted. Once the rats had had sufficient opportunity to explore this route, the apparatus was altered to the configuration shown in the right-hand panel of the figure: the original route was blocked off and a large number of alternative routes were offered in its place. Would the rats pick the alternative route that led most directly to the goal box? Tolman *et al.* found that indeed they did.

Unfortunately, in terms of interpreting how these rats found the shortest of the alternative routes, Tolman and his colleagues had made an error in the design of their experiment that simplified the task for the rats. Above the goal box they had fixed a light bulb. This light was visible to the rats from any position in the maze. Consequently there was no need for them to decide which alternative was the shortest way to the goal box – they could simply head straight for the light.

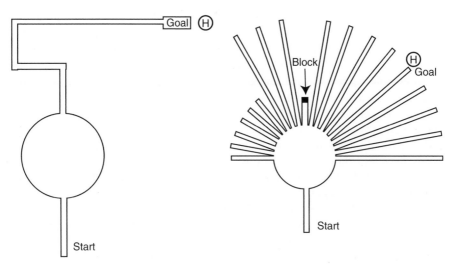

Figure 7.2   The mazes used in the two stages of the experiment described by Tolman *et al.* A light was located at position H (from Tolman *et al.*, 1946)

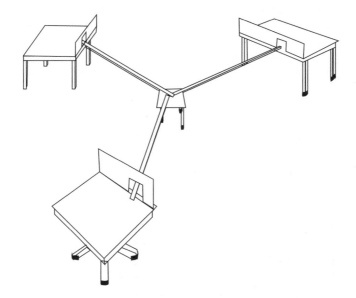

Figure 7.3   The layout for Maier's three-table task (from Maier, 1932)

Attempts by subsequent researchers to replicate Tolman *et al.*'s results without the presence of a light over the goal box were not successful.

Norman Maier (1932) developed a task that has proven useful in testing rats' ability to reason about space. The Maier three-table task (Figure 7.3) is simply three tables connected by runways. One of the three tables has food on it, but a screen blocks the rat's view of each table from the runway so it cannot see which table the food is on. At the beginning of a trial the rat is placed on the table that holds the food (this table is varied from trial to trial). After the rat has eaten a little of this food it is removed to one of the other tables. The question now is, can the rat find its way directly back to the table with the food on it? The answer to this question is generally 'yes', even after a delay of hours between eating and being given the opportunity to find its way back. There is, however, one criterion that must be met before a rat can successfully find the baited table – the animal must first have the opportunity to explore the three tables and the connecting runways. Rats that have had prior experience of only one of the three tables are quite unable to succeed at this task. Those with prior experience of two of the three tables are moderately successful – approximately what they might achieve by chance. Only rats with previous experience of all three tables and runways are clearly able to solve the problem of finding the food. The fact that rats need to have an opportunity to explore all three tables before they can choose the shortest route indicates that they are able to put together experiences to find the solution to new problems – a form of reasoning.

Another pioneer of animal cognition, Wolfgang Köhler (1925/1963), was also interested in the question of how different species cope with detour problems (though sometimes spelt 'Koehler', Wolfgang Köhler was not related to Otto Koehler mentioned in Chapter 5). His was a fairly informal method in which members of different species were placed in front of barriers of various shapes, behind which he placed a desirable food item. Two of Köhler's barrier problems are shown in Figure 7.4.

The subject was placed at the starting point, S; the desired food was placed at point G. The barriers marked in Figure 7.4 were transparent ones – a fence made of wire netting. The question of interest was, what would the animal do to get to the food? A dog placed in this arena immediately ran around the fence to get to the food. In a subsequent test the food was placed closer to the fence,

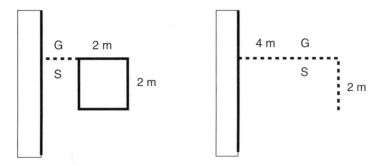

Figure 7.4   A barrier problem set by Köhler. S marks the starting point, and G the desired food (from Köhler, 1925/1963)

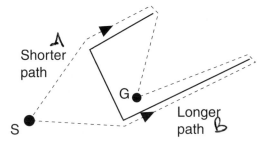

Figure 7.5   One of the barrier problems used by Poucet *et al.* S marks the cats' starting point and G shows where the food was placed (from Poucet *et al.*, 1983)

and according to Köhler the dog could not bring itself to move away from the close but unobtainable meat in order to go round the barrier to reach its ultimate goal. A girl of just over one year old could solve this problem, though also not without some hesitatation about first having to move away from the desired object in order to reach it. Likewise some chickens that Köhler tested had a great deal of difficulty moving away from the desired object and progressing around the fence. Köhler describes anecdotally how dogs and chimpanzees are capable of solving significantly more complex detour problems.

More recent experiments on detour problems in animals have broadened the range of species deemed capable of spatial reasoning and have identified some of the conditions that make detour problems easy or difficult for different species to solve. Bruno Poucet and his colleagues (1983) systematically examined the ability of cats to deal with detours of different types. One of their detour problems is shown in Figure 7.5. The cats started at the point marked S in the figure; food was placed at point G. To ensure they had an appreciation of the shape of the barrier and the relative distances involved in the testing area, each cat was given two opportunities to explore the area without there being any food reward present. Once a cat had explored both sides of the barrier, it was removed to the starting point and food was placed at the goal point, G, in such a way that the cat could see it being placed there. The question now was, would the cat choose the shorter route to the goal (route A in Figure 7.5); or would it choose route B, which though longer enabled the cat to stay closer to the target object on its way? Poucet *et al.* found that the route taken depended on whether the barrier was transparent or opaque. With an opaque barrier the cats were far more likely to take the shorter route, A, than the longer one. However with a transparent barrier the cats' choice of routes was about 50/50. As well as identifying the importance of transparency in identifying whether cats will take the shortest route to a goal, Poucet *et al.* also explored whether it is important how much the shortest route diverges from what would be the most direct route to a target object if no barrier were present. They found that cats were more likely to take the shorter alternative route if it lay close to the direct route to the goal – if it

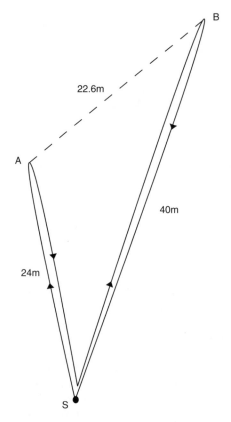

Figure 7.6   The triangular test area used by Chapuis and Varlet to test dogs' spatial reasoning ability (from Chapuis and Varlet 1987)

diverged too greatly from the direct route the cats were more likely to take a longer alternative route.

Similar studies were conducted on dogs (Breton spaniels) by Nicole Chapuis and her colleagues (including Bruno Poucet – see Chapuis *et al.*, 1983). Just as for cats, these researchers' dogs preferred the shorter route to a goal object when the barrier between their starting point and the object was opaque. When the barrier was transparent, however, the dogs, just like the cats, preferred the longer route if it enabled them to stay closer to the desired object.

Nicole Chapuis and Christian Varlet (1987) tested dogs' spatial reasoning ability by exploring their skill at taking short cuts in a large meadow. The task took place in a triangular test area, as shown in Figure 7.6. Food was placed in two positions (A and B in the figure), separated by an angle of 30° when viewed from the starting point (S). The food position, A, was 24 metres from the starting point, and position B was 40 metres from the starting point. After an experimenter had placed food at points A and B, a dog was led from S to A and back again; and then from S to B and back again (solid lines in the figure). This enabled the dog to see where the food was, although it was not allowed to take it. The critical question was, what would the dog do when it was let loose from S? Would it follow the lengthy route it had been taken on, or would it short-cut from A directly to B (or from B to A)? Ninety-six per cent of the dogs took the short cut, and in only one per cent of the trials did the dogs follow the lengthy route they had been shown originally.

Nicole Chapuis and Patricia Scardigli (1993) tested hamsters on some more complex versions of the task that Chapuis and Varlet had given to dogs. Using an apparatus that permitted a variety of alternative routes to the same target object, they found that hamsters were very able to deduce the shortest route under a variety of conditions.

Box 7.1   How to test the spatial reasoning ability of your dog or cat

Both Poucet *et al.*'s and Chapuis and Varlet's methods can very easily be adapted for use at home with your pet dog or cat (or other tame animal).

For Chapuis and Varlet's method, the only requirements are a suitably motivated dog or cat (as mentioned in Box 5.1 on object permanence, it is probably better to try this just before a feeding time than after), some suitable food, a fairly large open area (Chapuis and Varlet worked in a three-hectare meadow) and an assistant. Binoculars may help if you choose to work in a particularly large test area.

It is probably wise to get the ground measured out before your pet is brought onto the scene. The dimensions shown in Figure 7.6 worked well for Chapuis and Varlet in the case of young Alsatian dogs. For other species you will probably want to adjust the scale in proportion to the size and mobility of your animal. In addition, in order to be able to conduct repeated trials (Chapuis and Varlet tested each of seven animals twice a day for two days), you will need several of these testing triangles (otherwise the tracks left on one trial may tell the subject what to do on the next trial without the need for it to solve the problem anew). Eight of the triangles shown in Figure 7.5 can be fitted round a circle centred on the same starting point.

Be careful when setting up the test area to walk only from S to A and from S to B, never from A to B. Once you have your test area set up, walk your animal on a lead from the starting point to the first food item (S to A), then back to the starting point. Immediately go to the second food point and then return to the starting point (S to B to S). Without any delay, release your animal and observe where it runs. Without moving from the starting point yourself, record your animal's search route in as much detail as possible. Chapuis and Varlet gave their animals a maximum of ten minutes' search time. Although you may wish to alter this, depending on the

---

Box 7.1   (cont'd)

speed of your animal, it is wise to set a maximum time for the task, after which the animal is deemed to have failed.

Depending on the success of your animal at this task, you may wish to explore your animal's spatial reasoning ability in more detail. Theoretically interesting questions include the following. What difference does the angle between food points A and B make? The smaller the angle, the more efficient the short cut becomes – does this make a difference to your animal's behaviour? What about the delay between being led to the two food points and being released to get the food on its own – does increasing this delay improve or worsen your animal's performance? Finally, how would dogs or cats cope with more complex spatial reasoning problems such as those set out by Tolman, for example that shown in Figure 7.2? This investigation could also be conducted in an open field using modifications of the method developed by Chapuis and Varlet.

The method used by Poucet et al. needs only some suitable barriers in addition to the materials required for Chapuis and Varlet's method. Transparent barriers can be made easily out of chicken wire attached to posts stuck in the ground. Opaque barriers could be made from cardboard (except for taller dogs, in which case it might be better to work with preexisting walls and fences). Interesting modifications to Poucet et al.'s tests can be achieved by using barriers that present alternative routes of different lengths that pass closer to or further away from the target object. Intelligent dogs, for whom this task may be too easy, could be tested on detours that require more substantial backtracking before the goal can be reached, as well as more complicated routes to the goal.

Köhler's early finding that chicks have difficulty finding their way round barriers to reach a desired object inspired an interesting series of studies by Lucia Regolin et al. (1994). In line with Köhler's results and with those of modern research on dogs and cats, Regolin and her colleagues found that two-day-old chicks were more likely to reach a target object by going round a detour if the barrier was opaque rather than transparent. Likewise, in the case of a transparent barrier the chicks were more successful if the desired object was situated away from the barrier than they were if it was directly behind the barrier. In further tests Regolin et al. (1995) demonstrated that the chicks' problems with transparent barriers had less to do with the fact that they could see the desired object, and more to do with the chicks' inability to comprehend that a transparent object could be a barrier.

Successful navigation around barriers and via detours has been observed in several other species. *Portio fimbriata* is a species of spider from Queensland, Australia, that invades the webs of other spiders to feed. It has been observed in the field that *Portio* often take complex detours through webs to attack the resident web spider. Michael Tarsitano and Robert Jackson (1997) investigated the ability of these spiders to choose the correct route to a target object (a dead spider). They found that *Portio* are fully able to select the correct route even if that involves temporarily walking in the direction opposite to that required to reach their goal.

The mangrove swimming crab, a native of the Kenyan coast, can find its way back to its nest after being displaced by up to five metres from home. Stefano Cannicci and his coworkers (1995) observed that crabs would head straight for home even after displacements that involved a variety of detours.

Angelo Bisazza and his colleagues (1997) assessed the ability of pieciliid fish to swim around a barrier to obtain a desired object. Five related species of fish were tested in a very simple procedure. The males were separated from the females and made to swim along a narrow channel until they reached a transparent barrier. Behind the barrier four adult females of the same species were held captive in a transparent glass cylinder. All the fish tested were able to swim around the barrier to get to the females, but interestingly, each species had a distinct preference for swimming round either the left or the right side of the barrier.

Not all studies of detour performance in animals have reported equal success, however. Jacques Bovet (1995), in a study of the homing ability of red squirrels, found that these animals could only successfully return to their nests if they were displaced along straight paths. The squirrels in the study were displaced along routes of approximately 700 metres that involved two right-angled turns. These turns were either both to the left or both to the right, so that the displacement route described three sides of a rectangle – the shortest route home being the remaining fourth side of the rectangle. The squirrels did not pick the shortest route and their return bearings were essentially random.

All of the above examples of the ability to navigate detours and barriers required the integration of different aspects of experience in order to produce an efficient solution to a real world problem. Hence they were all examples of spatial reasoning.

Tool use

Although, like so many other skills, tool use was once considered a uniquely human ability, the use of tools is now recognized as being quite widespread among primates and has been demonstrated in several non-primate species as well. A tool can be defined as an external object used to help gain a desired end. Of course it must be acknowledged that not all the examples of tool use by animals that conform to this definition can also be considered as examples of 'reasoning'. Take, for example, the behaviour of the larvae of a species of *Neuroptera*. These larvae are called ant-lions because of their aggressive nature. To capture prey, ant-lions make use of the soil in which they live. They excavate funnel-shaped pits in suitably soft earth, and when prey fall into the pits, the ant-lions grab them and eat them. If the unfortunate animals so captured try to escape up the side of the pit, the ant-lions shower them with soil by means of rapid head and mandible movements in an attempt to hinder their escape. Fascinating as this behaviour certainly is, there is no suggestion that it can be flexibly adapted to circumstances. There is no integration of information going on that would fit any definition of reasoning.

Many of the most flexible examples of tool use come from primates, for example many wild primates use objects to threaten outsiders. But there are many examples of tool use by other mammals, as well as by birds and other types of animal. Tools are used by many species in the capture or preparation of food. Chimpanzees use sticks and poles to fish out ants and termites from their hiding places. Among the most complex tool use observed in the wild is the use of stones by Ivory Coast chimpanzees to crack open nuts. They select a large flat stone as an anvil and a smaller stone as a hammer. Stones suitable for use as anvils are not easy to find, and often a chimpanzee may carry a haul of nuts more than 40 metres to find a suitable anvil.

The use of tools by chimpanzees is especially interesting because these animals sometimes modify tools to make them better suited for their intended purpose. To make a twig more effective for fishing out termites, for example, a chimp may first strip it of its leaves.

Surprisingly, there is also a species of bird that uses sticks to probe holes in the search for insects. One of the species of Galapagos finch first noted by Darwin, the woodpecker finch, picks up or breaks off a twig, cactus spine or leaf stem. This primitive tool is then held in the beak and used to probe for insects in holes in trees that the bird cannot probe directly with its beak. Birds have been seen to carry twigs from tree to tree searching for prey, and a captive finch was even observed to shorten a twig or remove pieces that made it difficult to insert into insect-bearing holes.

Though not tool use by every definition (because the substance being utilized is not manipulated), water is used by some Japanese macaques to wash sand from sweet potatoes as well as to separate sand from food grains. This case has become famous because of the possible social transmission of the skill of potato washing by a young macaque to others in the group (see Chapter 2).

The need to break open mollusc shells brings out the tool user in two quite unrelated species. Sea otters smash them onto stone anvils that they hold against their chests, while gulls drop stones onto mollusc shells from a height. A similar technique is used by vultures to crack open ostrich eggs.

Tools may also be used for defence. Hermit crabs grab sea anemones with their claws and use them to repel their enemies. Laboratory studies have demonstrated that these crabs significantly improve their chances against predators such as octopus by means of this tactic. Forest-dwelling primates of many species throw objects, including stones, at intruders.

As so often in studies of animal behaviour, field studies raise the most interesting questions but do not enable the kind of situational control that is necessary to judge just how flexible the observed behaviour is. Since flexibility of response is one of the hallmarks of reasoning, we need to measure this property of a behaviour to see if it qualifies as reasoning. Some interesting cases of animals manipulating tools adaptively under controlled conditions are considered in the next section.

Insight

One of the few sets of studies of animal cognition to make it into almost all introductory psychology textbooks are those carried out by Wolfgang Köhler (1925) on chimpanzees. Köhler, a German citizen, was trapped by a British naval blockade on the island of Tenerife for the duration of the First World War. With his stay at the Prussian Anthropoid Research Station prolonged indefinitely, Köhler set about giving the chimps a series of problems that required reasoning for their solution.

One of the most famous of these problems was the so-called 'block-stacking' task. A banana was hung from the roof of an enclosure, out of reach of the chimps. The enclosure contained three packing boxes. Köhler describes what happened next:

> The objective hangs still higher up; Sultan has fasted all the forenoon and, therefore, goes at his task with great zeal. He lays the heavy box flat underneath the objective, puts the second one upright upon it, and, standing on the top, tries to seize the objective. As he does not reach it, he looks down and round about, and his glance is caught by the third box, which may have seemed useless to him at first, because of its smallness. He climbs down very carefully, seizes the box, climbs up with it, and completes the construction. (Köhler, 1925/1957, pp. 120–1)

Another of Köhler's apes – Grande – is pictured completing the box-stacking task in Figure 7.7.

In another of Köhler's tasks, Sultan was put inside an enclosure and some pieces of fruit were placed out of reach beyond the bars. Sultan was provided with two hollow bamboo sticks, each of which was too short to reach the highly desired food items. At first Sultan tried to reach the fruit with his hands, then with each of the sticks separately, and then with one stick pushed along by the other stick. All these efforts were futile and after about an hour Sultan gave up. Sultan's keeper then observed Sultan playing with the sticks for a while before inserting the thinner of the two sticks inside the thicker one. Armed with this now lengthened stick, Sultan rushed back to where the fruit was and raked it all in rapidly.

Köhler's emphasis in these studies was on the sudden change in the chimpanzees' behaviour from initial failure to sudden success. He felt that the very suddenness of the chimps' solutions to the problems suggested higher mental faculties – in particular insight. Our problem with Köhler's interpretation of his results is that we know so little about the animal's prior training. (We also have to contend with the fact that up to six chimps were working on any one problem at a time.) Köhler mentions that the chimpanzees were given many opportunities to play with packing boxes, hollow bamboo sticks, string and many other

Figure 7.7   Grande completing Köhler's block-stacking task while Sultan watches (from Köhler, 1921/1963. Copyright Springer-Verlag, Berlin)

things. There is little indication, however, of exactly what the different chimps did with these objects. It is possible, for example, that Sultan had previously stood on packing boxes to reach desired items; or inserted one stick inside another for some other purpose (Köhler does mention that he put his finger into the end of the larger stick to try to suggest to Sultan that objects could be inserted into it). Köhler was impressed that his chimps did not seem to be engaging in blind trial and error learning, but we have no way of knowing that the trial and error learning had not taken place earlier, when the chimps were playing with boxes and sticks while nobody was looking.

Sixty years after Köhler, Donald Premack and Guy Woodruff (1978) presented a chimpanzee named Sarah with updated versions of some of the problems Sultan had solved. Sarah was put in front of a television to watch videotapes of a person attempting to obtain a banana that was out of reach. In none of these brief videos did the person succeed. Having viewed a video Sarah was offered a choice between two photographs. One showed the person successfully obtaining the banana with the help of a tool; the other showed the person failing to reach the banana. In one of the videos, for example, Sarah could see a person attempting to reach a banana suspended out of reach from the ceiling – standing nearby was a large box. In this case Sarah chose the photograph that showed the person standing on the box and successfully reaching the banana, and not the alternative picture in which the person was unsuccessful. Sarah chose the photograph showing the person successfully reaching the banana in 21 of the 24 tests she was given.

Although Premack and Woodruff's results reinforced Köhler's earlier conclusion that chimpanzees can solve problems of this type, they too failed to tell us how such performances are achieved, particularly in terms of the types of prior experience that might enable a chimp or other animal to solve these kinds of reasoning problems.

The only experiment to study directly the issue of how prior experience leads to success in tasks such as the block-stacking problem was conducted on a species quite distant from the chimpanzee – the pigeon. Robert Epstein and his colleagues (1984) trained their pigeons to perform two tasks. First, the birds were trained to climb onto a small box and peck a picture of a banana, by being rewarded with food grains when they did so. Second, concurrently with this the pigeons were trained to push the box towards a spot on the wall. The starting position of the box and the position of the spot varied randomly from trial to trial. Here also the pigeons were rewarded with food grains for pushing the box. During the banana-pecking trials pushing the box was not rewarded; during the box-moving trials, attempts to climb on the box were not rewarded. Nonetheless when the pigeons were introduced to a chamber containing the picture of the banana with the box some distance away and no spot on the wall, the pigeons, after a minute or so's hesitation, pushed the box under the picture, climbed onto it and pecked at the banana.

Epstein *et al.* argued that when the pigeons first saw the box and the banana together in the chamber there were two possible responses: pecking the banana, and pushing the box. Pecking the banana without standing on the box had never been rewarded in this situation, so that left pushing the box as the only behaviour available to them that had been rewarded in the past. The pigeons were observed to line up the box with the banana, just as they had previously been trained to line it up with the spot on the wall. Once they had the box under the banana it is not surprising that the pigeons then climbed on top of it to peck the banana, since the situation at that point was the same as they had previously experienced.

This experiment by Epstein and his colleagues has been dismissed as only suggesting a mechanism for how pigeons – a species not noted for its cognitive abilities – can be tricked into doing something that only looks like reasoning. This, however, is to miss the point: here, for once, was complete knowledge of

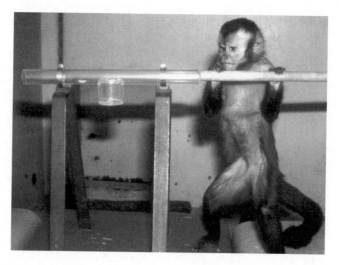

Figure 7.8   A capuchin monkey pushing a stick into Visalberghi and Limongelli's 'trap tube' to obtain a treat (photograph courtesy of E. Visalberghi)

the animals' prior experience with the objects in the task. It is this thorough knowledge of the animals' prior experience that gives their performance less of the almost magical quality we expect of abstract reasoning – not the fact that they were pigeons. More recent studies on insightful reasoning have followed this lead and have better controlled and recorded their subjects' experiences.

A more recent, well-controlled study on primate tool use failed to reveal such apparently insightful behaviour in its subjects. Elisabetta Visalberghi and Luca Limongelli (1994) tested capuchin monkeys on a quite simple task they called the 'trap tube' problem. The trap tube, shown in Figure 7.8, is a simple tube with a hole in the middle. A treat was placed in either the right or the left end of the tube, and the monkey was provisioned with a stick of just the right thickness to push through the tube and dislodge the treat. If the monkey pushed the treat out of either end of the tube, then it was allowed to consume it. If, however, the monkey pushed the treat so that it fell down the hole in the middle, it was lost to the monkey on that trial. In the course of over 140 trials, only one of the four monkeys learnt to push the treat consistently from the direction that ensured it would come out of the end and not fall down the 'trap'. Even this monkey's understanding of the task did not appear to have much depth, because if the tube was inverted so that the trap pointed upwards and was consequently quite harmless, the monkey continued to push the treat with the stick as if the 'trap' was still dangerous. It was concluded that this monkey had learnt by simple conditioning (see Chapter 3) always to push the treat from the end of the tube that was furthest from where the treat was resting.

When the same task was presented to a group of chimpanzees the performance was a little better and two of the five chimpanzees were successful (Limongelli

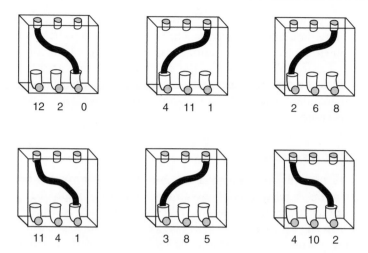

Figure 7.9   Six of the arrangements used by Hood et al. (1999) to test monkeys' understanding of gravity. The numbers beneath each outlet from the box indicate how often a monkey searched at that point for an object introduced at the top of the tube (the object always came out at the point to which the bottom of the tube was connected)

et al., 1995). These two chimps' understanding of the task was tested by presenting them with a version of the trap tube where the position of the trap hole was moved closer to one or other end of the tube. In this version the rule of always inserting the stick at the end of the tube furthest from the food item would sometimes cause the treat to fall through the hole. One of the chimps (Sheba, who as we saw in Chapter 6 performed well on some numerical reasoning tasks) consistently inserted the stick into whichever end of the tube would ensure the food did not fall down the hole. The second chimpanzee was also successful most of the time, but often achieved his successes by inserting the stick into the wrong end of the tube, and then pulling it out and trying from the other end when he could see that the treat was about to fall through the hole.

Another interesting failure to demonstrate insight was reported by Bruce Hood and his colleagues (1999). Hood developed a very simple task. Cotton top tamarins were shown objects being dropped down an opaque tube in the apparatus shown in Figure 7.9. As this figure shows, there were three points at the top of the box where the tube could be connected, and another three outlet points at the bottom of the box. The crucial point about this apparatus was that the end of the tube was never connected to the outlet directly beneath the point where the top of the tube was connected. Thus an object introduced at the top could never come out directly beneath where it had been put in. The tamarins failed to learn this and, as Figure 7.9 shows, seldom chose the outlet to which the opaque tube was connected.

Evidence of tool use and insightful behaviour both suggest that animals can sometimes draw on their experiences and put them together in novel ways to obtain desired ends – this is a form of reasoning. We must be careful, however, not to celebrate these apparent successes too soon. It needs to be demonstrated that the animal subject really is using insight and not relying on trial and error learning that took place before the experiment. With regard to tool use, we also need to be sure that the animal is demonstrating flexible exploitation of a tool that indicates an ability to reason and not just some instinctive or habitual behaviour.

Reasoning by analogy

To recognize that 'dog is to puppy as cat is to kitten' is to reason by analogy. We recognize that a relationship between two objects can imply the same relationship between two other objects. An interesting study was performed by Douglas Gillan and his colleagues (1981) on a chimpanzee, Sarah, who had been taught to use a variety of symbols as a means of communicating with her trainers (discussed in more detail in Chapter 8). Sarah was trained using pieces of coloured plastic. As shown in Figure 7.10, Sarah was shown two pieces that were the same colour but different sizes, and another piece that was a different shape but the same size as one of the first pair. The pair of pieces and the third piece were separated by a yellow shape bearing an equals sign, which was a sign that Sarah had been taught as meaning 'same'. Sarah was then given a choice between two alternative pieces (shown below the line in the left-hand panel of Figure 7.10). The correct response was to choose the piece that was the same shape as the one on the right, but the same size as the lower one on the left. Sarah was very successful at selecting the piece that ensured that the pieces in both pairs were in the same relationship to each other.

Sarah's most impressive successes came when she was given real-world objects in the same manner. In the first problem of this type, Sarah was shown a padlock

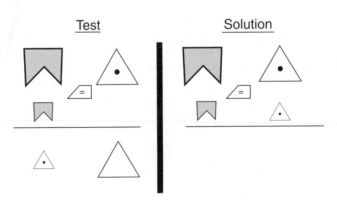

Figure 7.10   Examples of the items used to test Sarah's comprehension of analogy. Sarah had to choose the item below the line that stood in the same relationship to the object on the right as the two objects on the left. The right-hand side of the figure shows the correct solution (from Gillan et al., 1981)

and a key and then the 'same' symbol in front of a tin can. As alternative solutions she was offered a can opener and a paintbrush. Here the correct solution was the can opener ('padlock is to key as tin can is to can opener'). Given the same can and alternative solutions, but pencil and paper as the premises, Sarah selected the paint brush because the paint brush stood in the same relationship to the can as the pencil did to paper. Sarah was correct in 15 out of 18 trials using a variety of household objects.

Series learning – I: transitive inference

If Mary is taller than Susan, and Susan is taller than Jane, who is the tallest, Mary, Susan or Jane? If you answered 'Mary' then you successfully made a transitive inference. This form of reasoning is interesting because its successful solution requires you to go beyond the information given in order to deduce true relationships about the world. You were not told that Mary is taller than Jane and yet you can deduce this relationship.

Problems of the transitive inference type entered psychology in the early years of the twentieth century, and for a long time their solution was considered a uniquely human ability. In the 1970s, however, some developmental psychologists, interested in uncovering the earliest age at which children could solve these kinds of problem, developed a version of the transitive inference task that did not rely so heavily on language for its presentation. They did this by presenting children with rods of different lengths and colours, and asking the children which was the longest rod.

Brendan McGonigle and Margaret Chalmers (1977) recognized that, with a little more work, a completely non-verbal version of the transitive inference task could be developed for animals. McGonigle and Chalmers' subjects were squirrel monkeys. These monkeys were presented with pairs of containers of different colours placed on a tray (this tray goes by the name of the 'Wisconsin general test apparatus'). For each pair of containers, one had a peanut hidden underneath it and the other did not. So, for example, the monkey might be offered a choice between a blue and a red container. If it chose the blue container it would find the peanut; if it chose the red one it would get nothing. Once the monkeys knew what to do with the blue and red containers they were introduced to green and blue containers. The blue container no longer hid the peanut – it was now beneath the green container. Once the green–blue problem had been learnt the monkey was introduced to a yellow and green pair. Here it was the yellow and not the green container that hid the peanut. This pattern of training was extended to four overlapping pairs of five colours, as shown below:

Pair 1:	Blue–peanut	Red–nothing
Pair 2:	Green–peanut	Blue–nothing
Pair 3:	Yellow–peanut	Green–nothing
Pair 4:	Violet–peanut	Yellow–nothing

Once the monkeys had mastered each of the four problems separately, McGonigle and Chalmers intermixed them thoroughly, so that by the end of training the monkeys would choose, say, the green container on a green–blue trial, but on the very next trial would ignore the green container and choose the yellow one.

The point of this training scheme is that it is a non-verbal equivalent to the 'Mary is taller than Jane' scenario sketched at the beginning of this section. A monkey that chooses the violet container on a yellow–violet trial, the yellow container on a yellow–green trial, the green container on a green–blue trial and the blue container on a blue–red trial is indicating that violet is better than yellow, yellow is better than green, green is better than blue, and blue is better than red. If this training pattern is equivalent to telling the monkey that 'violet is better than yellow' and so on, what operation is equivalent to asking the monkey, 'Who is tallest, Mary, Susan or Jane?' McGonigle and Chalmers reasoned that if the monkeys had perceived the relationship they intended between the different coloured containers, then presenting yellow and blue containers together would be a valid test of whether the monkeys could form transitive inferences. Both yellow and blue containers had been rewarded with peanuts during training, but each had also, on occasion, been the container without a peanut hidden under it. Consequently, in terms of how often a peanut could be found under each container they should be equal. If a monkey understood the relationships between the different coloured containers that the experimenters had intended (violet is better than yellow, yellow is better than green, and so on), then it should prefer the yellow container to the blue one. In effect the monkey should reason, 'yellow is better than green, and green is better than blue; therefore yellow is better than blue'.

After a lengthy training period, McGonigle and Chalmers performed this test and found that the monkeys showed a spontaneous preference for yellow when presented with a choice between the yellow and blue containers. (The reason, by the way, that they used five colours in four pairs, rather than the three objects in two pairs used in tests on human subjects, is that tests containing either the first or the last items in the series would not be interesting. The monkeys would be expected to select the blue container in any test simply because, during training, it had been the only container that had *always* had a peanut under it. Similarly the yellow item would never be chosen during tests just because it had *never* had a peanut under it.)

McGonigle and Chalmers' successful demonstration of transitive inference formation in squirrel monkeys came as a shock. Previously it had been believed that even children had to reach a relatively high level of cognitive development before they could solve problems of this type – but now non-verbal monkeys were doing it. Soon after McGonigle and Chalmers' demonstration, other researchers used similar methods to demonstrate transitive inference in chimpanzees (Gillan *et al.*, 1981).

Lorenzo von Fersen and his colleagues (1991) modified McGonigle and Chalmers' method to make it suitable for pigeons. Using a modified Skinner box (see Chapter 3), their pigeons were trained to peck patterns projected onto two pecking keys. Here too, when tested on the critical second and fourth items from the implied series of stimuli, the pigeons chose correctly. Hank Davis (1992) demonstrated transitive inference formation in rats using a similar method.

These observations of the ability to solve transitive inference problems in such unrelated vertebrate species raise the question of why such animals would need such apparently advanced reasoning skills. Why do pigeons, rats, squirrel monkeys or chimpanzees need the skill to be able to deduce that Mary is taller than Jane? The answer turns out to be quite simple. The ability to form transitive inferences enables an animal to form rankings, and the need to form rankings is quite widespread in many species. Many social animals, for example, need to be aware of the hierarchy within their group. Figuring out who is dominant to whom is a process fraught with potentially dangerous interactions. An animal that was unable to form transitive inferences would have to interact with every member of the group to ascertain its own status. In order to understand the status of all members of the group, it would be necessary to observe all possible interactions between the various members. For a group of just 12 members, there would be 66 possible interactions between two individuals. On the other hand, if this animal was capable of forming transitive inferences, then it would only be necessary to observe 11 interactions in order to deduce the relationships between all the group members. The ranking of other objects, for example a hierarchy of food preferences, would also be made much more efficient by means of a transitive inference reasoning process.

Box 7.2   How do animals form transitive inferences?

The ability to form mental representations of complete series of objects seems unlikely in small-brained animals. Furthermore there is evidence from a different experimental paradigm (see the next section) to suggest that pigeons are unlikely to be able to form mental linear orderings of a series of stimuli. So how do they solve transitive inferences?

One proposal that has been put forward by Pat Couvillon and Jeff Bitterman (1992) and which I have been involved in developing, assumes only that each stimulus in a transitive inference experiment has a certain value to the animal being tested. Though complex in detail the principle behind this theory can be easily grasped.

Imagine that you are a pigeon in a transitive inference experiment. To capture the idea that each stimulus in the experiment has a certain value to a pigeon, give yourself 50 Monopoly dollars for each of the five stimuli. You are first confronted with the stimuli A and B — which should you choose? The usual choice is the stimulus

Box 7.2 (cont'd)

with the highest monetary value attached to it, but at the moment all the stimuli are of equal value ($50), so you choose by tossing a coin. If you choose A you can add $2 from the bank to A's $50. If you choose B you must return $2 from B's stash to the bank. As long as the difference in value between two stimuli is small (say, less than $9) you should continue to choose between them by tossing a coin. Once, however, the value difference is $10 or more, you should consistently choose whichever stimulus has the most value.

Train yourself first in this way on the AB pair. You should find that a $10 difference in value between A and B develops after five trials. Keep going until you have done ten AB trials. Now train yourself on BC trials. You will notice that when you start on this, the value of B has been reduced by your AB trials. Keep going as before until you have completed ten BC trials. Then proceed with CD trials. Here you may start by making incorrect D responses before picking up the correct, C, response, because C's value was depleted in the BC trials. Finally complete ten DE trials.

The following are the results I obtained at the end of ten training trials of each type:

- A – $66
- B – $58
- C – $54
- D – $52
- E – $40

Since the stimuli are now ranked in order of value an individual (person or animal) can always choose correctly whenever two stimuli are offered to it so long as it always chooses the stimulus with the higher value. The transitive inference problem can thus be solved without any mental ordering beyond the simple one that arises as a consequence of assigning values to stimuli in this way.

In this simplified example the pairs of stimuli were only presented one at a time. In the full model (Wynne, 1998) the transitive inference problem can be solved no matter which order the stimulus pairs are presented in.

Series learning – II: linear ordering

A form of learning about series that sounds superficially similar to the transitive inference problem, but has led to radically different results, was developed by Herb Terrace in the 1980s.

Terrace (1993) confronted pigeons with an array of eight pecking keys. Each of these keys could be illuminated with a red, green, blue, yellow or violet light. In any given trial five randomly chosen keys were illuminated, each with a different coloured light. The pigeon's task was to peck the five keys in a fixed order. For example it might have to peck red first, then green, then blue, then yellow, and finally violet. Since different pigeons were tested with different colour sequences it is easiest to denote the colours with letters of the alphabet, so we shall call this the sequence A-B-C-D-E. All the keys remained lit until the pigeon had successfully completed the sequence (when it was given a food reward). If the pigeon made a mistake (such as pecking the same colour twice or jumping ahead in the sequence), all the lights went out and the pigeon had to wait a few seconds for the trial to start again. Perhaps surprisingly, the pigeons found this task difficult to learn (it took around 120 daily sessions for a group of five pigeons to reach a satisfactory level). A further surprise was that the pigeons performed very poorly when tested on most subsets of stimuli from the original task. Terrace showed the pigeons different pairs of stimuli selected from the original five colours. Though the pigeons were successful with any pair that contained either the first (A) or the last (E) stimulus, their performance was around chance level with any other pair of stimuli. Quite unlike the case with transitive inference, this was as true for pairs that had occurred during training, such as BC or CD, as it was for the pair BD, which the pigeons had not been required to respond to during training.

Michael D'Amato and Michael Colombo (1988) tested cebus monkeys on Terrace's task. The monkeys were required to touch geometric shapes that appeared on a computer screen in a set order. The fact that the monkeys learnt the task much faster than Terrace's pigeons had done might be put down to procedural differences (the monkeys' screen had only five possible locations where the five stimuli could appear, compared with the eight response keys that the pigeons had to work with), but – more interestingly – the monkeys also had little difficulty solving subcomponents of the problem that did not involve the first (A) and last (E) stimuli. The monkeys were just as successful at the BC, CD and even BD pairs as they were at pairs such as AB and DE.

Why should pigeons' and monkeys' performance in this task be so different? One suggestion is that monkeys can form some kind of mental representation of a whole series of stimuli, but pigeons cannot. The way in which pigeons solve the task, Terrace proposes, is by learning a series of associations that can be expressed as simple rules. The first rule the pigeon learns is, 'when the stimulus lights come on – peck stimulus A'. The next rule that comes into play is, 'when you have pecked stimulus A – peck B'. This is followed by 'when you have pecked stimulus B – peck C' and 'when you have pecked stimulus C – peck D'. Finally, 'when you have pecked everything else – peck E'. This would explain why the pigeons can respond correctly to any stimulus pair that includes stimuli A or E, because the rules that include these stimuli do not refer specifically to any other stimuli – they just tell the pigeon to respond to A first and E last.

The difficulties that pigeons have when presented with groups of stimuli that contain just B, C or D stem from the fact that the simple associative rules that involve these stimuli start with stimulus A, which is not present in these trials. When, for example, a pigeon is confronted with the pair BC, the first rule that is activated is, 'when the stimulus lights come on – peck stimulus A'. But stimulus A is not available to be pecked. The only rule that instructs the pigeon to peck stimulus B is, 'when you have pecked stimulus A – peck B'. Since there is no stimulus A available this rule cannot be activated. Consequently the pigeons' behaviour appears very consistent with the theory that pigeons are unable to form a mental representation of a series of stimuli and instead act on the basis of simple associative rules.

Cebus monkeys, on the other hand, appear to work with a more structured representation of a series of stimuli – or at least a set of rules that can be applied more flexibly to novel circumstances.

Conclusions

The term 'reasoning' may not seem a particularly useful one when applied to animal behaviour. Many examples of animals acting in a problem situation in ways that have been viewed traditionally as cases of reasoning can be explained by their ability to detect cause and effect relationships according to the widespread rules of associative learning (discussed in Chapter 3). There remains, however, a difference between just detecting cause and effect relationships and applying that sensitivity to complex situations.

As we have seen so often in this book, there is no obvious pattern to the species that show more or less advanced reasoning abilities. In nature, primates, especially chimpanzees, are the most common tool users – tool use being one of the few field observations that occurs frequently and can imply reasoning. In the laboratory, on the other hand, rats and pigeons often perform as well as primates. Dogs and cats also perform excellently. Cases have also been observed of primates failing to reason appropriately, even in a completely natural situation of great adaptive importance to them.

Dorothy Cheney and Robert Seyfarth (1990) have conducted an intensive study of the vervet monkeys of West Africa (their work on the communication abilities of these animals is discussed in Chapter 8). One of the species that prey on vervet monkeys is the leopard. Leopards have the habit, unique among the species that prey on vervets, of dragging their kill into trees so that they can feed on it without harassment by other predators in the area. The sight of a carcass in a tree is a clear sign to human observers to be wary because a leopard is in the vicinity. The question is, do vervet monkeys reason in the same way when they see a carcass in a tree? Vervet monkeys certainly know they have to be afraid of leopards, and give a characteristic alarm call when they see one (see Chapter 8).

Each of the vervet monkeys Cheney and Seyfarth studied had had the opportunity to watch a leopard drag its kill into a tree. To test whether the monkeys had learnt the implications of a dead animal in a tree, Cheney and Seyfarth hid a stuffed carcass of a Thompson's gazelle at night in a tree close to where the monkeys were sleeping. Although the dead gazelle fooled a tourist bus driver into thinking that a leopard was in the vicinity, the monkeys were completely unfazed by the presence of a carcass so near by. They made no leopard alarm calls; there was not even any increase in vigilance by the group.

The vervet monkeys' failure to reason appropriately in this situation is doubly puzzling. It is puzzling first because of the importance of the task – there is no question here of the experimenters having created an unnatural problem for their subjects. It is also puzzling because it was not even a very difficult problem – it amounted to little more than the detection of cause and effect, which as we saw in Chapter 3 is a very widespread ability in the animal world.

The reason for the monkeys' failure at this task (a failure that extended to a similar inability to detect signs of other predators, and which was also found in baboons living nearby) remains a mystery. It is, however, a healthy reminder that animals do not always do what we expect them to do. Just as a relatively small-brained bird such as a pigeon can demonstrate the ability to perform a test (jumping on a box and pecking a banana) that in chimpanzees is considered as insight, so too can large-brained primates, with one of the most elaborate natural communication systems known to science, fail to pick up simple yet important signals in their natural environment.

FURTHER READING

Boakes, R (1984) *From Darwin to Behaviourism: Psychology and the Minds of Animals* (Cambridge: Cambridge University Press). This fascinating historical survey reviews the early research on spatial reasoning by Tolman, Maier, Köhler and others.

Köhler, W (1925/1963) *The Mentality of Apes* (London: Kegan Paul Trench & Trubner, trans. E. Winter). Köhler's research on spatial reasoning in a variety of species, as well as his work on insight and problem solving in chimpanzees is reported in his book.

Beck, B B (1980) *Animal Tool Behavior: The Use and Manufacture of Tools by Animals* (New York: Garland SPTM Press). This book presents a very thorough and wide-ranging review of tool use by animals.

WEBSITE

The following website includes video of a chimpanzee emulating Köhler's chimp Sultan trying to reach a banana by climbing on boxes:
http://www.pbs.org/wnet/nature/animalmind/intelligence.html

This lively website is the home page of the chimpanzee Ai whose numerical abilities are described above:
http://www.pri.kyoto-u.ac.jp/ai/index-E.htm

8
Communication and Language

> If we could talk to the animals, just imagine it
> Chatting to a chimp in chimpanzee
> Imagine talking to a tiger, chatting to a cheetah
> What a neat achievement that would be.
> (Leslie Bricusse, *Dr Doolittle*)

Who has not dreamed of one day waking up and being able to understand what the animals around us are saying? Children's stories, adults' daydreams and movies are full of speaking animals. Babe the pig, Flipper the dolphin, Mickey Mouse and countless others speak with distinctive but fully comprehensible voices. And don't imagine that the researchers whose ingenious work on the cognitive abilities of animals we have discussed in earlier chapters have not sometimes wished they could just ask their subjects directly: 'So, how many dots can you see?' 'Can you remember what I showed you yesterday?' How often have we looked our pigeon or rat subjects in the eye and wished we could cut through the elaborate experimental designs and just ask them straight out.

In this chapter we look at the question of animal communication. We first consider studies that have attempted to teach something like human language to other species. Then we look at a sample of the projects that have analysed the communication systems that some species use with each other.

Since the 1960s the various attempts to teach sign language to chimpanzees have generated a lot of excitement, but in reality it is unlikely that anything approximating a human language capacity has been demonstrated in any non-human species. As we shall see here, many of the claims made on behalf of these animals have been exaggerated. Viewed in an evolutionary perspective, it isn't really surprising that other species do not share our language. Modern human language probably came into being some time between 100 000 and half a million years ago. This estimate cannot be very precise for obvious reasons, but it is clearly a very short time in evolutionary terms. In comparison, human evolution diverged from that of our closest living relative, the chimpanzee, about five or six million years ago. Although five million years is also not long in evolutionary terms, it was well before hominids developed language.

Before we consider research that has looked at the language abilities of animals, it is prudent to remind ourselves of some of the cautionary tales from Chapter 1, as well as the impressive ability of many animals to notice cause and effect relationships that we considered in Chapter 3.

In Chapter 1 we discussed Clever Hans – the horse who was too clever by half. Hans appeared to be able to do quite complicated arithmetic and solve other sorts of problems too, but in reality his cleverness lay not in mathematical ability, but in a skill that was almost as clever but in a quite different way. Hans took note of tiny movements made by the people around him – movements so slight that they were not conscious of making them. These movements told Hans when he had made enough hoof stomps to answer correctly a question that had been put to him. In Chapter 3 we saw that abilities like those of Hans are the norm rather than the exception throughout the animal kingdom. All the species tested have shown an ability to learn about signals that indicate when important things (such as the arrival of food) are going to happen, and about what actions they should perform to obtain food and other items that are important to them. When we look at the attempts to teach human language to other animals we must keep in mind that these subjects were usually trained by the use of rewards (see Box 8.1), and we must ask ourselves whether these animals were really learning language or were just learning which signals were followed by a reward, or which

---

Box 8.1   Teaching apes to talk

The earliest attempts to teach human language to apes involved adopting an animal and encouraging it to talk, just like a human baby. However, unlike human infants the apes showed little inclination to imitate their caregivers and never got beyond about three words. All subsequent studies have used one of two methods: American Sign Language (ASL) or a system of symbols, the best known of which is 'Yerkish' – named after one of the early researchers in animal psychology, Robert Yerkes. Yerkish is a system of symbols, expressed by pressing keys on a keyboard.

ASL is the gestural language used by the deaf in North America. Probably the first person to suggest that it might be possible to communicate with apes using signs was the great seventeenth-century English diarist Samuel Pepys. The first to attempt this in practice were Allen and Beatrice Gardner, who in 1966 adopted a wild-born female chimpanzee, Washoe, when she was about one year old (Gardner and Gardner, 1969). Washoe was housed in the Gardners' backyard and was accompanied by human trainers who communicated with each other and with her entirely in ASL at all times. The Gardners had hoped that Washoe would spontaneously imitate ASL signs, but in practice they mainly taught her to use signs by moulding: a process of physically guiding the chimp's hand into the desired position. ASL was also used by Francine Patterson and her coworkers to communicate with a gorilla, Koko (Patterson, 1978). Unlike Washoe's trainers, Patterson combined spoken English with ASL in the hope that the use of two communication systems might enhance Koko's language acquisition. Again, training was by imitation and moulding of the correct signs. Herb Terrace's chimp, Nim Chimpsky (pictured in Figure 8.1 and named in joking honour of the linguist Noam Chomsky) was also trained in ASL in a manner roughly similar to Washoe (Terrace, 1979).

Box 8.1 (cont'd)

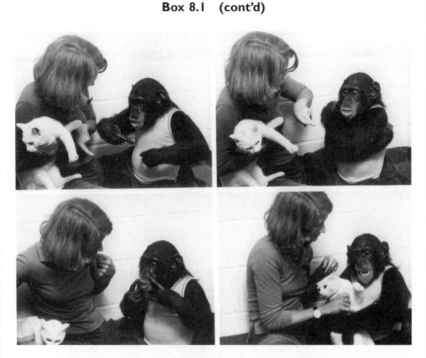

Figure 8.1   Nim signing 'Me hug cat' to a human trainer
(courtesy of H. Terrace)

Yerkish was developed by Duane Rumbaugh and his colleagues at the Yerkes Regional Primate Center in Atlanta Georgia. Lana, a chimpanzee, was the first subject trained in this system of communication (Rumbaugh and Gill, 1977). Lana was trained to press keys on large keyboards (Figure 8.2). The keys were of several different colours and each key was embossed with a different lexigram – a diagram that has symbolic value in the language system. Just as the word 'apple' has nothing about it that looks, sounds or tastes like an apple, so the Yerkish lexigram for apple (a blue triangle) is completely arbitrary and has no apple-like qualities. Lana was trained to press the keys in appropriate grammatical order by rewarding her with a favourite food when she got something right. First she was required only to press one key at a time in order to obtain a reward, but as training progressed, ever more complex sequences were required of her before she was given a reward.

A simpler symbolic language was used by Premack (1976) to communicate with the chimpanzee Sarah. This language was also based on symbols, but these symbols were made from metal-based plastic chips of different shapes and colours. Again, the appearance of the chip bore no resemblance to the item it named. The chips were stuck onto a magnetic board in sentences written vertically. Just like Lana, Sarah was

Box 8.1 (cont'd)

Figure 8.2   Lana operating a Yerkish keyboard (courtesy of D. Rumbaugh)

Figure 8.3   Kanzi with one of his trainers

rewarded with favourite foods for correctly responding to progressively longer and more complex instructions in the symbolic language.

Another study using Yerkish that deserves separate mention is that by Sue Savage-Rumbaugh and colleagues (1986) with Kanzi, a male bonobo (pygmy chimpanzee – Figure 8.3). Kanzi's case is interesting because he wasn't explicitly trained with Yerkish symbols. His mother, Matata, was the object of a study, and he just hung around and watched while she was trained. Matata was not a successful language student and was dropped from the project after about two years. At that point it was found that Kanzi quickly picked up how to use the Yerkish keyboard to indicate things that he wanted, and that he also quickly learnt to 'name' things he was shown by pressing the correct symbol.

actions they had to perform to obtain a reward (whether this was what their trainers intended or not). Similarly, we must consider whether there were human observers present who might have been offering almost imperceptible cues to indicate what response was required – just as Clever Hans picked up on the slight cues made by the people around him.

Remember also Lloyd Morgan's canon, according to which we should not ascribe a behaviour to a more complex cognitive process if a simpler one is sufficient to account for what we observe. This is a basic principle of all science – without it we can never be sure that we are not overinterpreting what we observe.

Ape language studies

Words

Box 8.1 summarizes the different methods that have been used to teach apes something resembling language. All of these methods resulted in some success in the teaching of words to the subjects in question. For example Washoe, the chimp trained in ASL by the Gardners, was able to produce 132 ASL signs by the time her training ended (after nearly five years). Koko (the gorilla trained in ASL by Francine Patterson) attained a vocabulary of 250 signs over four years, and Nim (the chimp trained by Herb Terrace and his colleagues) learnt some 125 ASL signs in three and a half years. These numbers may seem quite impressive, and they are certainly well in excess of anything that has been demonstrated in non-primates (though no comparable attempt has been made with any other species), but it is worth bearing in mind that a two-year-old child soaks up a vocabulary of about 10 words *every day*! Koko's four-year, 250-sign vocabulary would have been less then a month's work for a typical human two-year-old. Figure 8.4 compares the growth of Nim's vocabulary with that of a two-year-old child. Clearly there is a massive difference here.

Producing words or signs is one thing, but what about the use of these words? How much of what they were signing did the apes really understand? Although no other animals may have learnt so many signs, sign learning in itself is some-

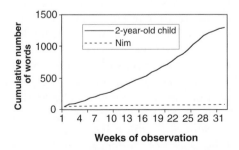

Figure 8.4   The growth of Nim's vocabulary over a 32-week period compared with that of a child just after her second birthday

thing many animals can do. The typical household mutt can understand three or four commands. The record for a dog – 53 different commands – is held by a German Shepherd called Fellow. Fellow was a movie star in the 1920s whose knowledge of commands was probably typical of the most that can be taught to a dog. In 1927 two animal psychologists from Columbia University tested his performance. They reported:

> We have just completed a test of an hour and a half on 'Fellow', the famous movie-actor dog and it is a most remarkable dog in many respects. It is certain that the dog obeys commands given by the human voice with remarkable speed and facility . . .
>
> One point is definitely settled – the dog does not require gesture in addition to the human voice, at least in many of its performances. Mr. Herbert gave commands from an adjoining room with the door closed, and with no one but total strangers in the room with the dog. The animal would go to the window, go into another room and do various things, pick out objects from among several, etc., when the commands were given from the room in which Mr. Herbert was concealed.
>
> . . . Personally we are of the opinion that the dog has learned to associate certain sounds, rather than words in the human sense, with the proper objects and commands. However, the large number of associations clearly marks the dog as most extra-ordinary. (Warden and Warner, 1928)

What evidence is there that apes are doing more than this, with an even longer list of signs? One phenomenon that has been pointed to as evidence that language-trained apes have a deeper understanding of the meanings of the signs they have been taught is their ability to come up with new words. The Gardners' chimp Washoe, for example, signed 'water bird', apparently to indicate a swan; Lucy (a chimpanzee who had received two years of language training) signalled 'drink fruit' for watermelon; and Lana (the chimp trained in Yerkish symbols) signed 'apple which-is orange-colour' to identify the fruit orange. In each case the ape did not know the correct word for the item, but it seems they could come up with a suitable name from their available lexicon. Or could they? How can we be sure that Washoe was coming up with a new word for swan when she signed 'water bird'? Could she not just have been signing for the two things she could see: 'water' and 'bird'? What evidence is there that she intended these two signs to refer to one thing, that she meant a type of bird, a water bird? Similarly, how do we know that Lucy's 'drink fruit' was her name for watermelon, rather than a request to be allowed to drink the fruit?

The problem is that anecdotes alone will not do the job – without carefully designed tests and complete contextual information, judgment must be suspended. Anecdotes typically suffer from the lack of critical background information, but they are also unreliable because of an insidious reporting bias. Anyone who observes the behaviour of animals is inevitably most drawn to the interesting, curious and exciting aspects of the animals' behaviour. What go unrecorded are the thousands of times the dog fails to open the gate, the cat does not knock her food down from the shelf, or the ASL-trained chimp strings two signs together in a totally meaningless or repetitive fashion. Without a record of the frequency of these failures the occasional anecdote of interesting success is quite uninterpretable. In the case of Lana signing 'apple which-is orange-colour,' a transcript is available (Rumbaugh and Gill, 1977):

> In this exchange, Tim, the trainer is holding an orange, which he finally gives Lana at the end. There is no apple present, nor is Shelly (another trainer) in the testing area.

Tim:	What color-of this?
Lana:	Color-of this orange
Tim:	Yes.
Lana:	Tim give cup which-is red.
Tim:	Yes.
Lana:	Tim give which-is shut?
	Shelly give?
Tim:	No Shelly.
Lana:	Eye.
	Tim give which-is orange?
Tim:	What which-is orange?
Lana:	Tim give apple which-is green.
Tim:	No apple which-is green
Lana:	Tim give apple which-is orange.
Tim:	Yes.

Viewed in full, Lana's production of 'apple which-is orange' seems much less compelling. The trainer initiated the 'color-of' dialogue, and even the 'apple' was not Lana's spontaneous name for the object Tim was holding. She refers to it as 'cup' and 'shut' (and possibly 'eye') before she first mentions apple; and when she does she calls it 'apple which-is green'. All of this is much more suggestive of her having learnt that certain sequences of symbols are likely to lead to a reward than of a real understanding of the meaning of these symbols at some deeper level.

An interesting example of the use of language in a novel way that suggests an understanding of the meaning of words is that of Sarah, the chimpanzee trained in a special symbolic language (Premack, 1976). She was taught new words by means of their relation to existing words being spelled out to her. She was taught the symbol for the colour brown with the sequence 'Brown colour-of chocolate'. 'Colour-of' and 'chocolate' were already known to her (though there was no chocolate visible at the moment of training), but brown was not. Sarah was then presented with four different coloured discs and asked to select the brown one, which she did successfully. This demonstration is interesting not just for the novel use of an unknown word, but also for the reference to an object (chocolate) that was not present. But there is a problem here because Sarah was extensively drilled with 'colour-of' constructions, and since she was using symbols on magnetic backgrounds (see Box 8.1) her trainers were able to restrict the number of symbols available to her so that the task was much easier than it might at first appear. Nonetheless this is an interesting demonstration.

Another important quality of human language is known as displaced reference – the ability to converse about things that are not immediately present. There are no chimps here in my office as I sit writing, and I suspect that there are no chimps where you are as you read this – and yet we can converse about chimps. Talking about objects that are not present is something we do all the time, and it is a very significant part of what makes human language so powerful. What evidence is there that this crucial feature of language was present in the ape language studies? In the above example of Sarah learning the colour brown by reference to chocolate, which was not physically present at the time, we have a suggestion of displaced reference. Other examples, however, are hard to find. The apes in these language studies were almost always signing about objects that were physically present at the moment they were being asked to sign about them. One of the exceptions is Kanzi, the bonobo (pygmy chimpanzee) trained by Sue Savage-Rumbaugh and her colleagues (1986). Kanzi regularly uses symbols to indicate places he would like to be taken to, places that are obviously not physically present until he is taken to them.

Sentences

Human language certainly involves a lot of words. Educated English speakers typically have a vocabulary of over 80 000 words. It is not, however, vocabulary that makes language so amazingly productive, rather it is the ability to string words together into sentences. Sentences link words together according to certain rules that determine their meaning – whether they mean anything at all and what that meaning is. The ability to construct sentences turns language from a tool that is able to express 80 000 ideas into something that can be used to express any idea at all. The number of possible sentences in English or any other language is potentially unlimited. Is there any evidence from the ape language studies that any of their subjects were able to construct anything akin to sentences?

The first item we can consider is the length of the expressions that the apes uttered. The vast majority of Nim's productions during the last year of his training were of just one word. Figure 8.5 compares the increase in the mean length of utterance for Nim with that for deaf and hearing children. While the children's curve shows a rapid spurt of longer and longer expressions in the second and third years of life, Nim just plods along using utterances with a mean length around 1.2 (Terrace, 1983). The vast majority (94 per cent) of the utterances of even the precocious bonobo, Kanzi, were just a single sign (Savage-Rumbaugh *et al.*, 1986).

But of course length of utterance is not everything. All these apes occasionally made longer utterances than just one or two symbols. Nim's longest utterance was 'Give orange me give eat orange me eat orange give me eat orange give me you' – not exactly hard to understand, but there is not much evidence of grammatical sense here either (Terrace, 1979).

Suppose your two-year-old son said to you, 'Please mummy give me an M&M' (a small chocolate). Assuming you are the child's mother, you would

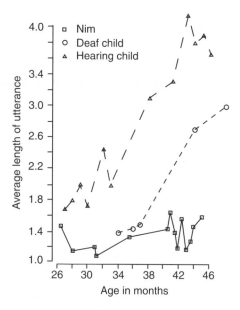

Figure 8.5 Changes in the length of utterance for Nim (the chimpanzee), a deaf child and a hearing child

have every right to be pleased – that is a fairly advanced sentence for a two-year-old. In comparison, let's consider an utterance of Lana's: 'Please machine give M&M period.' At first glance this would seem to suggest that Lana has an understanding of words and can formulate grammatical sentences with a high level of expertise. Before we leap to this conclusion, however, we should inform ourselves about what Lana is actually doing and how she achieved this feat.

As described in Box 8.1, Lana was trained to press keys on a keyboard in order to obtain a reward from a machine. At first Lana only had to press the key designating the reward (in this case an M&M) in order to obtain that reward. Next she was trained to prefix her request with the key that her trainers had chosen to designate 'please', followed by the key for 'period' (full stop) before her request would be granted. When your two-year-old remembers to say 'please' you are probably happy that he is beginning to understand some basic social niceties. However, when Lana learnt to press the key called 'please' there is no reason to assume that she had learnt anything other than that this key was necessary if the 'M&M' key was going to deliver her an M&M. Similarly, Lana was trained to press the key her trainers called 'machine' between pressing the 'please' key and the 'M&M' key, but there is simply no reason to assume that this key meant anything to Lana at all. During this training the machine connected to Lana's keyboard was the only thing offering M&Ms, so Lana was not discriminating between the machine and anything else that might have given her a treat. The 'machine' key was just another key that had to be pressed in the right order to obtain a reward. Remember also that Lana's 'sentences' were not spontaneous productions or imitations of the actions of her trainers, as a child's language typically is, but rather the result of thousands of trials of explicit training. Over and over again Lana was required to press keys in the correct order to receive the reward she wanted.

Interestingly, human infants do not appear to be given much direct training in grammar as such. Parents are much more likely to praise their children for honest, accurate speech than for grammatically correct utterances. Furthermore children do not usually respond very effectively to direct grammatical training. McNeill (1970, pp. 106–7) gives the following delightful example:

Child: Nobody don't like me.
Mother: No, say 'nobody likes me.'
Child: Nobody don't like me.

[Eight repetitions of the above exchange]

Mother: No, now listen carefully; say 'nobody likes me.'
Child: Oh! Nobody don't likes me.

Psychologists interested in the development of language in children, puzzle over why it is that when parents are so concerned with truth and so little with grammar, the usual result is children who tell lies that are grammatically correct!

Sue Savage-Rumbaugh (1993) and her colleagues tested Kanzi's understanding of syntax with 310 different sentences, such as 'Would you please carry the straw.' Of these 310, Kanzi responded correctly to 298. Savage-Rumbaugh acknowledges that there was no evidence to suggest that words such as 'would', 'please', 'the' and so on carried any meaning for Kanzi. She maintains, however, that Kanzi did understand the syntax of the remaining words. That Kanzi could understand, to take an example that was not used in the study, that 'dog bites man' means something different from 'man bites dog'. The problem with this interpretation is that very few of the commands on which Kanzi was tested were ambiguous as to what could be done to what. Consider the example above, 'Would you please carry the straw.' Kanzi could carry a straw, but could a straw carry Kanzi? Certainly not. Kanzi correctly responded to 'Grab Jeannine' and 'Give the trash to Jeannine.' In the first, Jeannine is the object of the sentence (the thing that is grabbed), in the second she is the subject (the person to whom the trash should be given): did Kanzi understand this difference when responding correctly to these two commands? The most likely answer is 'no'. In the first example the verb 'grab' does not permit any other interpretation than to grab the thing named. In the second example, Kanzi could hardly give Jeannine to the trash instead of the other way round. Unfortunately, the testing of Kanzi's sentence comprehension, though it showed he was able to put objects and actions together sensibly, provided very little evidence that he understood syntax.

Overall, evidence of grammatical structure in the spontaneous utterances of any of the language-trained apes is very slight. As we have seen, most of the spontaneous statements by these animals were extremely short (typically fewer than two signs) leaving little room for grammatical development. Some preferred patterns of word order were found in these studies. For example the Gardners reported that in combinations of 'you', 'me' and an action sign, Washoe preferred to put the sign for the subject before the sign for the action (Gardner and Gardner, 1971). She also preferred to put the sign for 'you' in front of the sign for 'me' in utterances that combined those two signs. Patterson (1978) reported that Koko usually put the sign 'more' in first position in most of the utterances that contained it. The problem here is that syntax is not a set of rules about where specific words or signs should appear in a sentence, but about the ordering of different types of word. If I placed the word 'more' at the beginning of every sentence that contains it, would that be grammatical? Obviously not. In English it is usual to place subject, action and object in that order. Consequently in this simple sentence structure the word 'more' only belongs at the beginning of a sentence if it refers to the subject of the sentence ('More water flooded into houses'). If I wanted 'more' to refer to the object of the sentence then it would belong towards the end ('Water flooded into more houses'). A habit of putting one word or another at some position in a sentence is not itself grammatical.

To summarize: the claims of their advocates notwithstanding, the ape language projects have generated very little evidence of linguistic comprehension or production. The labelling of the signs produced by chimpanzees and gorillas with English words has obscured a great deal more than it has revealed. Convincing evidence of even rudimentary features of what could be considered language 'understanding', such as displaced reference (using a sign to refer to an object that is not present), is extremely scarce. As for syntax and grammar, the typical ape's one- or two-word utterance hardly offers much scope for grammatical prowess, and very little has been observed.

Language training with other species

Communicating with dolphins

Because of their highly developed brains, aquatic mammals have sparked a lot of interest among psychologists. In addition, dolphins and other species spend a lot of time making noises at each other that suggest they may have some system for communicating among themselves. Though vocal mimicry has been demonstrated in dolphins, the technical problem of processing their very high pitched vocalizations has so far prevented anybody from training them to produce sounds on demand that could then be tested for language qualities. We shall look at what is known about spontaneous communication among dolphins below, but first let us consider a very interesting study conducted by Louis Herman and his colleagues (1984) at the University of Hawaii on language comprehension. (A report on a similar study by Robert Gisiner and Ronald Schusterman on sea lions was published in 1992.) Herman studied command comprehension by two bottle-nosed dolphins, Akeakamai and Phoenix. Phoenix was trained

Figure 8.6   Some of the commands used to train Akeakamai

on noises generated by computer; Akeakamai was trained to follow gestural commands.

Here we shall follow Akeakamai's training to understand a gestural language. A trainer standing at the side of the pool (and wearing goggles so that her eyes would not give anything away) made certain gestural commands and then rewarded Akeakamai if she followed the instructions correctly. Figure 8.6 shows some of the signs that Akeakamai was taught. In total she learnt over 50 signs. This was a relatively small number compared with the ape language projects, but these signs were carefully chosen so that interesting tests of displaced reference and syntax could be carried out. In displaced reference tests, Akeakamai was given a command that related to an object that was out of view and that she had to find before she could carry out the command. She successfully completed most of these tests.

Although the gestural language on which Akeakamai was trained had relatively few words, it had a strict grammar, and so a number of sentences could be constructed whose meaning depended on the ordering of the words. Akeakamai was tested on 193 novel sentences and performed 85 per cent of the commands successfully. For example in Akeakamai's gestural language, 'pipe hoop fetch' meant 'take the hoop to the pipe', whereas 'hoop pipe fetch' meant 'take the pipe to the hoop'. Akeakamai was clearly successful in differentiating between these two commands, and in comprehending similar sentences up to four words long. In further tests Akeakamai was presented some semantically nonsensical commands such as 'person water fetch', which meant 'take the stream of water to the person'. Akeakamai ignored such impossible requests, but carried out novel but possible commands of equal complexity without difficulty.

Irene Pepperberg and Alex

Alex, an African grey parrot who was trained by Irene Pepperberg (1987, 1994) for two decades, was mentioned in Chapter 5. Pepperberg exploited the wonderful vocal mimicry for which parrots are famous and trained Alex to speak (broken) English. Using her 'model–rival' technique (see Box 5.4), Alex was at first trained simply to name objects, but in subsequent exercises he successfully learnt to identify the colour, shape, material and even number of objects. Later Alex correctly answered questions of a high degree of complexity, such as 'What shape is the green wood?' Alex's need for human company makes it difficult to rule out the possibility that he picked up the correct answers from subtle cues given out by his human companions, perhaps like Clever Hans. The very wide range of responses that Alex produced makes this considerably less likely, however, than was the case with Hans, who just stomped his foot. Pepperberg did not pursue the question of Alex's understanding of grammar, preferring to exploit the parrot's language skills as a tool to uncover other cognitive abilities.

Animal communication in the wild

Vervet monkeys of Kenya

For all their ingenuity, studies that have attempted to teach language to animals in the laboratory do not address the question of what kinds of communication animals use in the wild. While it seems unlikely that laboratory studies could unearth abilities that the species studied do not actually use at some point in their lives, there is a possibility that laboratory studies might fail to find an ability that is used in the wild. One of the most thorough and fascinating studies of a spontaneous communication system among non-human primates was carried out over many years by Dorothy Cheney and Robert Seyfarth (1990) on East African vervet monkeys. Similar studies have been carried out on captive rhesus monkeys and Japanese macaques.

Cheney and Seyfarth built their research on an observation made by an earlier researcher. In 1963 Thomas Struhsaker (1967) spent a year among vervet monkeys in Kenya's Amboseli National Park. After many thousands of hours of careful observation and audio taping he transcribed 36 different kinds of vervet monkey sounds. He noted the contexts in which these different sounds were made so diligently that he was able to identify 21 of them as distinct messages that the monkeys sent to each other. For example vervet monkeys make distinct acoustic calls in the presence of three major predators: leopards, eagles and snakes. Each alarm call sounds different and produces a different response in the vervet monkeys who hear it. The first step Cheney and Seyfarth took was to investigate whether the monkeys really were responding to the alarm calls, and not to the predator itself or the behaviour of the monkey issuing the call. To do this the researchers taped the alarm calls and then played them back to the monkeys when the predators were absent. Their distinctive response to each type of alarm call in these playback experiments showed that they really were responding just to the calls.

Next Cheney and Seyfarth carried out a series of experiments to reveal as much as possible about what these alarm calls meant to the monkeys. Did the call made in response to a leopard, for example, mean something like, 'Watch out, there's a leopard!', or was it more like, 'Quick everybody, up into the trees!' Evidence that the calls referred to the predator rather than the action that a monkey should take to avoid the predator came from the observation that, when they heard the calls, monkeys in different places (on the ground, up a tree and so on) took different types of evasive action.

In order to investigate how deep the meanings of the vervet monkey alarm calls might be, Cheney and Seyfarth developed an experiment out of the story of the boy who cried 'Wolf!' once too often. They played back an alarm call made by monkeys when another group of monkeys was coming close. This was a long trilling 'wrr'. The first time they played this back with no other group present, the monkeys looked around for about six seconds. By the time the experimenters had played the tape eight times with no other group present, the monkeys looked up from what they were doing for just two seconds. They had learnt that there was no other group approaching, and somebody was just crying wolf (or rather 'wrr'). The next thing Cheney and Seyfarth did was to switch to a tape of a short staccato chutter. This chutter sounded completely different from the 'wrr', but it too was used by the monkeys to signal the approach of another group. Now, if the monkeys were just listening to sounds they would be expected to take renewed interest when the sound they heard changed, and look around much longer. On the other hand, if what they were doing was extracting the meaning of the 'wrr' call, then the change to a chutter call would not involve a change in meaning and so they would not be expected to pay any more attention to the chutter call than to the now discounted 'wrr' call. This is exactly what was found. The first chutter call was given even less attention than the last of the eight 'wrr' calls – the monkeys looked around for less than two seconds.

The possibility that vervet monkeys use alarm calls in a deceptive manner that might imply a theory of mind, as discussed in Chapter 2.

Dolphins

In the 1960s it was discovered that, in addition to the click sounds used for echolocation (see Chapter 4), bottlenose dolphins also produce relatively pure tone sounds. These pure tones are characteristic of the individual dolphin uttering them and are therefore labelled 'signature whistles'. It has also been known for some time that dolphins have an advanced ability to imitate sounds that they hear. This ability for vocal mimicry, combined both with the knowledge that they produce spontaneous whistles not used for echolocation, and the evidence (discussed above) that they can be taught to understand a human system of communication, raised the exciting possibility that dolphins might have some form of language-like communication system that they use in the wild.

Several researchers have found that both wild and captive dolphins develop their characteristic signature whistles in the first few months of life, and that these remain unchanged throughout their adult lives (Tyack, 1997). Juvenile female dolphins usually develop signature whistles that are quite different from those of their mother; interestingly, however, young male dolphins adopt whistles that differ little from those of their mother (ibid.). This might mean that it is not as important for male dolphins to form signature whistles that are distinct from their mother's because they leave the mother's group quite early in life to form all-male groups.

Not all the signature whistles that a dolphin makes are its own – some of the time (estimates range between 10 per cent and 50 per cent) dolphins imitate the signature whistles of other dolphins (ibid.). These imitated signature whistles are usually those of their close social contacts.

What could be the function of characteristic signature whistles and their imitation by others? It seems likely that the whistles are an important means of ensuring group cohesion in a social animal that lives in an environment where visual contact cannot always be maintained. Emitting signature whistles is a bit like calling out 'I'm over here!' in a darkened or smoke-filled room. In an interesting study, Vincent Janik and Peter Slater (1998) found that dolphins tend to increase the frequency of their signature whistles when they become visually separated from the rest of their group. It seems, therefore, that the signature whistles serve to help the group avoid becoming split up when they cannot see each other.

The practice of imitating others' signature whistles might also be a way of calling a group together – possibly to request the assistance of other group members. Peter Tyack (1997) reports how he and his colleagues temporarily captured a wild dolphin in order to record its whistles. They kept this dolphin in their corral for an hour. During the first half hour it produced its signature whistle 520 times, plus 39 variant whistles, but there was no imitation of any other dolphin's whistle that the researchers could identify. In the second half hour the dolphin suddenly started to imitate the signature whistle of the oldest dolphin in the group. The number of the dolphin's own signature whistles dropped to 472, the imitations rose to 47 and there were just six variant whistles. Tyack interprets this as the captive dolphin calling for assistance from the oldest member of the group.

Though dolphins' use of signature whistles is a very interesting example of a communication system in the wild, the nature of that system is not especially complex. Notwithstanding their large brains, dolphins' signature whistles are not really a form of language, but rather a simple system of identification calls.

The dance of the honey-bee

Honey-bee navigation was considered in Chapter 4. If the navigational ability of this small insect seems amazing enough, the dance 'language' of the honey-bee is even more astonishing. For his work on unravelling the dance language, Karl von Frisch shared the only Nobel Prize ever to be awarded for work on animal behaviour (in 1973 with Konrad Lorenz and Nikolaas Tinbergen).

When a bee returns to the hive after a successful foraging trip it performs a dance on the vertical surface of a honeycomb. If the nectar source was relatively close (less than about 100 metres), it performs what is known as a round dance. The worker bee runs around in a circle to its left and then to its right, alternating back and forth, as shown in Figure 8.7. This performance may continue for about half a minute. The sight of this dance makes the other worker bees very excited. First they troop around behind the dancing bee, keeping their antennae close to its body in a sort of bee conga, and pretty soon they fly off to find the food themselves. In the case of the round dance, the excitement with which the forager bee dances its way around the honeycomb gives some indication of how good a source of nectar it has found, and the bees it recruits pick up the odour of the nectar source with their antennae and use this information to find the right flowers.

The so-called waggle dance of the bee contains even more information. When the source is more than about 100 metres from the hive, the returning bee changes its dance slightly but significantly. Instead of dancing around in an approximate circle, it now dances in a figure of eight. As Figure 8.7 shows, the bee dances a short vertical run, before turning first to the left and then to the right to inscribe a figure of eight. As it dances the middle section of the eight, the bee energetically waggles its body from side to side and makes a buzzing

Figure 8.7   The round (left) and waggle (right) dances of the honey-bee

sound. As in the round dance, other bees start following the dancer around. According to von Frisch, as well as picking up the odour of the nectar source with their antennae, the waggle dance communicates to them both the distance of the source from the hive and the approximate bearing required to reach it. By means of an elegant series of experiments, von Frisch was able to demonstrate that the speed with which the forager bee dances the waggle dance indicates the distance of the food source from the hive.

Perhaps the most astonishing feature of the waggle dance is its signalling of the bearing needed to reach the food source. Von Frisch found that forager bees do not always dance their figures of eight with the central section strictly vertical. Rather the angle to the vertical can vary substantially. Von Frisch was able to show that the angle of the central part of the waggle dance to the vertical is actually the bearing to the sun that will lead to the nectar source.

Before we move on to consider criticisms of the idea that the dance of the honey-bee conveys information about the location of nectar sources, it is worthwhile first considering the claim that the dance constitutes a 'language'. The dance may offer information and act as a communication medium, but is it a form of language? It does refer to things that are not present (displaced reference), and the information it contains does depend on the structure of the communicative act (rather like grammar or syntax). However there are no individual units of the 'language' that can be reorganized in any way to refer to different things. Consequently if the dance is to be considered as a language, it is a language with just one statement: 'The nectar's over there guys!'

In more recent years there has been some controversy over what if anything the dance of the bee communicates. It has been pointed out that, in fact, rather few bees are directed to a nectar source by the performance of a dance, and many bees make their own way to the nectar without attending to the dance of a bee who has already been there (Wenner and Wells, 1990). Recruited bees are also in the air for a much longer time than is necessary for a direct flight to the nectar source if they really know what direction it is in. Additionally, in experimental conditions bees continue to turn up at a nectar source in significant numbers even if every single arriving bee is killed or put in a box so that none can fly back to the hive to communicate with the others.

Adrian Wenner (ibid.) has proposed that bees actually find food sources by relying on odour. All that is communicated by returning forager bees to their hive mates is the odour of the source they have returned from. Even the experiments by Axel Michelson and his colleagues (1992) using an artificial mechanical bee have failed to resolve this controversy.

What the ultimate outcome of this controversy will be we cannot say. It is instructive, however, to bear in mind that even theories of 50 years' standing can be overturned by new discoveries.

Conclusions

The popular media have encouraged the belief that animal psychologists have achieved Dr Doolittle's prowess with at least some species, such as chimpanzees and dolphins. It is often claimed, for example, that dolphins have a complex communication system, and there are those who even claim to understand what dolphins are saying. This is a case where the reality is a little less exciting. In the case of dolphins, no serious evidence has been reported of two-way communication with people. Certainly dolphins can be trained to carry out simple commands, but then so can dogs (dolphins' evident understanding of syntax has never been demonstrated in dogs, but it has never been attempted either). The spontaneous audible productions of dolphins – their signature whistles – amount simply to calling out their names.

Some of the early attempts to teach human language to apes look in retrospect somewhat misguided. It is far more informative to consider which structural aspects of language make it interesting (displaced reference and syntax, for example) and to focus on those components. Dolphins do appear to understand simple syntax, and some chimpanzees and dolphins have shown an awareness that symbols can refer to things that are not present.

There is also great value in studying how animals communicate with each other in the wild. The natural systems of communication in monkeys, dolphins and bees are adapted to the solution of communication problems of importance for survival: problems such as group cohesion, finding food and giving warning of predators. These skills are essential for survival, but unlike human language they are not open-ended communication systems of nearly infinite flexibility.

The idea of teaching something akin to our language to animals and uncovering direct evidence about their minds just by asking them has a deceptive simplicity to it. In fact interpreting what they 'say' is very difficult. This may be what the Austrian philosopher Ludwig Wittgenstein meant when he said: 'If a lion could speak, we could not understand him.'

FURTHER READING

Mithen, S (1997) *The Prehistory of the Mind: The Cognitive Origins of Art, Religion and Science* (London: Thames & Hudson). This book offers a fascinating speculative account of the origins of language. Mithen also comments on just why children's stories are so obsessed with talking animals.

Premack, D and Premack, A (1983) *The Mind of an Ape* (New York: Norton); Savage-Rumbaugh, S (1994) *Kanzi* (New York: Oxford University Press); Terrace, H (1979) *Nim* (New York: Knopf). These three books are fascinating personal accounts of teaching chimps to use sign language.

Wallman, J (1992) *Aping Language* (Cambridge: Cambridge University Press). This is a detailed and highly critical account of ape language studies.

Roitblat, H L, Herman, L M and Nachtigall, P E (eds) (1993) *Language and Communication: Comparative perspectives* (Hillsdale, NJ: Lawrence Erlbaum). This book contains much useful and interesting material on animal communication and language.

Von Frisch, K R (1967) *The Dance Language and Orientation of Bees* (London: Oxford University Press). Von Frisch's work on the communication system of the honey-bee is summarized in this fascinating volume.

—————————————————— **WEBSITES** ——————————————————

The following page from the Yerkes Regional Primate Center in Atlanta outlines Kanzi's biography and the research he has been engaged in
http://www.gsu.edu/~wwwlrc/biographies/kanzi.html

The following is the home page of the Dolphin Institute in Hawaii where Akeakamai and other dolphins in language experiments were trained
http://www.dolphin-institute.com/

An attractively illustrated article about the dance language of bees can be found at
http://www.apiculture.com/articles/bee_dance_2.htm

9
Conclusions and Comparisons

> What kind of a bird are you if you can't swim?
> What kind of a bird are you if you can't fly?
> (*Peter and the Wolf*, Prokofiev)

How do animals differ psychologically from each other, and from us? This question has fascinated comparative psychologists for over a century. It is not, unfortunately, a question that has proved easy to find a way of answering. Evolution teaches us to expect similarities in the psychology of closely related species and differences in the psychology of distantly related species, but it does not tell us what the appropriate measures of psychological similarity and dissimilarity might be. Evolution also teaches us that every species has adapted over countless generations to thrive in a particular part of the world around them – that species' ecological niche. The fact that every species is adapted to its own niche, with its own adaptive problems to deal with, means that it is difficult to compare meaningfully the cognitive talents of different species. As indicated by the interaction between the duck and the little bird quoted above from Prokofiev's *Peter and the Wolf*, each species is well adapted to its chosen environment and comparisons can be offensive.

While the task of comparing the psychological abilities of different species may be difficult both philosophically and practically, it is important enough to be worth making the attempt. Consequently in this final chapter I review various ways of comparing the cognitive abilities of different species.

Brain size

All forms of cognitive behaviour are governed by the central nervous system. Consequently, one might expect the size of the brain to have some influence on the complexity and intelligence of an animal's behaviour. A simple ranking of animals in terms of their brain size, however, would place elephants and whales, with brains often in excess of five kilos, at the top of the list. This does not sound right at all. Although we do not know much about the cognitive abilities of elephants and whales, there is little to suggest that they are exceptionally intelligent. Surely they have the largest brains at least in part because they have the largest bodies. All the parts of the body change size in proportion: feet, legs, arms, heads and brains too. An animal with a larger body will typically have a larger brain, in proportion with the rest of its body. Figure 9.1 shows the relationship between

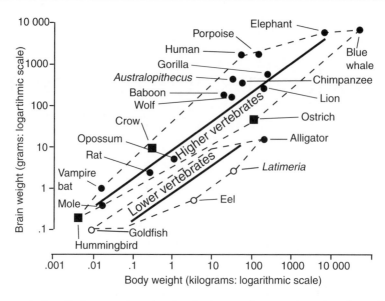

Figure 9.1   Brain mass plotted against body mass for several species of vertebrate
(from Jerison, 1973)

brain weight and body weight in many different species of vertebrate. Heavier
animals typically have heavier brains. It is also clear that the relationship between
brain weight and body weight is not the same in all animals in Figure 9.1. The
thick lines show the typical relationship between brain weight and body weight.
Some species, such as humans and porpoises, fall above the line – this means they
have larger than average brains for their body size. Other species, such as eels
and alligators, have smaller than average brains for their body size – they fall
below the line.

What we need is a measure of brain size *after taking account of* the differences
in body mass. Such a measure is the 'cephalization index' (known as K). A high
K value means that an animal has a larger than average brain for its body size,
and a small K value implies a smaller brain than the norm. In effect K is a measure
of how far an animal is from the solid line in Figure 9.1.

As shown in Figure 9.2, for 'simple' mammals K values of around 0.1 are
typical. Many mammals have K values of around 0.2. Primates' and whales' K
values are in the 0.2 to 0.3 range. At the top of the tree, dolphins have a K value
of 0.64, with humans right at the top with 0.89.

The simplicity of K is attractive, and K values generally coincide with popular
conceptions of the intelligence of different species (Beren *et al.*, 1999). This simplicity brings with it serious drawbacks, however. There are many factors beside
behavioural complexity that influence the size of brain a particular creature will
have (Kaas, 2000). For birds that fly, for example, weight is a very critical concern,
just as it is for machines that fly. Consequently the fact that birds have smaller
brains for their body size than land-based animals is not because of any limita-

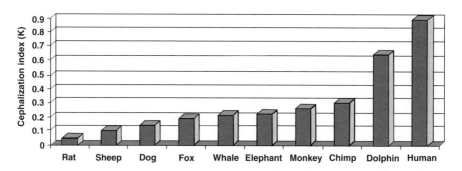

Figure 9.2   Cephalization indexes of several species (data from Russell, 1979)

tions in their psychological processes, but because they have evolved a more compact brain under evolutionary pressure to keep weight down. At the other end of the scale, the exceptionally large brains of dolphins may not have evolved because of the cognitive demands of their lifestyle, but because in water the weight of a large brain is relatively unimportant. Consequently the dolphin brain has evolved without the constraint that gravity imposes on the brains of land-dwelling and aerial animals.

In any case, all brain tissue is not created equal. Much of the brain is occupied with the control of breathing, movement, digestion and other essential but not very cognitive activities. To compare total brain sizes, even after allowing for different body sizes, is to confuse many different things with the psychological questions we are interested in. The part of the brain that is particularly well developed in humans is the neocortex. It has been argued that a large neocortex reflects advanced intelligence. Figure 9.3 compares a typical human brain with the brains of some other animals. You can see that the human neocortex has many characteristic folds. This is because in humans the neocortex has become so large that it can only fit inside the skull by folding. In most other species the neocortex is much smaller compared with the rest of the brain and consequently needs much less folding to make it fit. In lowly insectivores, the neocortex is only 13 per cent of the total brain weight; in rodents it is around 30 per cent, in primates above 50 per cent, and in humans it makes up a magnificent 80 per cent of total brain volume.

But even this measure has its own problems. For one thing, only mammals have a neocortex. Birds' brains, for example, have taken a different evolutionary track and have no neocortex at all. How, then, can we compare the size of different parts of the brain when different species have differently designed brains? Furthermore, how much can we learn from crude measures of the size of different parts of the brain? One thing that would seem important in calculating the processing power of a brain is the number of nerve cells the brain contains. Brain cells can vary greatly in size and in how densely they are packed, and consequently the size of a piece of brain tissue tells us little if anything about the number of

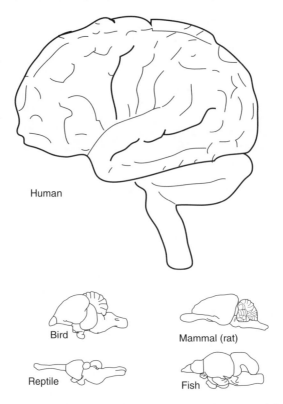

Human

Bird

Mammal (rat)

Reptile

Fish

Figure 9.3   The human brain compared with that of a reptile, fish, bird and rat

brain cells it contains. Take the neocortex of the dolphin, for example. Dolphins and other cetaceans (ocean mammals such as whales and porpoises) have particularly large neocortexes. As mentioned above, in humans the neocortex is so large that it has to be folded to fit inside the skull. The amount of folding is such that, when removed from the skull and spread out, it occupies more than twice the surface area it does when folded. In dolphins the neocortex is even more intensely folded: covering more than five times the surface area when spread out flat than when folded in the skull. But this does not mean that dolphins have more nerve cells in their neocortexes. Recent studies have found that the density of nerve cells in the neocortexes of marine mammals such as dolphins and whales is only a quarter of that in land-based mammals' neocortexes. Consequently dolphins' brains do not have nearly as many nerve cells as their large size would lead us to expect (Deacon, 1990).

In summary then, measures of brain size – even after allowing for body size, and even if we consider just the parts of the brain that might be more important for behavioural complexity – do not enable us to compare the intelligence and cognition of different species of animal. Our knowledge of the brains of different species is just too primitive and limited, although new discoveries are being made every day. Add to this our limited understanding of the cognition of any species and the relationship between cognition and brain structure, and it becomes clear that such an indirect approach is not likely to bear fruit for a long time to come.

Learning set

For many years, researchers interested in animal cognition struggled to find a standard test of cognitive ability or intelligence that would enable the direct comparison of different species. One technique that for some time seemed to offer a means of simple comparison is known as 'learning set'. Learning set is a higher order type of learning – a form of learning about learning.

Consider this very simple problem. A subject has a choice between a triangular and a square stimulus. It has to select the triangle to obtain a small food reward – selection of the square brings no reward. This is a simple form of instrumental conditioning (Chapter 3) known as concurrent discrimination, and a great many species can successfully solve a problem of this type. Once the subject has mastered this problem it is presented with a new choice: perhaps a circle versus a hexagon. Again the subject is trained until it masters this task, when it is presented with another, and then another, and so on for dozens or possibly hundreds of similar discrimination problems. The point of this long series of repetitions of very similar problems is to determine how much the subject improves with each new problem. When learning the very first problem, for example, the subject might make 20 errors before it consistently selects the triangle. With the second problem it might make 15 errors before consistently selecting the circle. When learning the third problem it might make slightly fewer errors again, and so on – making slightly fewer errors in each problem over the series of dozens or hundreds that are presented to it. The critical questions of interest are, what is the highest performance level that a subject can reach after extensive training, and how long does it take to reach that level?

For a subject that is capable of extracting the principle that all these discrimination problems have in common, there is no need to make more than one error in each problem. In the first trial the subject must choose at random (there is no way it can know in advance whether the choice of the triangle or the square is going to be rewarded), but as soon as it has experienced the consequences of that first trial, there is no logical reason why it need ever make a mistake again. In our example, an animal that chooses the triangle in the first trial and is rewarded should thereafter always choose the triangle. Conversely an animal that chooses the square in the first trial should never choose the square again. This ability to extract the principle at work in these experiments is a simple form of concept learning. An animal's success or failure at extracting this principle can most easily be seen by plotting its performance in the second trial of each problem. In the first trial the animal must choose at random, but in theory it can be 100 per cent correct in the second trial.

Obviously, at first, animals have little idea what is required of them and score about the level of chance (50 per cent) in the second trial of each new problem. With more experience however, some species begin to pick up the principle

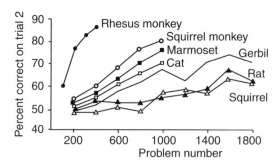

Figure 9.4   Percentage of correct responses in trial 2 of different discrimination problems plotted against successive problem number for several species (from Passingham, 1981)

underlying the task, and their performance in the second trial progressively improves. Figure 9.4 shows the second trial performance of several species trained in many successive problems in this way. It can be seen that rats and squirrels barely improved in the second trial, even though 1800 similar problems were presented. At the other extreme, rhesus monkeys reached a correct response level of nearly 90 per cent after 400 problems. Other species, such as cats, marmosets and squirrel monkeys, attained levels that were above chance but still included substantial numbers of errors. Part of the attraction of learning set as a method of comparing different species is the fact that performances such as those shown in Figure 9.4 correlate well with the relative brain size (as measured by the K index – see Figure 9.2) of the species in question.

There are, however, several problems with this seemingly simple method of directly comparing the intelligence of different species. The first is that data recently collected in my laboratory by Kathryn Bonney flatly contradicts this neat account. Bonney's study animal is a small marsupial called the fat-tailed dunnart (Figure 9.5a). Dunnarts are nocturnal mouse-like creatures that live throughout the arid southern parts of Australia in a variety of habitats, where they hunt small invertebrates and insects. Bonney studied the learning set ability of dunnarts in a simple apparatus where the animal had to choose between two tunnels with different visual stimuli at their ends. For the first problem, in order to obtain a mealworm food reward the dunnarts had to learn to approach stimulus bearing the outline of a circle and not the one bearing a uniform grey square. For the second problem the dunnarts were given a choice between a white square and a black square; and so on for 36 different discrimination problems. The dunnarts' performance in the second trial of each of these problems is shown in Figure 9.5b. Clearly, in the second trial of each problem these animals improved at an even faster rate than the rhesus monkeys in Figure 9.4. The dunnarts were achieving a more than 90 per cent success rate after just 18 discrimination problems. The brain of the dunnart, however, is very small. Their cephalization index is around 0.07, a lower value than that of any of the animals listed in Figure 9.2

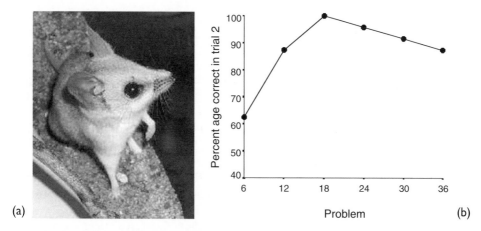

(a)   (b)

Figure 9.5   (a) Picture of a dunnart; (b) the dunnarts' trial 2 performance on 36 successive problems (courtesy of K. Bonney)

(Darlington *et al.*, 1999). Furthermore the part of the brain that is assumed to govern advanced problem solving – the neocortex – accounts for just 20 per cent of a dunnart's brain.

The most likely reason for the dunnarts' exceptional performance lies in their habitat. Fat-tailed dunnarts are one of the few small marsupial species to forage in open areas, where predation from the air is a much greater danger than it is in protected woodland environments. Catching fast-moving insects and small invertebrates in an arid and dangerous environment probably demands an ability to learn quickly about the signals in that environment.

More generally, the learning set task, indeed the whole notion of a 'magic bullet' task that would enable direct comparison of the intelligence of different species, has lost favour for a number of reasons. For one thing it has been found that performance can vary greatly with relatively minor procedural alterations. Dolphins, for example, were found to be completely incapable of forming learning sets with visual stimuli, but were well able to form learning sets with auditory stimuli (Herman and Arbeit, 1973). Since there are inevitable procedural differences between the ways in which members of different species are tested for the ability to form learning sets, these differences, rather than any more meaningful species differences, may be the reason for the varying results obtained from different species. There is also a problem with assuming that the different species tested possess equivalent perceptual abilities, or similar motivational states, when they are tested under what may appear to us to be similar conditions.

Are there really differences between species?

So difficult has it proved to find differences in the performance of different species that cannot be reduced to motivational or perceptual factors, that it has been seriously suggested that there may be *no* difference between the intelligence of *all* non-human species. Euan MacPhail (1987) has proposed that, with the exception of humans, whose intelligence is extended by the possession of language, all species have an approximately equal level of intelligence. Much, of course, depends here on how one defines 'intelligence'. MacPhail's assessment of intelligence emphasizes the kind of learning ability that we considered in Chapter 3 – learning about cause and effect. It certainly is the case that there is a surprising consistency of ability in this domain. As discussed in that chapter, a wide range of species have been found to be capable of learning about the consequences of their actions, and of learning about the relationship between the signals and the things signified in the environment around them. More detailed studies, not reviewed here in any detail but discussed by MacPhail (ibid.), show that a wide variety of species appear to learn about these things in similar ways.

But what about the other forms of animal cognition covered elsewhere in this book? What about spatial learning, perceptual abilities, communication and the great variety of cognitive skills we have discussed: can it really be argued that there are no (or minimal) species differences in these areas too?

Clearly, at one level the answer must be 'no'. In the perceptual domain the pigeon that can see ultraviolet light is doing something different from the cat that cannot. But perception might be considered a special case. Although perceptual abilities contribute to cognition, they might not be considered as representative cases of animal cognition. What about more obvious cognitive skills such as communication, reasoning, memory and the other faculties we have considered? In many of these cases, meaningful comparisons between species are very difficult because so few species have been studied, and the ways in which questions have been addressed by different researchers are so different.

With regard to the ability of animals to comprehend that other individuals have minds (Chapter 2), there is really only one task that has been tested on a wide range of species. This is the mirror self-recognition task – the test of whether an animal recognizes the image it sees in a mirror as being of itself. The tests conducted on numerous species indicate that only a very small group – humans, chimpanzees, pygmy chimps (bonobos) and possibly gorillas – recognize their mirror image as being of themselves. The many other species that have been tested, ranging from monkeys to fish, treat their mirror image either as another member of their species, or as nothing at all. The implications of this interesting comparative fact are still hotly disputed.

Other tests of theory of mind have not been studied in a useful cross-section of species. Daniel Povinelli's 'guesser–knower' experiments were only carried out on chimpanzees, so no comparisons can be drawn at all (Povinelli *et al.*, 1990). Experiments on imitation have been carried out on a very small range of species – two birds (pigeons and quail), some primates and a rodent (the rat) – and no meaningful differences in performance have been found.

Since I am not convinced that the mirror self-recognition studies have contributed to our understanding of animals' theory of mind, I would argue that, to date, no meaningful differences in theory of mind abilities have been demonstrated.

Studies of abstract conceptual abilities (Chapter 5) have been carried out on some of the species used in theory of mind studies, including pigeons, rats, monkeys and chimpanzees. In addition, studies of object permanence have been conducted on cats, dogs, other mammal species and birds. Most of the species tested succeeded at the visible displacement task (where an object is hidden while the subject watches – see Box 5.1 on testing your dog or cat for object permanence), but only four species are widely acknowledged as being successful at the hidden displacement task (where the object is hidden from view while in an opaque container). These four are humans, chimpanzees, gorillas and dogs. Were it not for the presence of dogs in this list we would be dealing just with a small group of very closely related animals. As things stand there is no obvious pattern – either in terms of evolutionary relatedness or ecological niche – that can explain why these four species should be the only ones to succeed at the invisible displacement task. Perhaps if more species are studied the pattern will become clearer.

Studies of concepts such as same–different, and perceptual concepts such as the concept of a tree or a person, have only been carried out on a very narrow range of species (pigeons, monkeys and recently horses) – far too few to be able to draw any conclusions about the distribution of these kinds of ability.

Research on animals' sense of time and number suggests that these concepts are fundamental to a wide range of species. Time of day seems to be something that a great many species are aware of, and there is evidence that the ability to time shorter time intervals is very widespread. Though few systematic studies have been carried out, there is little to suggest a difference in timing ability across species. Research on sensitivity to number has not been carried out on a wide range of species, but there is evidence that a variety of animals are sensitive at least to relative and absolute number. Species that have been studied in this regard include birds such as pigeons, crows and parrots; and mammals such as rats, a raccoon and several primates. More advanced number skills that contribute to counting have been demonstrated in chimpanzees and a parrot, but it seems unlikely that counting skills are restricted to these two species. It is to be hoped that further research will reveal the counting ability of other species.

Memory (Chapter 6) is one area of research where differences in ability based on ecological specialization have been found. Birds that store food over winter in many separate caches can remember many more locations than closely related birds that do not store food. Apart from this difference in memory capacity, it has not proven possible to demonstrate that food-storing birds have memory systems that function differently from those of other birds. Even pigeons, which are only used in memory research out of experimental convenience, have proved to have a quite prodigious ability to memorize hundreds of arbitrary stimuli. Another species extensively used in memory research because it is easy to house and test – the rat – also has an excellent memorization ability. A handful of other species, including invertebrates (honeybees) and primates have been tested on memory tasks. The tests used on different species are usually too different to allow comparisons across species, but the available evidence suggests that, although capacity may vary, the ways in which different species memorize things do not differ dramatically.

This problem of different species being tested in completely different ways makes it especially difficult to draw any comparative conclusions from the research that has been carried out on reasoning in different species (Chapter 7). While the range of species that has been studied on spatial reasoning tasks, for example, is commendably broad (from Australian spiders to chimpanzees), rarely have the same methods been used for more than one species. Similar problems beset the consideration of tool use. Serial learning, on the other hand, has been studied using fairly similar methods for pigeons, rats, monkeys, chimpanzees and humans. The results here indicate that transitive inferential reasoning (where a subject has to go beyond the evidence given to deduce relationships that have not been presented directly – see pages 153–6) may be solved in very similar ways by all the species that have been tested. In linear ordering tasks, on the other hand (where a subject is trained to respond to keys in a set order, and then tested on subsets of those keys – see pages 156–8), monkeys are far more successful than pigeons. It would be very interesting to see how other species respond to this problem so that we could identify which species behave like pigeons, and which like monkeys.

The results of research on communication (Chapter 8) present a very varied and eclectic picture. Different species communicate in many different ways. In terms of the spontaneous communication ability of animals observed in the wild, the most complex communication system would have to be that of the honey-bee. Honeybees, remember, are tiny flying insects with a brain of the most modest size. And yet the waggle dance of a honeybee communicates three different things to its hive mates: distance, direction and the quality of a food source. No other species, not even the great apes (except humans of course), communicates so much information to others. Vervet monkeys can communicate which of several sources of danger is approaching, but they do not have a system for communicating more than that one dimension of information.

Human language, of course, enables us to communicate any number of dimensions of information. Attempts to teach human language to other species may not have led to much mastery of language as such, but they have enabled these animals to communicate several dimensions of experience. Even Alex the parrot could identify the number, colour and identity of objects placed in front of him (Pepperberg, 1987, 1994). Since it is unlikely that animals demonstrate in the laboratory abilities they would never use in the wild, it is possible that examples of more complex communication in the wild will be found once we have developed better methods of studying them.

Overall then, comparative analysis of animal cognition suggests great diversity, but if we look at this diversity more closely, at the present time there is little evidence of clear differences between species. This may be because so few species have been studied on most questions, and where more than one species have been studied, the methods adopted have been too varied to permit meaningful comparisons. Certainly, in a couple of cases where comparable methods have been used, clearly differing results have been obtained (in mirror self-recognition, visible and invisible object displacement, and communication, for example). On the other hand, the reason why so few clear differences between species have been found could be because non-human species differ rather little in their cognitive abilities. This conclusion may seem intuitively unlikely, but the evidence is not strong enough at the moment to reject it.

Animal cognition is not a large field of scientific endeavour, and it is not growing as rapidly as we might like. This can be frustrating to those of us who want to find answers to questions such as the ones raised here. There is one attractive aspect of this state of affairs, however. It does mean that contributing to the big questions in animal cognition is something any reader of this book could do. You don't need fancy expensive equipment – just access to some animals, an inquiring and critical mind, a lot of patience and plenty of respect for your animals. I sincerely hope that some are inspired to join us in the struggle to understand animal minds.

FURTHER READING

MacPhail, E M (1987) The comparative psychology of intelligence, *Behavioral and Brain Sciences*, **10**, 645–95. Euan MacPhail's argument that non-human species do not differ in their intelligence is summarized in this article, which is accompanied by commentaries from many other leading scientists in the field.

Bitterman, M E (1975) The comparative analysis of learning: Are the laws of learning the same in all animals?, *Science*, **188**, 699–709. In this somewhat earlier article, Jeff Bitterman proposes that there are interesting differences between the learning abilities of different species.

Passingham, R E (1982) *The Human Primate* (Oxford: W. H. Freeman). This book discusses the relationship between brain size and intelligence in the evolution of humans.

Blumberg, M S and Wasserman, E A (1995) Animal mind and the argument from design, *American Psychologist*, **50**, 133–44; Kamil, A C (1987) A synthetic approach to the study of animal intelligence, *Nebraska Symposium on Motivation*, **35**, 257–308; Terrace, H S (1985) On the nature of animal thinking, *Neuroscience and Biobehavioral Reviews*, **9**, 643–52. These three papers present some other interesting views on how and why animal intelligence varies.

References

Able, K P (1996) The debate over olfactory navigation by homing pigeons. *Journal of Experimental Biology*, **199**, 121–4.

Akins, C K and Zentall, T R (1999) Imitation in Japanese quail: The role of reinforcement of demonstrator responding. *Psychonomic Bulletin & Review*, **5**, 694–7.

Au, W W L (1997) Echolocation in dolphins with a dolphin-bat comparison. *Bioacoustics*, **8**, 137–62.

Aydin, A and Pearce, J M (1994) Prototype effects in categorization by Pigeons. *Journal of Experimental Psychology: Animal Behavior Processes*, **20**, 264–77.

Baker, R (1980) *The Mystery of Migration*. London: MacDonald and Janes.

Balda, R P and Wiltschko, W (1995) Spatial memory of homing pigeons, Columba livia, tested in an outdoor aviary. *Ethology*, **100**, 253–8.

Barreto, G R and MacDonald, D W (1999) The response of water voles, Arvicola terrestris, to the odours of predators. *Animal Behaviour*, **57**, 1107–12.

Beatty, W W and Shavalie, D A (1980) Rat spatial memory: Resistance to retroactive interference at long retention intervals. *Animal Learning and Behavior*, **8**, 550–2.

Beren, M J, Gibson, K R and Rumbaugh, D M (1999) Predicting hominid intelligence from brain size. In M C Corballis and S E G Lea (eds) *The Descent of Mind: Psychological Perspectives on Hominid Evolution*. Oxford: Oxford University Press.

Berton, F, Vogel, E and Belzung, C (1998) Modulation of mice anxiety in response to cat odor as a consequence of predators diet. *Physiology and Behavior*, **65**, 247–54.

Biro, D and Matsuzawa, T (1999) Numerical ordering in a chimpanzee (Pan troglodytes): Planning, executing, and monitoring. *Journal of Comparative Psychology*, **113**, 178–85.

Bisazza, A, Pignatti, R and Vallortigara, G (1997) Laterality in detour behaviour: interspecific variation in poeciliid fish. *Animal Behaviour*, **54**, 1273–81.

Bloch, S and Martinoya, C (1982) Comparing frontal and lateral viewing in the pigeon. I. Tachistoscopic visual acuity as a function of distance. *Behavioural Brain Research*, **5**, 231–44.

Blough, D S and Blough, P M (1997) Form perception and attention in pigeons. *Animal Learning and Behavior*, **25**, 1–20.

Bolhuis, J J and van Kampen, H S (1988) Serial position curves in spatial memory of rats: primacy and recency effects. *Quarterly Journal of Experimental Psychology. B, Comparative and Physiological Psychology*, **40**, 135–49.

Bovet, J (1995) Homing red squirrels (Tamiasciurus hudsonicus): the importance of going straight. *Ethology*, **101**, 1–9.

Boysen, S T (1992) Counting as the chimpanzee sees it. In W K Honig and J G Fetterman (eds) *Cognitive Aspects of Stimulus Control*. Hillsdale, NJ: Lawrence Erlbaum.

Boysen, S T and Berntson, G G (1989) Numerical competence in a chimpanzee (Pan troglodytes). *Journal of Comparative Psychology*, **103**, 23–31.

Brannon, E M and Terrace, H S (2000) Representation of the numerosities 1–9 by Rhesus Macaques (Macaca mulatta). *Journal of Experimental Psychology: Animal Behavior Processes*, **26**, 31–49.

Brown, M F, McKeon, D, Curley, T, Weston, B, Lambert, C and Lebowitz, B (1998) Working memory for color in honeybees. *Animal Learning and Behavior*, **26**, 264–71.

Cannicci, S, Dahdouh-Guebas, F, Anyona, D and Vannini, M (1995) Homing in the mangrove swimming crab Thalamita crenata (Decapoda: Portunidae). *Ethology*, **100**, 242–52.

Carew, T J, Hawkins, R D and Kandel, E R (1983) Differential classical conditioning of a defensive withdrawal reflex in Aplysia californica. *Science*, **219**, 397–400.

Chapuis, N and Scardigli, P (1993) Shortcut ability in hamsters (Mesocricetus auratus): The role of environmental and kinesthetic information. *Animal Learning and Behavior*, **21**, 255–65.

Chapuis, N, Thinus-Blanc, C and Poucet, B (1983) Dissociation of mechanisms involved in dogs' oriented displacements. *Quarterly Journal of Experimental Psychology. B, Comparative and Physiological Psychology*, **35B**, 213–19.

Chapuis, N and Varlet, C (1987) Short cuts by dogs in natural surroundings. *Quarterly Journal of Experimental Psychology. B, Comparative and Physiological Psychology*, **39B**, 49–64.

Cheney, D L and Seyfarth, R M (1990) *How Monkeys See the World*. Chicago, IL: University of Chicago Press.

Church, R M (1978) The Internal Clock. In S H Hulse, M Fowler and W K Honig (eds) *Cognitive Processes in Animal Behavior* Hillsdale, NJ: Lawrence Erlbaum.

Clayton, N S and Dickinson, A (1998) Episodic-like memory during cache recovery by scrub jays. *Nature*, **395**, 272–4.

Connor, R C, Richards, A F, Smolker, R A and Mann, J (1996) Patterns of female attractiveness in Indian ocean bottlenose dolphins. *Behaviour*, **133**, 37–69.

Cook, R G (1992) The visual perception and processing of textures by pigeons. In W K Honig and J G Fetterman (eds) *Cognitive Aspects of Stimulus Control*. Hillsdale, NJ: Lawrence Erlbaum.

Cook, R G, Brown, M F and Riley, D A (1983) Flexible memory processing by rats: Use of prospective and retrospective information in the radial maze. *Journal of Experimental Psychology: Animal Behavior Processes*, **11**, 453–69.

Couvillon, P A and Bitterman, M E (1992) A conventional conditioning analysis of 'Transitive Inference' in pigeons. *Journal of Experimental Psychology: Animal Behavior Processes*, **18**, 308–10.

Cowie, R J, Krebs, J R and Sherry, D F (1981) Food storing by marsh tits. *Animal Behaviour*, **29**, 1252–9.

D'Amato, M R and Colombo, M (1988) Representation of Serial Order in Monkeys (Cebus apella). *Journal of Experimental Psychology: Animal Behavior Processes*, **14**, 131–9.

D'Amato, M R and Van Sant, P (1988) The person concept in monkeys (Cebus apella). *Journal of Experimental Psychology: Animal Behavior Processes*, **14**, 43–55.

Darlington, R B, Dunlop, S A and Finlay, B L (1999) Neural development in metatherian and eutherian mammals: Variation and constraint. *Journal of Comparative Neurology*, **411**, 359–68.

Darwin, C (1859) *On the Origin of Species by Means of Natural Selection*. London: John Murray.

Darwin, C (1872/1965) *The expression of the Emotions in Man and Animals.* Chicago, IL: University of Chicago Press.

Darwin, C (1877/1989) *The Descent of Man and Selection in Relation to Sex.* London: Pickering & Chatto.

Darwin, C (1987) *Charles Darwin's Notebooks 1836–1844* (P H Barnett, P J Gautrey, S Herbert, D Kohn and S Smith, eds). London and Ithaca, NY: British Museum (Natural History) and Cornell University Press.

Davis, H (1984) Discrimination of the number three by a raccoon (Procyon lotor). *Animal Learning and Behavior*, **12**, 409–13.

Davis, H (1992) Transitive inference in rats (Rattus norvegicus). *Journal of Comparative Psychology*, **106**, 342–9.

Davis, H and Albert, M (1986) Numerical discrimination by rats using sequential auditory stimuli. *Animal Learning and Behavior*, **14**, 57–9.

Davis, H and Bradford, S A (1986) Counting behavior by rats in a simulated natural environment. *Ethology*, **73**, 265–80.

Davis, H and Bradford, S A (1991) Numerically restricted food intake in the rat in a free-feeding situation. *Animal Learning and Behavior*, **19**, 215–22.

Davis, H, MacKenzie, K A and Morrison, S (1989) Numerical discrimination by rats (Rattus norvegicus) using body and vibrissal touch. *Journal of Comparative Psychology*, **103**, 45–53.

Davis, H, Taylor, A A and Norris, C (1997) Preference for familiar humans by rats. *Psychonomic Bulletin & Review*, **4**, 118–20.

Deacon, T W (1990) Rethinking mammalian brain evolution. *American Zoologist*, **30**, 629–705.

Delius, J D and Hollard, V D (1987) Orientation invariance of shape recognition in forebrain-lesioned pigeons. *Behavioural Brain Research*, **23**, 251–9.

Delius, J D, Perchard, R J and Emmerton, J (1976) Polarized light discrimination by pigeons and an electroretinographic correlate. *Journal of Comparative and Physiological Psychology*, **90**, 560–71.

Domjan, M (1998) *The Principles of Learning and Behavior*, 4th edn. Pacific Grove, CA: Brooks/Cole.

Duff, S J, Brownlie, L A, Sherry, D F and Sangster, M (1998) Sun compass and landmark orientation by black-capped chickadees (Parus atricapillus). *Journal of Experimental Psychology: Animal Behavior Processes*, **24**, 243–53.

Dyer, F C (1991) Bees acquire route-based memories but not cognitive maps in a familiar landscape. *Animal Behaviour*, **41**, 239–46.

Dyer, F C (1996) Spatial memory and navigation by honeybees on the scale of the foraging range. *Journal of Experimental Biology*, **199**, 147–54.

Eckerman, D A (1999) Scheduling reinforcement about once a day. *Behavioural Processes*, **45**, 101–14.

Emlen, S T (1970) Celestial rotation: Its importance in the development of migratory orientation. *Science*, **170**, 1198–201.

Emmerton, J (1998) Numerosity differences and effects of stimulus density on pigeons' discrimination performance. *Animal Learning and Behavior*, **26**, 243–56.

Emmerton, J, Lohmann, A and Niemann, J (1997) Pigeons' serial ordering of numerosity with visual arrays. *Animal Learning and Behavior*, **25**, 234–44.

Epstein, R, Kirshnit, C E, Lanza, R P and Rubin, L C (1984) 'Insight' in the pigeon: antecedents and determinants of an intelligent performance. *Nature*, **308**, 61–2.

Fersen, L von and Delius, J D (1989) Long-term retention of many visual patterns by pigeons. *Ethology*, **82**, 141–55.

Fersen, L von and Lea, S E G (1990) Category discrimination by pigeons using five polymorphous features. *Journal of the Experimental Analysis of Behavior*, **54**, 69–84.

Fersen, L von, Wynne, C D L, Delius, J D and Staddon, J E R (1991) Transitive inference formation in pigeons. *Journal of Experimental Psychology: Animal Behavior Processes*, **17**, 334–41.

Ferster, C B (1958) Intermittent reinforcement of a complex response in the chimpanzee. *Journal of the Experimental Analysis of Behavior*, **1**, 163–5.

Fitzke, F W, Hayes, B P, Hodos, W, Holden, A L and Low, J C (1985) Refractive sectors in the visual field of the pigeon eye. *Journal of Physiology*, **369**, 33–44.

Fullard, J H, Simmons, J A and Saillant, P A (1994) Jamming bat echolocation: The dogbane tiger moth Cycnia tenera times its clicks to the terminal attach calls of the big brown bat Eptesicus fuscus. *Journal of Experimental Biology*, **194**, 285–98.

Gagnon, S and Doré, F Y (1994) Cross-sectional study of object permanence in domestic puppies (Canis familiaris). *Journal of Comparative Psychology*, **108**, 220–32.

Gallup, G G (1997) On the rise and fall of self-conception in primates. In J G Snodgrass and R L Thompson (eds) *The self across psychology: Self-recognition, self-awareness, and the self concept*. New York: New York Academy of Sciences.

Garcia, J and Koelling, R A (1966) Relation of cue to consequence in avoidance learning. *Psychonomic Science*, **4**, 123–4.

Gardner, B T and Gardner, R A (1971) Two-way communication with a chimpanzee. In A Schrier and F Stollnitz (eds) *Behavior of non-human primates, Vol. 4*. New York: Academic.

Gardner, R A and Gardner, B T (1969) Teaching sign language to a chimpanzee. *Science*, **165**, 664–72.

Gill, F B (1988) Trapline foraging by hermit hummingbirds: Competition for an undefended, renewable resource. *Ecology*, **69**, 1933–42.

Gillan, D J, Premack, D and Woodruff, G (1981) Reasoning in the chimpanzee: I. Analogical reasoning. *Journal of Experimental Psychology: Animal Behavior Processes*, **7**, 1–17.

Gisiner, R and Schusterman, R J (1992) Sequence, syntax, and semantics: Responses of a language-trained sea lion (Zalophus californianus) to novel sign combinations. *Journal of Comparative Psychology*, **106**, 78–91.

Gould, J L (1986) The locale map of honey bees: do insects have cognitive maps? *Science*, **232**, 861–3.

Goulet, S, Doré, F Y and Lehotkay, R (1996) Activation of locations in working memory in cats. *Quarterly Journal of Experimental Psychology. B, Comparative and Physiological Psychology*, **49B**, 81–92.

Goulet, S, Doré, F Y and Rousseau, R (1994) Object permanence and working memory in cats (Felis catus). *Journal of Experimental Psychology: Animal Behavior Processes*, **20**, 347–65.

Grant, D S (1976) Effect of sample presentation time on long-delay matching in the pigeon. *Learning and Motivation*, **7**, 580–90.

Grant, D S and Roberts, W A (1976) Sources of retroactive inhibition in pigeon short-term memory. *Journal of Experimental Psychology: Animal Behavior Processes*, **2**, 1–16.

Grice, G R (1948) The relation of secondary reinforcement to delayed reward in visual discrimination learning. *Journal of Experimental Psychology*, **38**, 1–16.

Griffin, D R and Galambos, R (1941) The sensory basis of obstacle avoidance by flying bats. *Journal of Experimental Zoology*, **86**, 481–506.

Grossetete, A and Moss, C F (1998) Target flutter rate discrimination by bats using frequency-modulated sonar sounds: Behavior and signal processing models. *Journal of the Acoustical Society of America*, **103**, 2167–76.

Hamm, J, Matheson, W R and Honig, W K (1997) Mental rotation in pigeons (Columba livia)? *Journal of Comparative Psychology*, **111**, 76–81.

Hampton, R R, Shettleworth, S J and Westwood, R P (1998) Proactive interference, recency, and associative strength: Comparisons of black-capped chickadees and dark-eyed juncos. *Animal Learning and Behavior*, **26**, 475–85.

Hanggi, E B (1999) Categorization learning in horses (Equus caballus). *Journal of Comparative Psychology*, **113**, 243–52.

Hare, B, Call, J, Agnetta, B and Tomasello, M (2000) Chimpanzees know what conspecifics do and do not see. *Animal Behaviour*, **59**, 771–85.

Hare, B and Tomasello, M (1999) Domestic dogs (Canis familiaris) use human and conspecific social cues to locate hidden food. *Journal of Comparative Psychology*, **113**, 173–7.

Herman, L M and Arbeit, W R (1973) Stimulus control and auditory discrimination learning set in the bottlenose dolphin. *Journal of the Experimental Analysis of Behavior*, **19**, 379–94.

Herman, L M, Richards, D G and Wolz, J P (1984) Comprehension of sentences by bottlenosed dolphins. *Cognition*, **16**, 129–219.

Herrnstein, R J and de Villiers, P A (1980) Fish as a natural category for people and pigeons. In G H Bower (ed.) *The Psychology of Learning and Motivation: Advances in Research and Theory*, vol. 14. San Diego: Academic Press.

Herrnstein, R J, Loveland, D H and Cable, C (1976) Natural concepts in pigeons. *Journal of Experimental Psychology: Animal Behavior Processes*, **2**, 285–302.

Herz, R S, Zanette, L and Sherry, D F (1994) Spatial cues for cache retrieval by black-capped chickadees. *Animal Behaviour*, **48**, 343–51.

Heth, G, Todrank, J and Johnston, R E (1999) Similarity in the qualities of individual odors among kin and species in Turkish (Mesocricetus brandti) and golden (Mesocricetus auratus) hamsters. *Journal of Comparative Psychology*, **113**, 321–6.

Heyes, C M (1998) Theory of mind in nonhuman primates. *Behavioral and Brain Sciences*, **21**, 101–34.

Heyes, C M and Dawson, G R (1990) A demonstration of observational learning in rats using a bidirectional control. *Quarterly Journal of Experimental Psychology. B, Comparative and Physiological Psychology*, **42**, 59–71.

Hollis, K L, Pharr, V L, Dumas, M J, Britton, G B and Field, J (1997) Classical conditioning provides paternity advantage for territorial male blue gouramis (Trichogaster trichopterus). *Journal of Comparative Psychology*, **111**, 219–25.

Hood, B M, Hauser, M D, Anderson, L and Santos, L (1999) Gravity biases in a non-human primate? *Developmental Science*, **2**, 35–41.

Hume, D (1739/1978) *A Treatise of Human Nature: Book I Of the Understanding*. Oxford: Oxford University Press.

Ioalé, P, Nozzolini, M and Papi, F (1990) Homing pigeons do extract directional information from olfactory stimuli. *Behavioral Ecology and Sociobiology*, **26**, 301–5.

Janik, V M and Slater, P J B (1998) Context-specific use suggests that bottlenose dolphin signature whistles are cohesion calls. *Animal Behaviour*, **56**, 829–38.

Jennings, H S (1906) *Behavior of the Lower Organisms*. New York: Columbia University Press.

Jerison, H J (1973) *Evolution of the Brain and Intelligence*. New York: Academic Press.

Jones, R B and Roper, T J (1997) Olfaction in the domestic fowl: A critical review. *Physiology and Behavior*, **62**, 1009–18.

Kaas, J H (2000) Why is brain size so important: Design problems and solutions as neocortex gets bigger or smaller. *Brain and mind*, **1**, 7–23.

Kamil, A C (1978) Systematic foraging by a nectar-feeding bird, the amakihi (Loxops virens). *Journal of Comparative & Physiological Psychology*, **92**, 388–96.

Kamil, A C and Balda, R P (1990) Differential memory for different cache sites by Clark's nutcrackers. *Journal of Experimental Psychology: Animal Behavior Processes*, **16**, 162–8.

Kamin, L J (1968) 'Attention-like' processes in classical conditioning. In M R Jones (ed.) *Miami symposium on the prediction of behavior: aversive stimulation*. Miami. FL: University of Miami Press.

Kawai, N and Matsuzawa, T (2000) Numerical memory span in a chimpanzee. *Nature*, **403**, 39–40.

Köhler, W (1921/1963) *Intelligenzprufungen bei Menschenaffen*. Heidelberg: Springer.

Köhler, W (1925/1963) *The mentality of apes* (trans. E Winter). London: Kegan Paul Trench & Trubner.

Krebs, J R, Healy, S D and Shettleworth, S J (1990) Spatial memory of Paridae: comparison of a storing and a non-storing species, the coal tit, Parus ater, and the great tit, Parus major. *Animal Behaviour*, **39**, 1127–37.

Kreithen, M L and Keeton, W T (1974) Detection of changes in atmospheric pressure by the homing pigeon, Columba livia. *Journal of Comparative Physiology*, **89**, 73–82.

Kruczek, M (1998) Female bank vole (Clethrionomys glareolus) recognition: preference for the stud male. *Behavioural Processes*, **43**, 229–37.

Lieberman, D A, McIntosh, D C and Thomas, G V (1979) Learning when reward is delayed: A marking hypothesis. *Journal of Experimental Psychology: Animal Behavior Processes*, **5**, 224–42.

Limongelli, L, Boysen, S T and Visalberghi, E (1995) Comprehension of cause–effect relations in a tool-using task by chimpanzees (Pan troglodytes). *Journal of Comparative Psychology*, **109**, 18–26.

Lorenz, K (1935) Der Kumpan in der Umwelt des Vogels: Der Artgenosse als auslösendes Moment sozialer Verhaltungsweisen. *Journal für Ornithologie*, **83**, 137–213, 289–413.

Lorenz, K. (1977) *Behind the mirror*. London: Methuen.

Macphail, E M (1987) The comparative psychology of intelligence. *Behavioral and Brain Sciences*, **10**, 645–95.

Macreae, D and Trolle, E (1956) The defect of function in visual agnosia. *Brain*, **77**, 94–110.

Maier, N R F (1932) Cortical destruction of the posterior part of the brain and its effect on reasoning in rats. *Journal of Comparative Neurology*, **56**, 179–214.

Maki, W S and Hegvik, D K (1980) Directed forgetting in pigeons. *Animal Learning and Behavior*, **8**, 567–74.

Marchant, J (1975) *Alfred Russel Wallace: Letters and reminiscences*, vol. 1. New York: Arno Press.

Martinoya, C and Delius, J D (1990) Perception of rotating spiral patterns by pigeons. *Biological Cybernetics*, **63**, 127–34.

McFadden, S A and Reymond, L (1985) A further look at the binocular visual field of the pigeon (Columba livia). *Vision Research*, **25**, 1741–6.

McGonigle, B O and Chalmers, M (1977) Are Monkeys logical? *Nature*, **267**, 694–6.

McNeill, D (1970) *The acquisition of language: The study of developmental psycholinguistics*. New York: Harper and Row.

Mechner, F (1958) Probability relations within response sequences under ratio rein-forcement. *Journal of the Experimental Analysis of Behavior*, **1**, 109–21.

Menzel, R, Geiger, K, Chittka, L, Joerges, J, Kunze, J and Müller, U (1996) The knowledge base of bee navigation. *Journal of Experimental Biology*, **199**, 141–6.

Michelson, A, Andersen, B B, Storm, J, Kirchner, W H and Lindauer, M (1992) How honeybees perceive communication dances, studied by means of a mechanical model. *Behavioral Ecology and Sociobiology*, **30**, 143–50.

Miller, R R and Berk, A M (1977) Retention over metamorphosis in the African claw-toed frog. *Journal of Experimental Psychology: Animal Behavior Processes*, **3**, 343–56.

Mínguez, E (1997) Olfactory nest recognition by British storm-petrel chicks. *Animal Behaviour*, **53**, 701–7.

Morgan, C L (1894) *Introduction to Comparative Psychology*. London: Scott.

Morris, R G M (1981) Spatial localization does not require the presence of local cues. *Learning and Motivation*, **12**, 239–60.

Mossman, C A and Drickamer, L C (1996) Odor preferences of female house mice (Mus domesticus) in seminatural enclosures. *Journal of Comparative Psychology*, **110**, 131–8.

Nelson, B S and Stoddard, P K (1998) Accuracy of auditory distance and azimuth perception by a passerine bird in natural habitat. *Animal Behaviour*, **56**, 467–77.

Nishida, T (1987) Local traditions and cultural transmission. In B B Smuts, D L Cheney, R M Seyfarth, R W Wrangham and T T Stuhsaker (eds) *Primate Societies*. Chicago, IL: University of Chicago Press.

Olton, D S (1985) A comparative analysis of memory. *Journal of Experimental Psychology: Learning, Memory, and Cognition*, **11**, 480–4.

Palacios, A G and Varela, F J (1992) Color mixing in the pigeon (Columba livia) II: A psychophysical determination in the middle, short and near-UV wavelength range. *Vision Research*, **32**, 1947–53.

Papi, F and Luschi, P (1996) Pinpointing 'Isla Meta': The case of sea turtles and alba-trosses. *Journal of Experimental Biology*, **199**, 65–71.

Passinghan, R E (1981) *Primate Specializations in Brain and Intelligence*, Symposia of the Zoological Society of London, **46**, 361–88.

Patterson, F G (1978) The gesture of a gorilla: Language acquisition in another pongid. *Brain and Language*, **5**, 72–97.

Pavlov, I P (1954) *Sämtliche Werke*, band II/2. Berlin: Akademie Verlag.

Pepperberg, I M (1987) Evidence for conceptual quantitative abilities in the African gray parrot: Labeling of cardinal sets. *Ethology*, **75**, 37–61.

Pepperberg, I M (1994) Numerical competence in an African gray parrot (Psittacus erithacus). *Journal of Comparative Psychology*, **108**, 36–44.

Pfungst, O (1911/1965) *Clever Hans: (The horse of Mr. von Osten)*. New York: Holt, Rinehard and Winston.

Piaget, J (1952) *The origins of intelligence in children*. (trans. M Cook, originally published 1936) New York: International Universities Press.

Poucet, B, Thinus-Blanc, C and Chapuis, N (1983) Route planning in cats, in relation to the visibility of the goal. *Animal Behaviour*, **31**, 594–9.

Povinelli, D J and Eddy, T J (1996) What young chimpanzees know about seeing. *Monographs of the society for research in child development*, **61**, v–247.

Povinelli, D J, Nelson, K E and Boysen, S T (1990) Inferences about guessing and knowing by chimpanzees (Pan troglodytes). *Journal of Comparative Psychology*, **104**, 203–10.

Povinelli, D J, Rulf, A B, Landau, K R and Bierschwale, D T (1993) Self-recognition in chimpanzees (Pan troglodytes): Distribution, ontogeny, and patterns of emer-gence. *Journal of Comparative Psychology*, **107**, 347–72.

Premack, D (1976) *Intelligence in ape and man*. Hillsdale, NJ: L. Erlbaum and Associates.

Premack, D and Woodruff, G (1978) Chimpanzee problem-solving: A test for comprehension. *Science*, **202**, 532–5.

Real, P G, Iannazzi, R and Kamil, A C (1984) Discrimination and generalization of leaf damage by blue jays (Cyanocitta cristata). *Animal Learning & Behavior*, **12**, 202–8.

Reaux, J E, Theall, L A and Povinelli, D J (1999) A longitudinal investigation of chimpanzees' understanding of visual perception. *Child Development*, **70**, 275–90.

Regolin, L, Vallortigara, G and Zanforlin, M (1994) Perceptual and motivational aspects of detour behaviour in young chicks. *Animal Behaviour*, **47**, 123–31.

Regolin, L, Vallortigara, G and Zanforlin, M (1995) Object and spatial representations in detour problems by chicks. *Animal Behaviour*, **49**, 195–9.

Reid, S L and Spetch, M L (1998) Perception of pictorial depth cues by pigeons. *Psychonomic Bulletin & Review*, **5**, 698–704.

Remy, M and Emmerton, J (1989) Behavioral spectral sensitivities of different retinal areas in pigeons. *Behavioral Neuroscience*, **103**, 170–7.

Rescorla, R A (1967) Pavlovian conditioning and its proper control procedures. *Psychological Review*, **74**, 71–80.

Rilling, M and McDiarmid, C (1965) Signal detection in fixed-ratio schedules. *Science*, **148** (whole no. 3669), 526–7.

Roeder, K D and Treat, A E (1961) The detection and evasion of bats by moths. *American Scientist*, **49**, 135–48.

Romanes, G J (1884) *Animal intelligence*, London: Kegan Paul, Trench.

Rumbaugh, D M and Gill, T V (1977) Lana's acquisition of linguistic skills. In D M Rumbaugh (ed.) *Language Learning by a Chimpanzee: The LANA Project*. New York: Academic Press.

Russell, S (1979) Brain size and intelligence: a comparative perspective. In D A Oakley and H C Plotkin (eds) *Brain, Behavior and Evolution*. London: Methuen.

Sacks, O (1990) *The Man who Mistook his Wife for a Hat*. New York: HarperCollins.

Savage-Rumbaugh, S (1988) A new look at ape language: Comprehension of vocal speech and syntax. In D W Leger (ed.) *Comparative Perspectives in Modern Psychology (Nebraska Symposium on Motivation, 1987)*. Lincoln, NA: University of Nebraska Press.

Savage-Rumbaugh, S, McDonald, K, Sevcik, R A, Hopkins, W D and Rubert, E (1986) Spontaneous symbol acquisition and communicative use by Pygmy Chimpanzees (Pan paniscus). *Journal of Experimental Psychology: General*, **115**, 211–35.

Savage-Rumbaugh, S, Murphy, J, Sevcik, R A, Brakke, K E, Williams, S L and Rumbaugh, D M (1993) Language comprehension in ape and child. *Monographs of the Society for Research in Child Development*, **58**, 1–221.

Schmidt-Koenig, K, Ganzhorn, J U and Ranwaud, R (1991) The sun compass. In P Berthold (ed.) *Orientation in birds*. Basel, Switzerland: Birkhauser Verlag.

Schrier, A M, Angarella, R and Povar, M L (1984) Studies of concept formation by stumptailed monkeys: Concepts humans, monkeys, and letter A. *Journal of Experimental Psychology: Animal Behavior Processes*, **10**, 564–84.

Sherry, D F (1982) Food storage, memory and marsh tits. *Animal Behaviour*, **30**, 631–3.

Sherry, D F (1984) Food storage by black-capped chickadees: Memory for the location and contents of caches. *Animal Behaviour*, **32**, 451–64.

Sherry, D F (1992) Landmarks, the hippocampus, and spatial search in food-storing birds. In W H Honig and J G Fetterman (eds) *Cognitive Aspects of Stimulus Control*. Mahwab, NJ: Lawrence Erlbaum.

Sherry, D F, Krebs, J R and Cowie, R J (1981) Memory for location of stored food in marsh tits. *Animal Behaviour*, **29**, 1260–6.

Shimp, C P (1981) The local organization of behavior: Discrimination of and memory for simple behavioral patterns. *Journal of the Experimental Analysis of Behavior*, **36**, 303–15.

Shimp, C P (1982) On metaknowledge in the pigeon: An organism's knowledge about its own behavior. *Animal Learning and Behavior*, **10**, 358–64.

Simmons, J A, Ferragamo, M J and Moss, C F (1998) Echo-delay resolution in sonar images of the big brown bat, Eptesicus fuscus. *Proceedings of the National Academy of Sciences*, **95**, 12647–52.

Skinner, B F (1948) 'Superstition' in the pigeon. *Journal of Experimental Psychology*, **38**, 168–72.

Skinner, B F (1962) Two 'synthetic social relations'. *Journal of the Experimental Analysis of Behavior*, **5**, 531–3.

Spetch, M L (1990) Further studies of pigeons' spatial working memory in the open-field task. *Animal Learning and Behavior*, **18**, 332–40.

Spetch, M L and Honig, W K (1988) Characteristics of pigeons' spatial working memory in an open-field task. *Animal Learning and Behavior*, **16**, 123–31.

Srinivasan, M V, Zhang, S W, Lehrer, M and Collett, T S (1996) Honeybee navigation en route to the goal: Visual flight control and odometry. *Journal of Experimental Biology*, **199**, 237–44.

Staddon, J E R (1970) Effect of reinforcement duration on fixed-interval responding. *Journal of the Experimental Analysis of Behavior*, **13**, 9–11.

Staddon, J E R and Higa, J J (1999) Time and memory: Towards a pacemaker-free theory of interval timing. *Journal of the Experimental Analysis of Behavior*, **71**, 215–51.

Staddon, J E R and Simmelhag, V L (1971) The 'superstition' experiment: A re-examination of its implications for the principles of adaptive behavior. *Psychological Review*, **78**, 3–43.

Struhsaker, T T (1967) Auditory communication among vervet monkeys (Cercopithecus aethiops). In S A Altmann (ed.) *Social communication among primates*. Chicago, IL: University of Chicago Press.

Swaisgood, R R, Lindburg, D G and Zhou, X (1999) Giant pandas discriminate individual differences in conspecific scent. *Animal Behaviour*, **57**, 1045–53.

Tarsitano, M S and Jackson, R R (1997) Araneophagic jumping spiders discriminate between detour routes that do and do not lead to prey. *Animal Behaviour*, **53**, 257–66.

Terrace, H (1979) *Nim*. New York: Knopf.

Terrace, H (1983) Apes who 'talk': Language or projection by their teachers? In J De Luce and H T Wilder (eds) *Language in Primates: Perspectives and Implications*. New York: Springer Verlag.

Terrace, H S (1993) The phylogeny and ontogeny of serial memory: List learning by pigeons and monkeys. *Psychological Science*, **4**, 162–9.

Thompson, R K R and Herman, L M (1977) Memory for lists of sounds by the bottlenosed dolphin: Convergence of memory processes with humans? *Science*, **195**, 501–3.

Thorndike, E L (1898) Animal intelligence: An experimental study of the association processes in animals *Psychological Review Monograph*, **2** (whole no. 8).

Thorndike, E L (1911) *Animal Intelligence: Experimental Studies*. New York: Macmillan.

Tolman, E C and Honzik, C H (1930) 'Insight' in rats. *University of California Publications in Psychology*, **4**, 215–32.

Tolman, E C, Ritchie, B F and Kalish, D (1946) Studies in spatial learning. I. Orientation and the short-cut. *Journal of Experimental Psychology*, **36**, 13–24.

Tyack, P L (1997) Development and social functions of signature whistles in bottlenose dolphins Tursiops truncatus. *Bioacoustics*, **8**, 21–46.

Uexküll, J von (1957) A stroll through the world of animals and men. In C H Schiller (ed.) *Instinctive behavior: The development of a modern concept* (trans. C H Schiller). New York: International Universities Press.

Urcioli, P J, Zentall, T R, Jackson-Smith, P and Steirn, J N (1989) Evidence for common coding in many-to-one matching: Retention, intertrial interference, and transfer. *Journal of Experimental Psychology: Animal Behavior Processes*, **15**, 264–73.

Vander Wall, S B (1982) An experimental analysis of cache recovery in Clark's nutcracker. *Animal Behaviour*, **30**, 84–94.

Varela, F J, Palacios, A G and Goldsmith, T H (1993) Color vision of birds. In H P Zeigler and H-J Bischof (eds) *Vision, Brain, and Behavior in Birds*. Cambridge, MA: MIT Press.

Vaughan, W J and Greene, S L (1984) Pigeon visual memory capacity. *Journal of Experimental Psychology: Animal Behavior Processes*, **10**, 256–71.

Visalberghi, E and Limongelli, L (1994) Lack of comprehension of cause–effect relations in tool-using capuchin monkeys (Cebus apella). *Journal of Comparative Psychology*, **108**, 15–22.

Von der Emde, G, Schwarz, S, Gomez, L, Budelli, R and Grant, K (1998) Electric fish measure distance in the dark. *Nature*, **395**, 890–4.

Walcott, C (1991) Magnetic maps in pigeons. In P Berthold (ed.) *Orientation in birds*. Basel, Switzerland: Birkhauser Verlag.

Walker, M M and Bitterman, M E (1985) Conditioned responding to magnetic fields by honeybees. *Journal of Comparative Physiology A-Sensory Neural & Behavioral Physiology*, **157**, 67–71.

Wallace, A R (1869) Principles of geology [review]. *Quarterly Review*, **126**, 359–94.

Wallraff, H G (1980) Olfaction and homing in pigeons: Nerve-section experiments, critique, hypotheses. *Journal of Comparative Physiology*, **139**, 209–24.

Wallraff, H G (1990) Navigation by homing pigeons. *Ethology, Ecology and Evolution*, **2**, 81–115.

Ward, J F, MacDonald, D W and Doncaster, C P (1997) Responses of foraging hedgehogs to badger odour. *Animal Behaviour*, **53**, 709–20.

Warden, C J and Warner, L H (1928) The sensory capacities and intelligence of dogs, with a report on the ability of the noted dog 'Fellow' to respond to verbal stimuli. *The Quarterly Review of Biology*, **3**, 1–28.

Wasserman, E A (1993) Comparative cognition: Toward a general understanding of cognition in behavior. *Psychological Science*, **4**, 156–61.

Watanabe, S, Sakamoto, J and Wakita, M (1995) Pigeons' discrimination of paintings by Monet and Picasso. *Journal of the Experimental Analysis of Behavior*, **63**, 165–74.

Wenner, A M and Wells, P H (1990) *Anatomy of a controversy: The question of a 'Language' among bees*. New York: Columbia University Press.

Wiltschko, R (1996) The function of olfactory input in pigeon orientation: Does it provide navigational information or play another role? *Journal of Experimental Biology*, **199**, 113–19.

Wiltschko, W and Wiltschko, R (1996) Magnetic orientation in birds. *Journal of Experimental Biology*, **199**, 29–38.

Woodruff, G and Premack, D (1979) Intentional communication in the chimpanzee: The development of deception. *Cognition*, 7, 333–62.

Wright, A A, Cook, R G, Rivera, J J, Sands, S F and Delius, J D (1988) Concept learning by pigeons: Matching-to-sample with trial-unique video picture stimuli. *Animal Learning and Behavior*, **16**, 436–44.

Wynne, C D L (1998) A minimal model of transitive inference. In C D L Wynne and J E R Staddon (eds) *Models for Action*. Hillsdale, NJ: Lawrence Erlbaum.

Zentall, T R (1996) An analysis of imitative learning in animals. In C M Heyes and B G J Galef (eds) *Social learning in animals: The roots of culture*. New York: Academic Press.

Zentall, T R (2000) Symbolic representation by pigeons. *Current Directions in Psychological Science*, **9**, 118–22.

Index

Entries in *italics* are to references and further reading.